CW01617706

Risk and Compliance Questions and Answers

Other titles available from Law Society Publishing:

Anti Money Laundering Toolkit, 3rd edition
Alison Matthews

Assessing and Addressing Risk and Compliance in Your Law Firm
Rebecca Atkinson

Compliance and Ethics in Law Firms, 2nd edition
Tracey Calvert

Financial Crime: A Compliance Manual
Rebecca Atkinson

Regulation and In-house Lawyers, 2nd edition
Tracey Calvert and Bronwen Still

Solicitors and the Accounts Rules, 4th edition
Andrew Allen and Janet Taylor

Titles from Law Society Publishing can be ordered from all good bookshops or direct (telephone 0370 850 1422, or visit our online shop at **www.lawsociety.org.uk/bookshop**).

RISK AND COMPLIANCE QUESTIONS AND ANSWERS

Rebecca Atkinson and Tracey Calvert

The Law Society

All rights reserved. No part of this publication may be reproduced in any material form, whether by photocopying, scanning, downloading onto computer or otherwise without the written permission of the Law Society except in accordance with the provisions of the Copyright, Designs and Patents Act 1988. Applications should be addressed in the first instance, in writing, to Law Society Publishing. Any unauthorised or restricted act in relation to this publication may result in civil proceedings and/or criminal prosecution.

The authors have asserted the right under the Copyright, Designs and Patents Act 1988 to be identified as authors of this work.

Whilst all reasonable care has been taken in the preparation of this publication, neither the publisher nor the authors can accept any responsibility for any loss occasioned to any person acting or refraining from action as a result of relying upon its contents.

The views expressed in this publication should be taken as those of the authors only unless it is specifically indicated that the Law Society has given its endorsement.

To ensure you are relying upon the correct version and most up-to-date version of the SRA Principles, Codes, Rules, warning notices and guidance, please refer to www.sra.org.uk/solicitors/standards-regulations/.

© The Law Society 2022

Crown copyright material is reproduced with the permission of the Controller of Her Majesty's Stationery Office

ISBN-13: 978-1-78446-198-0

Published in 2022 by the Law Society
113 Chancery Lane, London WC2A 1PL

Reprinted 2023

Typeset by Data Standards Ltd, Frome, Somerset
Printed and bound by CPI Group (UK) Ltd, Croydon, CR0 4YY

FSC
www.fsc.org
MIX
Paper | Supporting responsible forestry
FSC® C013604

The paper used for the text pages of this book is FSC® certified. FSC (the Forest Stewardship Council®) is an international network to promote responsible management of the world's forests.

Contents

Preface xv
About the authors xvi
Table of cases xvii
Table of statutes xviii
Table of statutory instruments xix
Table of European legislation xxi
Table of other enactments xxii
Abbreviations xxvi

PART I: ANTI-MONEY LAUNDERING

1 Anti-money laundering legislation 3

1.1 What is money laundering? 3
1.2 Generally speaking, what are the obligations on law firms? 4
1.3 What is POCA 2002 and what are the offences under it? 6
1.4 What are the defences to offences under POCA 2002? 8
1.5 What is the Terrorism Act 2000 and what are the offences and defences under it? 10
1.6 What is a BOOM? How do I register a BOOM? When do I need to register a BOOM? 14
1.7 What is an MLRO and what is their role? Who should be the MLRO? 16
1.8 What is a MLCO and what is their role? Who should be the MLCO? 17
1.9 What crossover is there between the MLRO/MLCO and the COLP and COFA? 19
1.10 What is the definition of tax adviser and why does it matter? 20
1.11 We do not give tax advice, so do we need to apply for supervision with the SRA under the AML Regulations? 22

2 Risk assessments 24

Practice-wide risk assessments

2.1 What is the obligation to conduct a practice-wide risk assessment? 24
2.2 What format should a practice-wide risk assessment take? 25

2.3 What should be included in the practice-wide risk assessment? 26
2.4 Once the risk assessment is done, what should happen to it? 29

Client and matter risk assessments

2.5 What is the requirement to undertake a client and matter risk assessment? 30
2.6 What should a client and matter risk assessment cover? 31
2.7 What is the crossover between the practice-wide risk assessment and the client and matter risk assessment? 35
2.8 Do I need to repeat my risk assessment for a new matter or during a matter? 36
2.9 What are the consequences of not completing the client and matter risk assessment? 37

3 Client due diligence 38

Client due diligence

3.1 What is the requirement to undertake client due diligence and why do we need to undertake it? 38
3.2 What ID do I need to obtain on my clients, and can it differ depending on work type? 39
3.3 What is meant by independent verification of ID? 45
3.4 What is electronic identification and verification, and can I use it? What needs to be considered? 46
3.5 What are the consequences of not undertaking CDD on clients? 47
3.6 What is a politically exposed person, and how can I check if my client is one? 48
3.7 What other checks might I want to take on clients? 49
3.8 What is simplified due diligence? 50
3.9 What is enhanced due diligence? Under what circumstances must enhanced due diligence be done? 51
3.10 What is ongoing monitoring? When should it be done, and what methods could be used to undertake it? 53
3.11 My client cannot provide the 'normal' ID documents – what can I ask for? 55
3.12 I cannot verify my client's identity – can I still act? 56
3.13 What work can I do whilst I am in the process of obtaining CDD? 57
3.14 What is a high-risk third country and what do I have to do if I am dealing with someone in such a country? 58
3.15 What is an occasional transaction and am I undertaking one? 59
3.16 Do I need to identify an intermediary, agent or representative of the client? 59
3.17 I am being referred a matter from another law firm and that law firm wants to be my client instead of the underlying client of theirs – can the law firm be the client? 60

3.18 A partner in the firm is saying that he or she knows the client and therefore we do not need to obtain ID documentation or undertake any form of risk assessment – is this correct? 62
3.19 What the client is telling me does not match the people with significant control register – what do I need to do? 63

Funds

3.20 What are source of funds and source of wealth? 64
3.21 Why do I need to be concerned with source of funds and source of wealth? 65
3.22 How can I investigate source of funds and wealth, and what do I need to obtain? 66
3.23 I cannot get clarity on my client's source of funds and wealth – should I be suspicious? Can I proceed? 68
3.24 My client's source of funds and wealth is cryptocurrency – what do I need to consider? 68
3.25 What happens if I undertake source of funds and wealth enquiries and I am satisfied, but it later turns out that the monies used were proceeds of crime? 70
3.26 Can my central onboarding team deal with source of funds and wealth investigations? 70
3.27 A deposit of monies has been made unsolicited and now the sender wants the monies back – what steps should we take? 71
3.28 Our client wants to pay us in cash – should we accept? 72
3.29 Just before completion our client informs us that funds are to come from a separate corporate entity – what do we need to do? 73
3.30 My client's family member/friend wants to pay our fees – what do I need to do? 74
3.31 My client's family/friend wants to pay all/part of the transaction monies – what do I need to do? 75

Reliance

3.32 What does reliance mean under the AML Regulations? What should be obtained? 76
3.33 What is the problem with reliance? 77
3.34 A regulated entity has asked to rely on our assessment of the CDD – should we agree? 78
3.35 We want to rely on the CDD assessment of another regulated entity – what do we need to think about? 79

Records

3.36 What is the requirement to maintain records under the AML Regulations? 80
3.37 How can we vary the timescale by which we maintain records? Why would we want to? 81

4 **Suspicion and suspicious activity reports** 83

4.1 What is suspicion? 83
4.2 When I am suspicious, what should I do? 84
4.3 What is the role of the MLRO? 85
4.4 What is a SAR, what does it do and what is the timescale for a response? 86
4.5 What is the best way to draft a SAR? What should it cover? 87
4.6 How does privilege come into play when it comes to SARs? 89
4.7 I have made a SAR – what can I tell the client? 91
4.8 The NCA haven't come back to me on my SAR – can I act? 92
4.9 The NCA have refused to provide a defence – what does this mean? 92
4.10 I have made a SAR but the facts or proposed activity has changed – what do I need to do? 93
4.11 My client is sending money from China in contravention of the local laws there – is this a problem? 94
4.12 My client's source of funds is investment in cannabis growing abroad where it is legal – is this a problem? 95
4.13 My client has breached a legal requirement which is a criminal offence and the proceeds they have gained from this activity is £500. Do I still need to make a SAR? Can I act? 97

5 **Practice management and HR** 98

Employee screening

5.1 What do the regulations say? 98
5.2 What steps could I take to screen my firm's people? 99
5.3 Should everyone be screened, including consultants and suppliers? 100
5.4 Can I outsource screening? Who remains responsible? 102
5.5 Our screening has shown an adverse result – what now? 102

Training

5.6 What do the AML Regulations say in relation to training? Who should undertake training? 103
5.7 What methods of training are appropriate? How can we train our people most effectively? 104
5.8 Should the MLRO and MLCO receive additional training? 105

Auditing – internal and external

5.9 What do the AML Regulations say in relation to audits? 106
5.10 Should the independent audit be done by an external person? What should it include? 107

Red flags and warning signs

5.11 What are the red flags/warning signs of money laundering? 108
5.12 How can I make sure that those in the firm understand these red flags/warning signs? 109

SRA AML visits

5.13 The SRA is visiting to review our AML compliance – what is it likely to ask? 110
5.14 What steps can I take to prepare for an SRA visit? 112
5.15 What are the possible outcomes for an SRA visit? 113

PART II: FINANCIAL CRIME

6 Anti-bribery and corruption 117

6.1 What offences does the Bribery Act 2010 create? 117
6.2 Is there a corporate offence? 118
6.3 What are the penalties for a BA 2010 offence? 119
6.4 What is the best way to assess a firm's bribery risk? 119
6.5 Should my firm have an anti-bribery and corruption policy? How could that policy be implemented and its implementation checked? 120
6.6 Should we have an anti-bribery and corruption officer? 121
6.7 What are the best methods of training? 122
6.8 What might my firm's stance on gifts and hospitality be? 123
6.9 We are acting for a client in a jurisdiction where we have been informed 'grease payments' are common and expected. What are 'grease payments' and should we make them? 124
6.10 What due diligence should be done on third party suppliers? 125
6.11 What should we do if bribery is suspected? What needs to be considered? 126
6.12 My firm currently gives Christmas gifts each year to local estate agents who refer work to us. Is this a problem? 127
6.13 My firm is considering setting up an overseas operation in a country which has a high level of corruption. What risks should we consider? 128
6.14 My firm has instructed a professional firm based overseas on behalf of a client regarding a dispute in another country. There is a high level of corruption within this country. The firm is concerned that a bribe may have been paid by the professional firm in order to resolve the dispute. The firm is not clear on whose behalf the bribe has been paid. What is the position? 128
6.15 A client has informed the solicitor acting in the sale of his business that contracts with those the business supplies to came about after a grease payment was made. The business and contracts are in the UK. What does the firm need to do and think about? 129

7 Tax evasion and the Criminal Finances Act 2017 **131**

7.1 What offences does the Criminal Finances Act 2017 create? Who is an associated person? 131
7.2 What is an unexplained wealth order? 133
7.3 What is an account freezing order? 133
7.4 What are the penalties for an offence under CFA 2017? 134
7.5 What is the best way to assess my firm's CFA 2017/tax evasion risk? 135
7.6 Should my firm have an anti-tax evasion policy? How could that policy be implemented and its implementation checked? 137
7.7 What are the best methods of training? 138
7.8 What are examples of the types of tax evasion that could be happening in mainstream practice areas? 139
7.9 What warning notices has the SRA published on this subject and what Law Society guidance will help me? 140
7.10 What should we do if tax evasion is suspected? What needs to be considered? 141
7.11 How often should training and messaging be repeated? 142
7.12 The client is asking that we do not include certain assets in the form E which needs to be completed for their matrimonial matter. Their reason is because 'they didn't pay tax on it'. What should we do? 143
7.13 The client has asked the firm to bill their company for a will that was made. Can we amend the bill? 143
7.14 The client has asked that we readdress the bill to their parent company. Our client is the parent company's subsidiary. Can we do this? 144

8 Sanctions **145**

8.1 What are sanctions, why are they imposed, what types are there and who needs to comply? 145
8.2 Who are the sanction regime key players, and what do they do? 147
8.3 What is OFAC and does it affect me and my firm? 148
8.4 Where can I find sanctions lists? 149
8.5 When should I check clients for sanctions? Whom, in respect of corporate clients, should I check? 150
8.6 What is the obligation to report to OFSI? 152
8.7 How does privilege work when it comes to sanctions? 153
8.8 For what do I need a licence? How do I apply for a licence? 153
8.9 My client is sanctioned and I am applying for the appropriate licence – what can I do whilst I wait for it? Can my client pay my bill? 155
8.10 My client is sanctioned by a non-UK country – can I act? 156

PART III: REGULATION AND COMPLIANCE

9 **Regulatory framework** **161**

9.1 What is the significance of the Legal Services Act 2007 to us? 161
9.2 What is the Legal Services Board? 162
9.3 What is the Solicitors Regulation Authority? 163
9.4 What disciplinary action can the SRA take against us? 165
9.5 What do we need to know about the Solicitors Disciplinary Tribunal? 167
9.6 What is the role of the Law Society of England and Wales? 169
9.7 What do we need to know about the Legal Ombudsman? 170
9.8 What are the different types of law firms which the SRA authorises? 172
9.9 What are the reserved legal activities, and why do we need to be aware of these? 173
9.10 How can solicitors practise? 174
9.11 What is a freelance solicitor? 176
9.12 Do we need to register new partners, directors or members with the SRA? 179
9.13 What compliance training should we deliver to support staff/lateral hires/temporary staff/qualified lawyers, and why? 181
9.14 Do we need to help non-solicitors understand the importance of the SRA and professional ethics? 183
9.15 Do we need to maintain training records and why? 185

10 **Practising certificates, certificate renewals and continuing competency regime** **188**

10.1 Do solicitors always need a practising certificate to work in the law firm? 188
10.2 Can we ask retired solicitors to provide locum or similar support? 189
10.3 What are the requirements on firms to reauthorise each year with the SRA and renew solicitors' practising certificates? 191
10.4 What should we expect from our solicitors in relation of continuing competency? 192
10.5 How do we manage the SRA annual renewal exercise effectively? 193

11 **SRA Accounts Rules** **195**

11.1 Who needs to know about the SRA Accounts Rules and why? 195
11.2 Should we send client monies to an in-house solicitor? 197
11.3 Can we round up disbursements in bills to clients? 198
11.4 If we hold client money in respect of our costs, does this have to be placed in a client account? 199
11.5 Can we retain completion funds in our client account if our client intends to use the money to buy another property? 201
11.6 Can we donate small client balances to charity? 202

11.7 What is a third party managed account, and what should we take into account when considering whether it is appropriate to use this type of account? 203

12 Data protection **207**

12.1 What should be included in an effective firm-wide data protection response? 207
12.2 Do we need to appoint a data protection officer? 209
12.3 How should we respond to a data subject access request? 211
12.4 What steps must we take if we have a data breach incident? 212

13 Financial services **215**

13.1 Do we need to include financial services in our compliance response? 215
13.2 What is the appropriate compliance response when considering how to provide financial services correctly? 217
13.3 Must we appoint an insurance distribution officer, and what does this role involve? 219
13.4 What financial services training should we provide to colleagues? 222

14 Modern slavery **225**

14.1 What is the aim and purpose of the Modern Slavery Act 2015? 225
14.2 Which firms must comply with the annual statement requirement? 226
14.3 Should we have a modern slavery/anti-slavery policy? 227
14.4 What should be placed in our Modern Slavery Act statement? Who should endorse it/sign it? Where should it be published? 227
14.5 What are the sanctions for non-compliance? 229
14.6 How should compliance with MSA 2015 be approached? 229

15 Price transparency **232**

15.1 What are the regulatory requirements in respect of price transparency? 232
15.2 What complaints information must be on our website? 233
15.3 What else are we required to publish? 234
15.4 We have acted on a conveyancing transaction and charged more than the price published on our website – is this a problem? 235

16 Conflicts of interest **237**

16.1 How does the SRA define a significant risk for the purposes of the conflict of interest duties? 237
16.2 How does the SRA define a related matter for the purposes of the conflict of interest duties? 238
16.3 Can we act for buyer and seller of a property if they instruct different offices of our firm? 239

16.4 Can we act for seller and buyer of a property using the 'substantially common interest exception'? 241
16.5 Can we act in a contract race using the 'competing for the same objective exception'? 243
16.6 Is it a conflict to continue acting for a client after we have discovered that we have made a mistake? 244
16.7 Is it a conflict to act against the interests of a former client? 245

17 Confidentiality, disclosure and conflict of duties 248

17.1 What is the proper use of an information barrier, and how do we manage the associated risks? 248
17.2 When does the duty of confidentiality end? 250
17.3 What are the issues if we have sent an email to the wrong recipient? 251
17.4 What do we need to consider when seeking a client's informed consent to disclosure of their confidential information? 253
17.5 What do we need to consider when seeking a client's informed consent to non-disclosure of information material to their retainer? 254
17.6 We are acting on a joint retainer. What is our duty of confidentiality in respect of the clients' affairs? 256
17.7 Can we disclose a will document to the testator's attorney or another family member? 257
17.8 We have recently hired a solicitor who was acting for our client's opponent whilst employed in their previous law firm. What are the solicitor's and our own ethical duties? 259
17.9 How does the SRA define 'adverse interests' for the purposes of the conflict of duties and para.6.5 of the SRA Codes? 260
17.10 What policies help us to comply with duties relating to conflicts of interest and conflicts of duties? 261

18 Acting on a client's matter 265

18.1 What are the pros and cons of using a limited retainer? 265
18.2 What are the risks when supporting a client with unbundled legal services and how do we manage them? 266
18.3 Is it unethical to contact another lawyer's client directly? 268
18.4 We are acting for a client and the other side is unrepresented. Do we have a duty to help the other side? 269
18.5 We are an authorised law firm. The solicitor on the other side of a matter describes themselves as a freelancer. Should we deal with them in the same way as we would with a recognised sole practitioner or a solicitor employed in private practice? 270
18.6 The solicitor on the other side of a matter works in an unauthorised business. Can we correspond with them? 271
18.7 Our client has misled the court – what must we do? 273

19 Client care **275**

19.1 What are the dos and don'ts of contacting prospective clients? 275
19.2 What should we tell clients about equality? 277
19.3 Do we need to send client care/terms of engagement literature when acting on repeat instructions for a regular client? 279
19.4 Do we need to include a detailed description of the legal services we are providing in our client care letter? 280
19.5 Who is our client? 282
19.6 Can we open a general file to deal with a particular client's matters? 284
19.7 Can we enter into a long-term service agreement with our clients? 285
19.8 Do we have to accept all new instructions? 286

20 Running a law firm – compliance questions **288**

20.1 What job titles should we avoid and why? 288
20.2 The SRA talks about 'effective supervision'. What does this mean? 290
20.3 What compliance response supports effective supervision and risk management? 291
20.4 How do we deal with a complaint of discrimination raised by a member of staff? 294
20.5 We are acting for a client or manager/employee seeking reasonable adjustments. What is the correct compliance response? 296
20.6 Must undertakings be in writing? 297
20.7 What should our firm's risk management manual contain and why? 298
20.8 How do we manage referral and introductions effectively? 300
20.9 What services can we outsource to third parties and what are the risk and compliance challenges? 301
20.10 What documented procedures and policies will help us to demonstrate effective governance of regulatory requirements? 302

Index 307

Preface

Navigating the breadth of risk and compliance topics can be time consuming and challenging. For those who want a quick answer to a specific question, this book will help. Presented in the form of over 200 questions and answers, readers of this book will find easily attainable information about a wide breadth of topics including money laundering and financial crime, regulatory duties and the relationship with the Solicitors Regulation Authority and other regulatory bodies, professional ethics and professional values, and matters concerning legal compliance. The book can be read cover to cover or dipped in to when the need arises. The questions and answers provide guidance to everyone in a law firm and particularly those who are working in the risk and compliance space whether they are the COLP or COFA or someone in a risk and compliance team.

The law is stated as at February 2022.

About the authors

Rebecca Atkinson is Director of Risk and Compliance at Howard Kennedy LLP and is their COLP, MLRO, MLCO and DPO. Rebecca leads the firm's internal risk and compliance function and sets the risk and compliance vision and strategy. Rebecca was called to the English Bar, is a solicitor of England and Wales, a New York Attorney and a risk and compliance professional with over a decade of experience. She is the author of *Assessing and Addressing Risk and Compliance in Your Law Firm* (2020) and *Financial Crime: A Compliance Manual* (2021), both published by the Law Society. Rebecca is also a regular practice note-writer for Practical Law Company, sits on a PLC Consultation Board, as well as the Law Society Regulatory Processes Committee, the editorial board for the Law Society's Legal Compliance bulletin and is an editor for the AML chapter of *Cordery on Legal Services*. Rebecca also provides webinars and seminars for the Law Society and MBL.

Tracey Calvert is a lawyer who has worked both in private practice and in-house. She has been a senior ethics adviser and then a policy executive with the Law Society and the SRA. She now runs her own consultancy business which provides regulatory, compliance and ethics services. She is the author of several books, including *Compliance and Ethics in Law Firms* (2019) published by the Law Society, contributes to *Cordery on Legal Services*, is on the board of the Law Society's Legal Compliance bulletin and is the current Co-Chair of the International Bar Association's Professional Ethics Committee.

Table of cases

Prince Jeffrey Bolkiah *v.* KPMG [1998] UKHL 52 .... 17.9
R *v.* Da Silva [2007] 1 WLR 303 .... 4.1

Table of statutes

Administration of Justice Act 1985
s.9 .... 9.8
Anti-terrorism, Crime and Security Act 2001 .... 1.5.3
Bribery Act 2010 ..... 6.1, 6.2, 6.3, 6.4, 6.5, 6.6, 6.8, 6.9, 6.10, 6.11, 6.12, 6.13, 6.14, 6.15
s.7 .... 6.2
Building Societies Act 1986 .... 11.7
Criminal Finances Act 2017 .... 7.1, 7.2, 7.3, 7.4, 7.5, 7.6, 7.7, 7.8, 7.9, 7.10, 7.11, 7.12, 7.13, 7.14
Data Protection Act 2018 .... 3.36, 12.1
Economic Crime (Transparency and Enforcement) Act 2022 .... 7.2
Equality Act 2010 .... 9.11, 19.8
Financial Services (Banking Reform) Act 2013 .... 8.9
Financial Services and Markets Act 2000 .... 13.1, 13.2, 13.3, 13.4
Part 4A 8.1
Legal Aid Sentencing and Punishment of Offenders Act 2012 .... 20.8
s.56 .... 20.8
Legal Services Act 2007 .... 9.1, 9.2, 9.3, 9.4, 9.6, 9.7, 9.8, 9.9
s.1 .... 9.3
s.12 .... 9.9, 9.11, 10.2, 20.9
(1) 9.9
s.71(2) 9.8
Sched.2, para.4 .... 9.9
Sched.13 .... 9.12
Mental Capacity Act 2005 .... 17.7
Modern Slavery Act 2015 .... 14.1, 14.2, 14.3, 14.4, 14.6
Proceeds of Crime Act 2002 .... 1.1, 1.3, 1.4, 1.5.5, 1.10, 3.7, 4.1, 4.6, 4.8, 4.9, 4.10, 4.11, 4.12
ss.327, 329 .... 1.3, 1.4, 4.5, 4.11, 4.12
s.328 .... 1.3, 1.4, 1.5.1, 4.5, 4.11, 4.12
s.330 .... 1.3, 1.4, 4.5
(7A) 4.12
ss.331, 332, 333 .... 1.3
s.338 .... 1.4
s.342 .... 1.3
Rehabilitation of Offenders Act 1974 .... 9.3
Sanctions and Anti-Money Laundering Act 2018 .... 8.1
Solicitors Act 1974 .... 10.1, 11.7, 20.1
s.1A 10.1, 10.2
s.43 .... 9.5
Terrorism Act 2000 .... 1.5, 1.5.1, 1.5.2, 1.5.3, 1.5.4, 1.5.5, 1.10
ss.15, 16, 17, 18 .... 1.5.1, 1.5.2
s.19 .... 1.5.3
s.21 .... 1.5.2
s.21A 1.5.3
s.21D, (1), (3) 1.5.5
s.21E, (4) 1.5.5
s.21F(2)(a) 1.5.5
s.21G 1.5.5
ss.21ZA, 21ZB, 21ZC 1.5.2

Table of statutory instruments

European Communities (Lawyer's Practice) Regulations 2000, SI 2000/1119 .... 20.1
Extraterritorial US Legislation (Sanctions against Cuba, Iran and Libya) (Protection of Trading Interests) (Amendment) Order 2018, SI 2018/1357 .... 8.3
Money Laundering and Terrorist Financing (High-Risk Countries) (Amendment) Regulations 2022, SI 2022/393 .... 3.9, 3.14
Money Laundering, Terrorist Financing and Transfer of Funds (Information on the Payer) Regulations 2017, SI 2017/692 .... 1.2, 1.5, 1.6, 1.8, 1.10, 1.11, 2.1, 2.5, 2.6, 2.9, 3.5, 3.6, 3.8, 3.9, 3.11, 3.12, 3.14, 3.15, 3.17, 3.18, 3.19, 3.25, 3.26, 3.32, 3.35, 3.36, 4.3, 5.2, 5.3, 5.4, 5.7, 5.8, 5.9, 5.13, 5.14, 5.15, 7.5, 8.5, 9.3, 9.14, 13.3, 19.6, 19.8
reg.3 .... 3.9, 3.15
reg.6(1) 3.2
reg.11 .... 1.10
reg.12 .... 1.2
reg.18 .... 1.2, 2.1, 2.3, 5.10
reg.19 .... 1.2, 5.10
reg.20 .... 1.2
reg.21 .... 1.2, 5.9, 5.10
(1) 1.8
(b) 5.1
(3) 1.7, 4.3
reg.24 .... 1.2, 5.6, 5.10, 9.13, 9.15
reg.25 .... 9.15
reg.26 .... 1.6
reg.27 .... 1.2, 3.1, 3.5, 3.14, 5.10
reg.28 .... 1.2, 3.1, 3.5, 3.10, 3.12, 5.10
(2)–(6) 3.32
(3), (4), (5) 3.2
(6)–(8) 3.12
(9) 3.3
(10) 3.16, 3.32
(11) 3.10
(13) 2.5, 2.6
(19) 3.4
reg.30 .... 1.2, 3.13, 5.10
(7) 3.2
reg.30A 3.19, 3.32
reg.31 .... 3.13
(1) 3.12
reg.33 .... 1.2, 3.9, 5.10

Money Laundering, Terrorist Financing and Transfer of Funds (Information on the Payer) Regulations 2017 – *continued*
reg 33(3)(c) 3.14
reg.35 .... 1.2, 3.6, 3.9, 5.10
reg.37 .... 1.2, 5.10
(3)(b)(iii) 3.2
reg.39 .... 1.2, 3.32, 3.33, 3.34, 3.35, 5.10
(2) 3.32
reg.40 .... 1.2, 3.32, 3.36, 3.37, 5.10
(3), (5) 3.36
reg.86 .... 3.5
Sched.3 .... 1.6
Money Laundering and Terrorist Financing (Amendment) Regulations 2019, SI 2019/1511 .... 3.34, 9.15
Payment Services Regulations 2017, SI 2017/752 .... 11.7
Terrorism Act 2000 and Proceeds of Crime Act 2002 (Amendment) Regulations 2007, SI 2007/3398 .... 1.5.2

Table of European legislation

Directive (EU) 2018/843 Fifth Directive on Money Laundering 1.10

Table of other enactments

Solicitors' Code of Conduct 2007 .... 16.2, 17.9
SRA Accounts Rules 1.9, 9.11, 9.13, 9.14, 11.1, 11.2, 11.3, 11.4, 11.5, 11.6, 11.7, 13.3, 18.5
rule 2.1 .... 11.4
(d) 9.11, 11.4
rule 2.2 .... 11.4
rule 2.3 .... 11.4
rule 2.4 .... 11.4
rule 2.5 .... 11.6
rule 3.3 .... 1.9, 11.5
rule 4.1 .... 11.4
rule 5.1(c) 11.6
rule 7 .... 11.4
rule 8.1(b), (c) 11.4
rule 11 .... 11.7
rule 11.1 .... 11.7
rule 11.2 .... 11.7
rule 12 .... 11.4
SRA Authorisation of Firms Rules 9.8, 9.10, 9.12
rule 13.1 .... 9.12
rule 13.2 .... 9.12
SRA Authorisation of Individuals Regulations 9.10, 9.11, 10.1, 10.2, 18.5, 18.6
reg.10.2 .... 9.10, 9.11
(b)(vii) 11.2
SRA Code of Conduct for Firms 1.9, 4.11, 6.11, 7.10, 9.3, 9.4, 9.5, 9.7, 9.10, 9.13, 9.14, 10.2, 11.1, 11.7, 12.1, 12.2, 12.3, 12.4, 13.3, 15.1, 15.4, 16.1, 16.2, 16.3, 16.4, 16.5, 16.6, 16.7, 17.1, 17.2, 17.3, 17.4, 17.5, 17.6, 17.7, 17.8, 17.9, 17.10, 18.1, 18.2, 18.3, 18.4, 18.7, 19.1, 19.2, 19.3, 19.4, 19.5, 19.6, 19.7, 19.8, 20.1, 20.2, 20.3, 20.4, 20.5, 20.6, 20.7, 20.8, 20.9, 20.10
section 1
para.1.1 .... 19.2, 20.4
para.1.2 .... 18.3, 18.4, 19.2, 20.4
para.1.3 .... 20.6
para.1.4 .... 18.7
section 2 .... 9.13, 10.2, 12.4, 17.10, 20.2, 20.4, 20.7, 20.9, 20.10
para.2.1 .... 12.4, 20.10
(b) 20.4
para.2.2 .... 12.4, 17.3, 20.7
para.2.3 .... 20.9

para.2.5 .... 12.1, 12.2, 12.4, 20.7
section 3 .... 9.3, 9.4
para.3.1 .... 9.9, 12.1, 20.5
para.3.2 .... 9.3, 9.4, 9.5, 9.7
para.3.3 .... 9.3, 9.4
para.3.5 .... 16.6
para.3.6 .... 9.3
para.3.9 .... 9.3, 20.4
para.3.10 .... 9.3, 20.4
para.3.11 .... 9.3, 9.5, 9.7
para.3.12 .... 9.3
section 4 .... 13.1, 19.5
para.4.1 .... 17.7, 19.4, 19.5, 19.7
para.4.2 .... 10.2, 13.4, 19.2, 19.3, 19.4, 19.5
para.4.3 .... 9.13, 9.14, 9.15, 13.4, 19.1
para.4.4 .... 19.5, 20.2, 20.3
section 5
para.5.2 .... 11.1
section 6 .... 17.10, 19.5
para.6.1 .... 16.1, 16.2, 16.6, 16.7, 17.10
para.6.2 .... 16.1, 16.2, 16.3, 16.5, 16.7, 17.10, 18.1
para.6.3 .... 12.4, 16.7, 17.1, 17.2, 17.3, 17.4, 17.6, 17.7, 17.8, 17.9, 17.10
para.6.4 .... 16.7, 17.5, 17.8, 17.9, 17.10, 18.1
(b), (d) 17.5
para.6.5 .... 16.7, 17.1, 17.5, 17.9, 17.10
(a), (b) 17.1
section 7
para.7.1(b) 20.8
(c) 11.7, 19.1, 19.2, 19.3, 19.4, 19.5, 19.7, 20.1
section 9
para.9.1(d) 20.4
SRA Code of Conduct for Solicitors, RELs and RFLs 1.9, 4.11, 6.11, 7.10, 9.3, 9.4, 9.5, 9.7, 9.10, 9.11, 9.13, 9.14, 10.2, 11.1, 11.4, 11.7, 12.1, 12.2, 12.3, 12.4, 13.3, 15.1, 15.4, 16.1, 16.2, 16.3, 16.4, 16.5, 16.6, 16.7, 17.1, 17.2, 17.3, 17.4, 17.5, 17.6, 17.7, 17.8, 17.9, 17.10, 18.1, 18.2, 18.3, 18.4, 18.5, 18.6, 18.7, 19.1, 19.2, 19.3, 19.4, 19.5, 19.6, 19.7, 19.8, 20.1, 20.4, 20.5, 20.6, 20.8, 20.9
section 1
para.1.1 .... 19.2, 20.4
para.1.2 .... 18.3, 18.4, 19.2, 20.4
para.1.3 .... 20.6
para.1.4 .... 6.11, 18.7
section 3 .... 13.1, 19.3, 19.5
para.3.1 .... 17.7, 19.3, 19.4, 19.5, 19.7
para.3.2 .... 10.2, 13.4, 19.5
para.3.3 .... 9.13, 9.15
para.3.4 .... 10.2, 19.2, 19.3, 19.4, 19.5
para.3.5 .... 9.13, 20.2, 20.3
para.3.6 .... 9.13

SRA Code of Conduct for Solicitors, RELs and RFLs – *continued*
section 4
para.4.1 .... 19.3
para.4.2 .... 11.1, 11.2
para.4.3 .... 11.2
section 5 .... 20.8
para.5.1(a), (b), (c), (e) 20.8
section 6 .... 17.10, 19.5
para.6.1 .... 16.1, 16.2, 16.6, 16.7, 17.10
para.6.2 .... 16.1, 16.2, 16.3, 16.5, 16.7, 17.10, 18.1
para.6.3 .... 12.4, 16.7, 17.1, 17.2, 17.3, 17.4, 17.6, 17.7, 17.8, 17.9, 17.10
para.6.4 .... 16.7, 17.5, 17.8, 17.9, 17.10, 18.1
(b), (d) 17.5
para.6.5 .... 16.7, 17.1, 17.5, 17.9, 17.10
(a), (b) 17.1
section 7 .... 9.3, 9.5
para.7.1 .... 9.9, 12.1
para.7.2 .... 9.3
para.7.3 .... 9.3, 9.4, 9.5, 9.7
para.7.4 .... 9.4
para.7.5 .... 9.3, 9.7
para.7.6 .... 9.3
para.7.7 .... 1.9, 9.3
paras.7.8, 7.9, 7.10 .... 9.3
para.7.11 .... 16.6
para.7.12 .... 1.9
section 8 .... 11.7, 19.3, 19.5
para.8.1 .... 3.16, 19.5
para.8.3 .... 19.3, 19.5
para.8.4 .... 19.5
para.8.5 .... 19.2
para.8.6 .... 11.7, 19.3, 19.4, 19.5, 19.7
para.8.7 .... 11.7, 15.4, 19.3, 19.5, 19.7
para.8.8 .... 9.11, 11.8, 20.1
para.8.9 .... 19.1
SRA Financial Services (Conduct of Business) Rules 13.1, 13.2, 13.3, 13.4
Part 2
rule 2 .... 13.2
rule 2.2 .... 13.3
rule 4 .... 13.2
rule 5 .... 13.2
rule 7 .... 13.2
Part 3 .... 13.1, 13.2
rule 9.1 .... 13.3
rule 10 .... 13.3
rule 11 .... 13.3
rule 12 .... 13.3
rule 13 .... 13.3
rule 14 .... 13.3
rule 15 .... 13.3

rule 16 .... 13.3
rule 17 .... 13.3
rule 18 .... 13.3
rule 19 .... 13.3
rule 20 .... 9.15, 13.3
rule 20.1 .... 13.4
rule 21 .... 9.13, 13.3
Part 4 .... 13.1
SRA Financial Services (Scope) Rules 13.1, 13.2, 13.3, 13.4
rule 2 .... 13.2
rules 3, 4 .... 13.1
rule 5 .... 13.1, 13.2
rule 5.1 .... 13.3
rule 5.2, (b) 13.3
rule 6 .... 13.1
SRA Indemnity Insurance Rules 9.11
SRA Overseas and Cross-border Practice Rules 9.10
SRA Principles 1.9, 4.11, 6.11, 7.10, 9.10, 9.11, 9.13, 9.14, 11.2, 12.4, 13.3, 17.2, 17.3, 17.4, 17.5, 17.6, 17.10, 18.1, 18.2, 18.4, 18.5, 18.6, 18.7, 19.1, 19.2, 19.3, 19.4, 19.5, 19.7, 19.8, 20.4, 20.5, 20.8, 20.9, 20.10
Principle 1 .... 1.9, 4.11, 6.11, 7.10, 12.1, 18.7, 20.5, 20.9
Principle 2 .... 1.9, 4.11, 6.11, 7.10, 11.2, 11.3, 12.4, 17.2, 17.4, 17.5, 18.4, 19.1, 19.2, 20.4, 20.8
Principle 3 .... 20.8
Principle 4 .... 1.9, 6.11, 7.10, 11.2, 19.1
Principle 5 .... 1.9, 4.11, 6.11, 7.10, 11.2, 11.3, 17.2, 17.4, 17.5, 18.4, 19.1
Principle 6 .... 19.2, 20.4
Principle 7 .... 11.3, 11.6, 17.2, 17.4, 17.5, 18.4, 18.5, 19.5, 20.8
SRA Regulatory and Disciplinary Rules 9.4, 9.5
rule 6 .... 9.5
SRA Transparency Rules 9.11, 11.3, 15.1, 15.2, 15.3, 15.4, 18.2, 19.2, 19.3, 19.4, 19.7
rule 1.5(f) 19.4
UK General Data Protection Regulation 12.1, 12.2, 12.4, 17.3

Abbreviations

5AMLD	Fifth Anti-Money Laundering Directive (EU) 2018/843
ABO	anti-bribery officer
ABS	alternative business structure
AFO	account freezing order
AML	anti-money laundering
AML Regulations	Money Laundering, Terrorist Financing and Transfer of Funds (Information on the Payer) Regulations 2017, SI 2017/692
BA 2010	Bribery Act 2010
BOOM	beneficial owner, officer or manager
CDD	client/customer due diligence
CFA 2017	Criminal Finances Act 2017
CFT	counter financing of terrorism
CGT	capital gains tax
COB Rules	SRA Financial Services (Conduct of Business) Rules
COFA	compliance officer for finance and administration
COLP	compliance officer for legal practice
CPD	continuing professional development
CPS	Crown Prosecution Service
DOB	date of birth
DPO	data protection officer
DSAR	data subject access request
EDD	enhanced due diligence
EEA	European Economic Area
FATF/GAFI	Financial Action Task Force/Groupe d'action financière
FCA	Financial Conduct Authority
FCDO	Foreign, Commonwealth and Development Office
FSMA 2000	Financial Services and Markets Act 2000
HMRC	Her Majesty's Revenue and Customs
HR	human resources
IDO	insurance distribution officer
IHT	inheritance tax
KPI	key performance indicator
LASPO 2012	Legal Aid Sentencing and Punishment of Offenders Act 2012

LeO	Legal Ombudsman
LLP	limited liability partnership
LSA 2007	Legal Services Act 2007
LSAG	Legal Sector Affinity Group
LSB	Legal Services Board
MLCO	money laundering compliance officer
MLRO	money laundering reporting officer
MSA 2015	Modern Slavery Act 2015
NCA	National Crime Agency
OFAC	Office of Foreign Assets Control
OFSI	Office of Financial Sanctions Implementation
OLC	Office for Legal Complaints
OPBAS	Office for Professional Bodies Approved Supervisors
PA	personal assistant
PC	practising certificate
PCPs	policies, controls and procedures
PEP	politically exposed person
POCA 2002	Proceeds of Crime Act 2002
PQE	post qualified experience
PSC	people with significant control
REL	registered European lawyer
RFL	registered foreign lawyer
SAMLA 2018	Sanctions and Anti-Money Laundering Act 2018
SAR	suspicious activity report
SDD	simplified due diligence
SDLT	stamp duty land tax
SDT	Solicitors Disciplinary Tribunal
SRA	Solicitors Regulation Authority
TA 2000	Terrorism Act 2000
TF	terrorist financing
TPMA	third party managed account
UN	United Nations
UWO	unexplained wealth order
VAT	value added tax

PART I

Anti-money laundering

CHAPTER 1

Anti-money laundering legislation

1.1 What is money laundering?

Put very simply, money laundering is the process by which proceeds of crime are cleaned. The stages of money laundering in general terms are:

(a) placement of monies into non-cash items;
(b) layering transactions to complicate tracing; and
(c) integration of the funds.

The proceeds of crime can crop up in unexpected ways. However, it is important to understand that without a criminal offence and the production of proceeds of crime (or criminal property, as it is known) there cannot be money laundering. Therefore if a criminal act has taken place but no proceeds have been gained, then there cannot be any money laundering.

The money laundering offences are set out in the Proceeds of Crime Act 2002 (POCA 2002) and explained at **1.3** below.

What are the compliance challenges?

It is important that personnel in firms understand what money laundering is and how it can crop up in their work so that they are able to prevent it from happening, spot it when it does happen and make the necessary report to the money laundering reporting officer (MLRO) if they are suspicious or know money laundering is or could be occurring.

What resources will help?

- Legal Sector Affinity Group (LSAG) guidance, 'Anti-money laundering guidance for the legal sector' (**www.lawsociety.org.uk/en/topics/anti-money-laundering/anti-money-laundering-guidance**), published January 2021. Provides clear guidance on money laundering and also provides a useful flowchart for determining whether a criminal offence under POCA 2002 may be occurring.

- Law Society guidance:
  - 'Quick guide to the Money Laundering Regulations 2017' (17 January 2020, **www.lawsociety.org.uk/topics/anti-money-laundering/quick-guide-to-the-mlrs**);
  - 'Warning signs of money laundering' (20 January 2020, **www.lawsociety.org.uk/topics/anti-money-laundering/money-laundering-warning-signs**).
- Online training and face-to-face (virtual or in-person) training will also assist.

Compliance tips – how to mitigate the risk of getting it wrong

- As set out above, it is vital that those within the firm understand the basic elements of what money laundering is and how it can occur in their work.
- To ensure that this is understood, the firm must mandate that training is undertaken by all those who have a role in spotting and mitigating risk (see **5.6**).
- The firm must have clear policies, controls and procedures (PCPs) which not only set out what money laundering is where appropriate but also address the risk of money laundering occurring (see **2.1**).

1.2 Generally speaking, what are the obligations on law firms?

Law firms and those within the firm including solicitors (called 'relevant persons' in the Money Laundering, Terrorist Financing and Transfer of Funds (Information on the Payer) Regulations 2017, SI 2017/692 (AML Regulations)), as 'independent legal professionals' (defined by reg.12), are obligated to follow the requirements of the regulations for certain activities.

These activities are as follows:

- the buying and selling of real property or business entities;
- the managing of client money, securities or other assets;
- the opening or management of bank, savings or securities accounts;
- the organisation of contributions necessary for the creation, operation or management of companies; and
- the creation, operation or management of trusts, companies, foundations or similar structures.

Further, law firms – through their activities in forming companies or acting or arranging for another person to act as an office holder of a company or a trustee of a trust or providing a registered office service – are classed as a 'trust or company service provider' (reg.12). Trust and company service providers are also required to meet the requirements of the regulations.

At a very high level, the regulations require firms and individuals to undertake the following:

- Undertake a firm-wide risk assessment to assess anti-money laundering (AML) risk in their firm and put in appropriate measures to mitigate it (reg.18).
- Have PCPs (regs.19, 20) to include:
  - risk management practices;
  - internal controls (see below);
  - undertaking customer due diligence (CDD) (regs.27, 28, 30, 33, 35, 37);
  - following the requirements for reliance (reg.39) and record keeping (reg.40);
  - monitoring and management of compliance with the PCPs and internally communicate the PCPs.
- Have internal controls (reg.21) to include:
  - appointment of MLRO and money laundering compliance officer (MLCO) with both being approved by the Solicitors Regulation Authority (SRA);
  - screening of employees;
  - implement an independent audit function;
- Undertake/implement AML and anti-terrorist financing training (reg.24).

What are the compliance challenges?

- The breadth of the AML Regulations can seem daunting. They need to be understood by MLROs and MLCOs to ensure that they are implemented properly.
- Sufficient time should be afforded to those who hold the roles of MLRO and MLCO to enable them to understand the regulations and carry out their role effectively.

What resources will help?

- The LSAG guidance 'Anti-money laundering guidance for the legal sector' (20 January 2021, **www.lawsociety.org.uk/topics/anti-money-laundering/anti-money-laundering-guidance**) sets out all of the requirements and is a very useful resource.
- Law Society guidance, e.g. 'Anti-money laundering (AML) compliance for small firms' (16 January 2020, **www.lawsociety.org.uk/topics/anti-money-laundering/aml-compliance-for-small-firms**) covering conducting an AML risk assessment; PCPs; and CDD and warning signs.
- SRA warning notice: 'Money laundering and terrorist financing' (updated 25 November 2019, **www.sra.org.uk/solicitors/guidance/money-laundering-terrorist-financing/**).
- *Financial Crime: A Compliance Manual* (Rebecca Atkinson, Law Society Publishing, 2021).

Compliance tips – how to mitigate the risk of getting it wrong

- MLROs and MLCOs are encouraged to read the regulations (they are not long and this will give the best understanding of what the regulations require) and the LSAG guidance.

1.3 What is POCA 2002 and what are the offences under it?

POCA 2002 creates money laundering offences and the regime of reporting suspicious activities to authorities.

Perhaps obviously given its name, POCA 2002 is concerned with criminal property. This is defined as a person's benefit from criminal conduct and the alleged offender knows or suspects that it constitutes or represents such benefit.

Where there is no criminal property, no money laundering offence can follow – though it is still possible to commit an offence of failure to report suspicions.

The offences created by POCA 2002 are listed below.

POCA 2002, s.327 – Concealing

A person commits an offence if he or she conceals, disguises, converts, transfers criminal property or removes criminal property from England and Wales, Scotland or Northern Ireland.

POCA 2002, s.328 – Arrangements

A person commits an offence if he or she enters into or becomes concerned in an arrangement which he or she knows or suspects facilitates (by whatever means) the acquisition, retention, use or control of criminal property by or on behalf of another person.

POCA 2002, s.329 – Acquisition, use and possession

A person commits an offence if he or she acquires, uses or has possession of criminal property.

POCA 2002, ss.330, 331 and 332 – Failure to disclose offences

For a section 330 offence (failure to disclose: regulated sector) to be committed, the following conditions need to be met. A person commits an offence if:

- he or she knows or suspects, or has reasonable grounds for knowing or suspecting, that another person is engaged in money laundering; and

- the information on which his suspicion is based comes in the course of business in the regulated sector; and
- he or she fails to disclose that knowledge or suspicion, or reasonable grounds for suspicion, as soon as practicable to a nominated officer or the National Crime Agency (NCA).

For a section 331 offence (failure to disclose: nominated officer in the regulated sector) to occur the nominated officer (MLRO), having received a disclosure under section 330 and forming the required knowledge or suspicion or reasonable grounds to know or suspect money laundering, fails to disclose this as soon as practicable to the NCA.

For a section 332 offence (failure to disclose: nominated officer in the non-regulated sector) to occur a nominated officer appointed in a firm that conducts non-regulated activities who fails to make a disclosure when they know or suspect that another person is engaged in money laundering will commit an offence. This test is a subjective and not objective. Practically it means that where an MLRO receives information in relation to a piece of non-regulated work, for example litigation, the MLRO needs to consider whether they have an obligation to make a disclosure and not simply to decide not to on the basis that the work is unregulated.

POCA 2002, s.333 – Tipping off

A person commits an offence if he or she discloses to another that he or she has made a suspicious activity report (SAR) to a constable, HM Revenue and Customs (HMRC), the MLRO of the person's firm or the NCA, and that disclosure is likely to prejudice any investigation that might be conducted following the SAR. For this offence to occur, the information needs to come to the person in the course of business in the regulated sector.

POCA 2002, s.342 – Prejudicing an investigation

For this offence to occur, the person knows or suspects that an appropriate officer is acting in connection with a confiscation investigation, civil recovery investigation or a money laundering investigation which is being or about to be conducted and makes a disclosure about it which is likely to prejudice an investigation or that person falsifies, conceals, destroys or otherwise disposes of, or causes or permits the falsification, concealment, destruction or disposal of, documents which are relevant to the investigation.

What are the compliance challenges?

- All relevant personnel in a firm must understand the POCA 2002 offences.

What resources will help?

- Law Society guidance, e.g.:
  - 'Tipping off a client' (21 January 2020, **www.lawsociety.org.uk/en/topics/anti-money-laundering/tipping-off-a-client**);
  - 'Responding to a financial crime investigation' (24 January 2022, **www.lawsociety.org.uk/topics/anti-money-laundering/responding-to-a-financial-crime-investigation**);
  - Law Society 'question and answers guidance' e.g. 'Is outlining our reporting obligations in client care letters "tipping off"?' (**www.lawsociety.org.uk/Contact-or-visit-us/Helplines/Practice-advice-service/Q-and-As** and under 'Topic' choose 'Anti-money laundering');
  - 'Anti-money laundering in the property market' (9 September 2019, **www.lawsociety.org.uk/topics/property/anti-money-laundering-in-property**);
  - see also the Law Society's AML resource page (**www.lawsociety.org.uk/topics/anti-money-laundering/**).
- The firm's policy should make the above offences clear, and all relevant personnel must receive appropriate training.

Compliance tips – how to mitigate the risk of getting it wrong

- Firms must ensure that their AML policy clearly spells out the POCA 2002 offences and that personnel receive training on a regular basis. See **5.6–5.8**.

1.4 What are the defences to offences under POCA 2002?

POCA 2002 provides defences to the money laundering offences that it creates. Below is a high-level overview of these defences.

POCA 2002, s.338 – Authorised disclosure

In order to avoid committing an offence under sections 327, 328 and 329, section 338 allows an authorised disclosure of the actual or suspected money laundering in defence of a principal money laundering offence. The section sets out that the disclosure must be made either before money laundering has occurred, whilst it is occurring but as soon as there is suspicion or after it has occurred if there was good reason not to disclose earlier and the disclosure is made as soon as practicable. Where a disclosure is an authorised one, regulatory requirements (such as confidentiality) will not be breached.

Reasonable excuse not to make a disclosure

Here a defence to a principal money laundering offence is available if a person intended to make an authorised disclosure but had a reasonable excuse not to do so. Reasonable excuse has not been defined by the courts and LSAG advises that in its view information giving rise to knowledge or suspicion of money laundering which is privileged (and where the crime/fraud exception does not apply) will afford the relevant person a reasonable excuse defence to not making a disclosure.

LSAG also sets out the following possible reasonable excuses:

- if it is clear that a regulator or enforcement authority (in the UK or elsewhere) is already aware of the suspected criminal conduct or money laundering and the reporter does not have any additional information which might assist the regulator or enforcement authority;
- if the only information that a reporter would be providing for the purposes of an authorised disclosure or a report under section 330 is information entirely within the public domain; or
- if all the suspected predicate offending occurs outside the UK and all the suspected money laundering occurs outside the UK and there is otherwise no UK nexus to the suspected criminality.

Adequate consideration defence

This defence applies if there was adequate consideration for acquiring, using and possessing the criminal property, unless the person knows or suspects that those goods or services may help another carry out criminal conduct.

Privileged circumstances

This applies to an offence of failure to disclose. Information being provided in privileged circumstances is not the same as legal professional privilege and is a design of POCA 2002 to comply with the exemptions from reporting set out in the European directives.

Privileged circumstances means information communicated:

- by a client, or a representative of a client, in connection with the giving of legal advice to the client; or
- by a client, or by a representative of a client, seeking legal advice from you; or
- by a person in connection with legal proceedings or contemplated legal proceedings.

If the goal of the giving of the information is to further a criminal purpose, then the exemption will not apply.

Lack of training

This defence is available for those employees within the regulated sector.

What are the compliance challenges?

- As above, all relevant personnel in a firm must understand the POCA 2002 offences.

What resources will help?

- The firm's policy should make the above offences clear, and all relevant personnel must receive appropriate training.

Compliance tips – how to mitigate the risk of getting it wrong

- Firms must ensure that their AML policy clearly spells out the POCA 2002 offences and that personnel receive training on a regular basis. See **1.3**.

1.5 What is the Terrorism Act 2000 and what are the offences and defences under it?

The Terrorism Act 2000 (TA 2000) criminalises the participation in terrorist activities and also the provision of monetary support for such activities. Firms need to be aware of the requirements under TA 2000 as well as under the AML Regulations. LSAG provide a thorough run-through of the offences and defences – these are set out below at a high level.

1.5.1 Principal offences under TA 2000

TA 2000, s.15 – Fundraising

Section 15 sets out that a person commits an offence if:

- the person invites another to provide money or other property; or
- the person receives money or other property; or
- the person provides money or other property; and
- in the case of inviting or receiving monies or other property, the person intends that it should be used; or
- the person has reasonable cause to suspect that it may be used for the purposes of terrorism; and
- when providing money or other property, the person knows or has reasonable cause to suspect that it will or may be used for the purposes of terrorism.

It is not a defence that the monies or other property is payment for goods and services.

TA 2000, s.16 – Use and possession

Here a person commits an offence if the person uses money or other property for the purpose of terrorism. The offence is committed if the person possesses money or other property and intends that it should be used, or has reasonable cause to suspect that it may be used, for the purposes of terrorism.

TA 2000, s.17 – Funding arrangements

Here a person commits an offence if the person enters into or becomes concerned in an arrangement as a result of which money or other property is made available or is to be made available to another, and that person knows or has reasonable cause to suspect that it will or may be used for the purposes of terrorism.

TA 2000, s.18 – Money laundering

Here a person commits an offence if the person enters into or becomes concerned in an arrangement which facilitates in the following ways the retention or control by or on behalf of another person of terrorist property:

- by concealment;
- by removal from the jurisdiction;
- by transfer to nominees; or
- in any other way.

It is a defence for a person charged with an offence to prove that the person did not know and had no reasonable cause to suspect that the arrangement related to terrorist property.

For the purposes of this offence, the meaning of arrangement is the same as under POCA 2002 (s.328).

1.5.2 Defences to principal offences under TA 2000

The Terrorism Act 2000 and Proceeds of Crime Act 2002 (Amendment) Regulations 2007, SI 2007/3398 created three new defences to the principal offences under TA 2000 (ss.21ZA, 21ZB and 21ZC) in addition to an existing defence of police cooperation (s.21). The defences are as follows.

TA 2000, s.21 – Police cooperation

A person does not commit an offence under TA 2000, ss.15–18 if the person acts with the express consent of a constable and a disclosure is made as to the person's suspicion or belief that the money or other property is terrorist property and provides the information on which that suspicion or believe is based. The defence does not apply if the constable forbids the person to continue involvement in the transaction or arrangement and the person continues that involvement. The section also sets out that this defence is also available to employees who report their suspicions internally using the procedure set out by their employer.

TA 2000, s.21ZA – Prior consent

A person does not commit an offence under TA 2000, ss.15–18 if the person made a disclosure of his or her suspicion and consent is given to becoming involved in the transaction or arrangement. The disclosure has to have been made prior to involvement. This disclosure would be made by way of a SAR.

TA 2000, s.21ZB – Consent

A person does not commit an offence under TA 2000, ss.15–18 if after becoming involved a disclosure is made and there is a reasonable excuse for the person's failure to make the disclosure before becoming involved. Again, this disclosure would be made by way of a SAR. The defence does not apply if an authorised person forbids the person to continue involvement in the transaction or arrangement and the person continues that involvement.

TA 2000, s.21ZC – Reasonable excuse for failure to disclose

It is a defence for a person charged with an offence under TA 2000, ss.15–18 if they intended to make a disclosure but had a reasonable excuse for not doing so.

1.5.3 Failure to disclose offences under TA 2000

There are two offences for failing to disclose a terrorism offence. One relates to the non-regulated sector and one to the regulated sector.

TA 2000, s.19 sets out that anyone commits an offence if they do not disclose as soon as reasonably practicable a belief or suspicion that another person is committing a terrorist financing offence and the information on which that belief or suspicion is based.

TA 2000, s.21A (inserted by the Anti-terrorism, Crime and Security Act 2001) creates an offence for those in the regulated sector who fail to make a disclosure to a constable or the firm's nominated officer where they know or suspect or have reasonable grounds to suspect that another person is committing or attempting to commit an offence under the Act.

1.5.4 Defences to the failure to disclose offences under TA 2000

There are two defences available to those who stand accused of failure to disclosure offences under TA 2000. These are:

1. Reasonable excuse for not making a disclosure.
2. The information on which the belief or suspicion is based was given in privileged circumstances without an intention to further a criminal purpose. This defence applies to those who are employed by or are in partnership with a professional legal adviser and the information is given in privileged circumstances.

1.5.5 Tipping off offences and defences under TA 2000

Offences

1. **Disclosing a SAR**

   Under TA 2000, s.21D(1) a person commits an offence if they disclose that a SAR was made and that disclosure is likely to prejudice any investigation that might be conducted following the SAR. The information which is disclosed should have come to the person in the course of business in the regulated sector.

2. **Disclosing an investigation**

   Under TA 2000, s.21D(3) it is an offence to disclose that an investigation into allegations that an offence under the Act has been committed is being contemplated or is being carried out and that disclosure is likely to prejudice that investigation and the information on which the disclosure is based came to the person in the course of a business in the regulated sector. The person does not need to be aware that a SAR has been submitted.

Defences

1. **Disclosures within an undertaking or group**

   TA 2000, s.21E sets out that it is not an offence for an employee, officer or partner of a practice to disclose a SAR if the disclosure is to an employee, officer or partner of the same undertaking. Further, under section 21E(4) a legal professional adviser will not commit an offence under section 21D if:

   (a) the disclosure is to a professional legal adviser or a relevant professional adviser,
   (b) both the person making the disclosure and the person to whom it is made carry on business in the United Kingdom or an EEA state or in a country or territory imposing equivalent money laundering requirements, and
   (c) those persons perform their professional activities within different undertakings that share common ownership, management or control.

2. **Other permitted disclosures between institutions**

Under TA 2000, s.21F(2)(a), a legal professional will not commit the offence of tipping off if the disclosure relates to:

(i) a client or former client of the institution or adviser making the disclosure and the institution or adviser to whom it is made,
(ii) a transaction involving them both, or
(iii) the provision of a service involving them both ...

The disclosure must be made for the purpose of preventing an offence under the Act and the person to whom the disclosure is made must be situated in a European Economic Area (EEA) state or country/territory imposing equivalent money laundering requirements. Further both parties must have equivalent duties of confidentiality and protection of personal data.

3. **Other permitted disclosures**

Under TA 2000, s.21G, a person will not commit an offence of tipping off if the disclosure is to a client for the purposes of dissuading the client from engaging in conduct that amounts to an offence. This only applies to the regulated sector.

What are the compliance challenges?

- Like offences under POCA 2002, all relevant personnel in a firm must understand the TA 2000 offences. Law firms are seen to be at low risk of being utilised for terrorist financing. However, the firm's policy must still make reference to TA 2000 and set out the offences.

What resources will help?

- The firm's policy should make the above offences clear and all relevant personnel must receive appropriate training.

Compliance tips – how to mitigate the risk of getting it wrong

- Firms must ensure that their AML policy clearly spells out the TA 2000 offences, and that personnel receive training on a regular basis.

1.6 What is a BOOM? How do I register a BOOM? When do I need to register a BOOM?

A BOOM is a 'beneficial owner, officer or manager' of a law firm. Under AML Regulations 2017, reg.26, no person may be a BOOM in a firm without the approval of their supervisory authority. For most firms this will be the SRA.

The BOOM regime was first introduced under the AML Regulations and the SRA took the decision to treat all partners in law firms as BOOMs and approve them as such. Therefore, when firms look at their partners in the mySRA platform, they may find that all the partners have been approved as BOOMs and are designated as 'money laundering officers'.

However, not all partners are a BOOM.

A BOOM is:

- a beneficial owner who exercises ultimate control over management of the firm or someone who owns or controls more than 25 per cent of the shares or voting rights in the firm;
- an officer is someone who is a director, secretary, chief executive, member of the committee of management or a person purporting to act in such capacity or an individual who is acting as controller. In relation to a partnership an officer is a partner, a manager, secretary or similar officer of the partnership or someone purporting to act in such a capacity;
- a manager is a person who has control, authority or responsibility for managing the business of that firm and includes the nominated officer i.e. the MLRO and also the MLCO (see **1.7** and **1.8**, respectively).

To register a BOOM, an application to the SRA must be made in the prescribed format and approval given before the individual who is to become a BOOM can take post if their post will bring them into the scope of the regulations. The applicant will give the SRA enough information for a criminal record check to be conducted, and provided no conviction of the offences under AML Regulations 2017, Sched.3 has occurred, the SRA must approve the BOOM.

If later the BOOM is convicted of a criminal offence listed under Sched.3, the approval of the BOOM will cease to be valid and those activities the person was conducting that brought him or her within scope of the regulations must cease. The individual and firm should report the conviction to the SRA within 30 days of the conviction (if the person convicted is reporting) or from when they became aware (if the firm is reporting).

If a person ceases to be a BOOM, then the SRA must be notified within 14 days.

What are the compliance challenges?

- A person must not act in their capacity as a BOOM until approved. Breaching the AML Regulations is a criminal offence. It is therefore vital that each firm firstly undertakes a stock take of their BOOMs and seeks any approval needed and a new BOOM obtains approval before undertaking their role. The BOOM regime is arguably not well known and it is important that those in the firm are aware of it, for example human resources (HR).

What resources will help?

- AML Regulations 2017, reg.26.
- LSAG guidance, 'Anti-money laundering guidance for the legal sector' (20 January 2021, **www.lawsociety.org.uk/topics/anti-money-laundering/anti-money-laundering-guidance**).
- Firms should check mySRA to see who is noted as a BOOM, and if it is incorrect, correct it as soon possible.

Compliance tips – how to mitigate the risk of getting it wrong

- Make sure relevant people in the firm (such as HR and senior leadership) understand what a BOOM is and that supervisory approval needs to be given (i.e. by the SRA) before the BOOM can take post.
- Make sure the firm has a method of spotting when a BOOM is taking post and a process for applying for BOOM approval in good time.

1.7 What is an MLRO and what is their role? Who should be the MLRO?

AML Regulations 2017, reg.21(3) requires law firms to appoint a nominated officer known as an MLRO. The role of the MLRO is to receive reports made internally by those within the firm, and where appropriate make SARs to the NCA. See **Chapter 4** for further detail.

The MLRO should be of sufficient seniority to be able to make decisions about when to make a report to the NCA without being restrained from doing so. Further, if the MLRO needs to make a decision about whether the firm can continue acting, the MLRO will need to be of sufficient seniority to make such a decision. As such, often MLROs are partners or those who hold senior management roles in firms.

What are the compliance challenges?

- Making sure to appoint the right person to the role of MLRO is vital. If the MLRO is not sufficiently senior they may find they are challenged when making decisions on whether to continue acting in a matter or making a SAR.
- The MLRO also needs to have a thorough grasp of the concepts of suspicion of money laundering, when suspicion can and should arise, how to make a report to the NCA together with how to draft the same, as well as what the reporting regime is designed to do. To that end, MLROs need to receive adequate regular training.
- Firms must ensure that the MLRO has sufficient time to undertake the role. Firms must understand that being the MLRO is a job and not just a job title.

What resources will help?

- LSAG provides guidance on the role of the MLRO and reporting suspicions and should be consulted: 'Anti-money laundering guidance for the legal sector' (20

January 2021, **www.lawsociety.org.uk/topics/anti-money-laundering/anti-money-laundering-guidance**).

- External MLRO training should also be sought out, unless an internal AML expert within the firm is available to provide training.
- Law Society materials:
  - The Law Society produces many guidance pieces – see its AML resources page at **www.lawsociety.org.uk/topics/anti-money-laundering/**.
  - The Law Society also has useful 'questions and answers' guidance (**www.lawsociety.org.uk/Contact-or-visit-us/Helplines/Practice-advice-service/Q-and-As** and under 'Topic' choose 'Anti-money laundering').
- The MLRO should read the SRA guidance:
  - 'Improper use of client account as a banking facility' (updated 25 November 2019, **www.sra.org.uk/solicitors/guidance/improper-use-client-account-banking-facility/**);
  - 'Money laundering and terrorist financing suspicious activity reports' (updated 25 November 2019, **www.sra.org.uk/solicitors/guidance/money-laundering-terrorist-financing-suspicious-activity-reports/**).

Compliance tips – how to mitigate the risk of getting it wrong

- Make sure the MLRO is suitable and of sufficient seniority, and clearly communicate within the firm who the MLRO is and what their role encompasses.
- Ensure that the MLRO has sufficient knowledge and time to dedicate to the role, and adequate training to undertake the role.

1.8 What is a MLCO and what is their role? Who should be the MLCO?

AML Regulations 2017, reg.21(1) requires firms to appoint a person who is a member of the firm's board (or equivalent management body if there is no board) or instead is a member of the firm's senior management as an officer responsible for the firm's compliance with the regulations. This role is known as the firm's money laundering compliance officer (MLCO).

The need to appoint an MLCO is dependent on the nature of the business and size of the firm. It follows therefore that not all firms will need to appoint an MLCO. Certainly, very small practices are unlikely to need to appoint an MLCO. Alternatively, it may be that the MLRO already fulfils this function but is not designated as the MLCO too but should be. See **1.9** below for an explanation of how the roles may overlap.

The regulations do not define what aspect of the regulations the MLCO is responsible for, and in this sense the regulation here must be interpreted widely, and as such it is the MLCO's role to be responsible for compliance with all aspects of the AML Regulations. This therefore has to include the firm-wide AML risk assessment (see **Chapter 2**) and all PCPs (see **2.1**).

What are the compliance challenges?

- Like the MLRO role, it is important to make sure to appoint the right person to the role of MLCO. If the MLCO is not sufficiently senior, they may find they are challenged when implementing AML compliance in the firm.
- The MLCO also needs to have a thorough grasp of all aspects of AML compliance, and as such, unless they are already well versed in the regulations, they should be provided with training.
- Firms must ensure that the MLCO has sufficient time and resources to undertake the role (including additional personnel where needed). Firms must understand that being the MLCO is a job and not just a job title.

What resources will help?

- Any MLCO would be very wise to read the AML Regulations from start to finish, and then read the LSAG guidance 'Anti-money laundering guidance for the legal sector' (20 January 2021, **www.lawsociety.org.uk/topics/anti-money-laundering/anti-money-laundering-guidance**).
- The Law Society has a wealth of guidance that can be found at:
  - its AML resources page at **www.lawsociety.org.uk/topics/anti-money-laundering/**;
  - 'Anti-money laundering in the property market' (9 September 2019, **www.lawsociety.org.uk/topics/property/anti-money-laundering-in-property**);
  - the Law Society also has useful 'questions and answers' guidance (**www.lawsociety.org.uk/Contact-or-visit-us/Helplines/Practice-advice-service/Q-and-As** and under 'Topic' choose 'Anti-money laundering').
- MLCOs should also read the relevant SRA guidance materials (see **www.sra.org.uk/solicitors/guidance/topic/money-laundering/**).

Compliance tips – how to mitigate the risk of getting it wrong

The consequences of getting the MLCO appointment wrong could be very serious. If the MLCO doesn't understand the regulations or fails to dedicate time to ensuring that the firm's PCPs meet the regulatory requirements and that they are followed, money laundering could occur, resulting in criminal prosecutions and regulatory action by the SRA. Below are some quick-fire tips on how to ensure that this doesn't happen:

- appoint an MLCO that is sufficiently senior in the firm (i.e. sits on the board or is board level);
- ensure that the MLCO understands the AML Regulations, and in particular the PCPs requirements;
- ensure that the MLCO receives any required training;
- conduct an audit of compliance on a regular basis (in one form or another, every one to two years) – see **5.9–5.10**. This will ensure that the firm is maintaining compliance and that any changes can be made as necessary.

1.9 What crossover is there between the MLRO/MLCO and the COLP and COFA?

In addition to an MLRO/MLCO, firms may have a compliance officer for legal practice (COLP) and/or compliance officer for finance and administration (COFA). It is often the case that one individual will take on some or all of these roles, depending on the size of the firm. These roles certainly overlap, and if undertaken by more than one person can provide an environment of often much-needed support amongst role-holders.

It is the MLRO's sole decision as to whether there exists suspicion or knowledge such that a report to the NCA needs to be made. How that information came to the attention of the MLRO is of interest to the MLCO, as they are tasked with making sure that relevant members of staff are aware of their regulatory obligations and also that the MLRO undertakes their role effectively. Likewise, this will be of interest to the COLP, who has an interest in ensuring that the relevant SRA Principles and aspects of the SRA Codes of Conduct (all available at **www.sra.org.uk/solicitors/standards-regulations/**) are complied with. In terms of the SRA Principles, that may be relevant to a suspicion of money laundering, these could be to act 'in a way that upholds the constitutional principle of the rule of law, and the proper administration of justice' (Principle 1); to act 'in a way that upholds public trust and confidence in the solicitors' profession and in legal services provided by authorised persons' (Principle 2); to act 'with honesty' (Principle 4); and to act 'with integrity' (Principle 5).

Of relevance also are the reporting requirements of solicitors who are obliged to report to the SRA any facts or matters which they reasonably believe are capable of amounting to a serious breach of the regulatory requirements (SRA Code of Conduct for Solicitors, registered European lawyers (RELs) and registered foreign lawyers (RFLs), para.7.7). A solicitor will have discharged this obligation by reporting the same to the COLP on the understanding that the COLP will make a report to the SRA (SRA Code of Conduct for Solicitors, RELs and RFLs, para.7.12).

The COFA is mainly concerned with compliance with the SRA Accounts Rules (available at **www.sra.org.uk/solicitors/standards-regulations/**), and as such will need to ensure adherence to SRA Accounts Rules, rule 3.3 in particular and it must be remembered that the genesis of that rule was in fact money laundering. This rule sets out that no monies must come through the firm's client account that do not relate to the delivery of regulated services. In essence this means that monies cannot be received by the client or other party for the purchase of goods or payments that do not relate to the work at hand. If money laundering is occurring through the firm, it is possible that this rule is also being breached. Thus, the COFA has a role to play in the fight against money laundering within the firm also.

Understanding how these roles overlap highlights that ensuring that money laundering does not occur never sits in one place within the firm, and instead is a collective responsibility in practice.

What are the compliance challenges?

- It is important that each role-holder understands their role and has the time and capability to fulfil the role to the best of their ability. If the role-holder is not able to do this, non-compliance in the firm could occur.

What resources will help?

- For MLROs and MLCOs:
  - the AML Regulations themselves;
  - the LSAG guidance 'Anti-money laundering guidance for the legal sector' (20 January 2021, **www.lawsociety.org.uk/topics/anti-money-laundering/anti-money-laundering-guidance**);
  - the Law Society guidance; and
  - SRA warning notices and guidance;

  should be considered (see **1.7** and **1.8** above at '*What resources will help?*').
- For COLPs, a full understanding of the SRA Codes of Conduct and regulatory framework is necessary (**www.sra.org.uk/solicitors/standards-regulations/**).
- For COFAs, a full understanding of the SRA Accounts Rules (**www.sra.org.uk/solicitors/standards-regulations/accounts-rules/**).

Compliance tips – how to mitigate the risk of getting it wrong

- Appoint role-holders that are sufficiently senior in the firm to fulfil their roles.
- Ensure that each role-holder understands the area of regulation or law he or she is responsible for ensuring the firm comply with.
- Ensure that each role-holder receives required training.

1.10 What is the definition of tax adviser and why does it matter?

On 10 January 2020, the Fifth Anti-Money Laundering Directive (5AMLD) (EU) 2018/843 brought in a new definition of tax adviser. This is important because those that are deemed to be undertaking work within the definition of tax adviser are regulated for AML purposes and must undertake full CDD on their client and matter.

The definition of tax adviser is now: 'a firm or sole practitioner who by way of business provides material aid, or assistance or advice, in connection with the tax affairs of other persons, whether provided directly or through a third party, when providing such services' (AML Regulations 2017, reg.11).

This definition is much wider than the previous iteration, and as such the SRA issued 'Tax adviser guidance' (**www.sra.org.uk/globalassets/documents/solicitors/tax-adviser-guidance.pdf?version=4aade6**). This guidance is useful in understanding the SRA's interpretation of the legislation and should be consulted.

Below are some useful extracts from the SRA guidance (p.3):

> Recognising tax adviser services that are in scope can be challenging because this is so broadly defined in the regulations. Services that are normally out of scope may, with a subtle change, be brought within scope. For example, employment law would generally be seen as out of scope. But advising on the tax implications of a settlement between the employer and employee could draw the matter into scope.
>
> Being able to determine when this happens, and when you may need to apply the requirements in the regulations is very important so that you are able to appropriately risk assess the client and undertake fully compliant customer due diligence. Failure to do so might mean you are risking facilitating money laundering and might be opening yourself to criminal sanctions and disciplinary action. This can also help mitigate against the risk of committing an offence under the Proceeds of Crime Act (2002) or Terrorism Act (2000).
>
> You might choose to protect against this risk by applying AML-compliant onboarding procedures (client and matter risk assessments, customer due diligence etc) for all clients, whether the service you are asked to provide is in scope or not. This can help mitigate the risk of, subsequently providing your client with a service where the regulations apply (also known as 'passporting'), without maintaining AML compliance.

The SRA guidance also has a table which sets out how work that was out of the scope of the regulations might become in scope.

It is clear that work that might be considered to be out of scope of the AML Regulations can become in scope during the retainer due to this wider definition of tax adviser and as such, areas that were once considered safely outside of the reach of the AML Regulations no longer have that comfort. It is therefore important to understand the definition and apply PCPs accordingly. One option is to treat all work regardless of type as falling within the scope of the AML Regulations. This would ensure that there was no responsibility on fee earners to understand when out of scope work has come in scope and minimises the risk of a failure to follow the AML Regulations and in particular conduct CDD.

What are the compliance challenges?

- Understanding when a piece of work that was out of scope of the AML Regulations has become in scope and what this means. For example, if a piece of litigation work was to be undertaken and was therefore outside the scope of the AML Regulations, but then settlement was being negotiated which had a tax element, this is likely to mean that the work has become in scope. If no due diligence was undertaken up to that point, then full CDD would need to be undertaken. This could cause delay to the work being conducted and upset the client.
- The fee earner needs to understand and spot that the work has now become in scope of the AML Regulations and undertake CDD. The risk here is that the fee earner may not spot that the work has become regulated.
- Thought needs to be given as to whether to adopt the same level of CDD for all matters regardless of whether they are in scope or not as a safeguard to CDD not be undertaken when the work changes.

What resources will help?

- The SRA have published guidance on the definition of tax adviser: 'Tax adviser guidance' (**www.sra.org.uk/globalassets/documents/solicitors/tax-adviser-guidance.pdf?version=4aade6**) and this is a very useful resource.
- The SRA have also produced a webinar on this topic: 'Anti-money laundering: what tax advisers need to know' (16 February 2021, **www.sra.org.uk/sra/news/events/on-demand-events/aml-tax-advisers/**).

Compliance tips – how to mitigate the risk of getting it wrong

- If your firm has decided not to adopt the same level of CDD regardless of the work that is being undertaken then it is vital that fee earners working in the areas that are considered not to be caught by the AML Regulations (broadly speaking litigation, some advisory work and will writing) understand when their matter becomes in scope of the regulations.
- Fee earners must understand that they do not need to be providing the tax advice themselves, but can be caught by simply assisting in the implementation of the advice given by others.

1.11 We do not give tax advice, so do we need to apply for supervision with the SRA under the AML Regulations?

All firms that undertake activities within the scope of the AML Regulations must apply to the SRA (or another supervisor if not regulated by the SRA, such as HMRC) to be supervised under the AML Regulations. Those who do not take AML regulated work do not need to apply for such supervision. As outlined above, the definition of tax adviser is very wide. It is therefore foreseeable that work that starts life outside of scope of the AML Regulations can become in scope.

The wider definition of tax adviser came into force on 10 January 2020. The SRA gave law firms until 10 January 2021 to apply for the required supervision. Those firms who were already supervised by the SRA for their work in scope of the regulations should check with the SRA via its contact centre (because it is not possible to check via mySRA portal) whether the firm is also supervised for tax adviser work.

Failure to apply for or be supervised when undertaking such work could lead to enforcement action by the SRA and prosecution by the authorities.

Every firm who considers that it does not provide work that is in scope must consider the widened definition of tax adviser and if it is foreseeable that their work could come within scope they need to make the appropriate application to the SRA for supervision.

What are the compliance challenges?

- Determining whether work may or may not come into scope later in a retainer may be challenging. Firms are encouraged to err on the side of caution and consider applying for supervision by the SRA.

What resources will help?

- The SRA has published guidance on the definition of tax adviser: 'Tax adviser guidance' (**www.sra.org.uk/globalassets/documents/solicitors/tax-adviser-guidance.pdf?version=4aade6**) and this is a very useful resource.
- Further, the SRA has produced a webinar on this topic: 'Anti-money laundering: what tax advisers need to know' (16 February 2021, **www.sra.org.uk/sra/news/events/on-demand-events/aml-tax-advisers/**).

Compliance tips – how to mitigate the risk of getting it wrong

- Firms need to carefully read the SRA guidance, watch the webinar and consider if they need to apply for supervision under the AML Regulations.

CHAPTER 2

Risk assessments

PRACTICE-WIDE RISK ASSESSMENTS

2.1 What is the obligation to conduct a practice-wide risk assessment?

Money Laundering, Terrorist Financing and Transfer of Funds (Information on the Payer) Regulations 2017, SI 2017/692 (AML Regulations), reg.18 sets out that firms must take appropriate steps to identify and assess the risks of money laundering and terrorist financing in their practice. The regulation further sets out that the firm must consider information available from their supervisory body, in the case of most firms the Solicitors Regulation Authority (SRA), and risk factors relating to:

- its clients;
- the countries and geographic areas in which the firm operates;
- the firm's products or services;
- the firm's transactions; and
- the delivery channels of that service.

The regulation also sets out that the firm must consider the size and nature of the firm and keep a record of all steps undertaken to assess the above-mentioned risk factors. Finally, the regulation goes on to state that the SRA can request sight of a firm's risk assessment.

The purpose of the practice-wide risk assessment is to assess the anti-money laundering (AML) risk in the firm's practice and as a consequence of that risk assessment put in place policies, controls and procedures (PCPs) to mitigate those risks.

What are the compliance challenges?

- The person undertaking the risk assessment must have full understanding and knowledge of the firm's practice in order to assess the AML risk within it.
- The person must therefore have an appropriate position within the firm to undertake the assessment and speak to various stakeholders. Ordinarily, the firm's money laundering reporting officer (MLRO) or money laundering compliance officer (MLCO) will conduct the assessment or oversee it if conducted by someone else.
- The assessment should be shared with the firm's board or equivalent.

What resources will help?

- Since the implementation of the AML Regulations 2017, the SRA has increased its focus on AML compliance significantly, and to that end has conducted a number of firm visits as well as requested firms' AML risk assessment for their review. As a consequence of these visits and reviews, the SRA has issued the following resources:
    - SRA warning notice: 'Compliance with the money laundering regulations – firm risk assessment' (updated 25 November 2019, **www.sra.org.uk/solicitors/guidance/compliance-money-laundering-regulations-firm-risk-assessment/**);
    - SRA guidance: 'Firm risk assessments' (updated 25 November 2019, **www.sra.org.uk/solicitors/guidance/firm-risk-assessments/**).
- The Legal Sector Affinity Group (LSAG) guidance, 'Anti-money laundering guidance for the legal sector' (20 January 2021, **www.lawsociety.org.uk/topics/anti-money-laundering/anti-money-laundering-guidance**) has a very useful guide outlining what a firm's AML risk assessment should cover and how that might be approached.

Compliance tips – how to mitigate the risk of getting it wrong

- Practice-wide risk assessments are only as good as the implementation behind them. There is little point in spending time and energy putting together a practice-wide risk assessment if that does not then feed into the firm's PCPs whether that be deciding client due diligence (CDD) to be undertaken based on risk or screening of employees (see **5.1–5.5**). It is important to therefore see the risk assessment as a first stage document which leads on to actions to mitigate AML risk. To not see it this way may well mean the risk assessment is not as effective as it should be.

2.2 What format should a practice-wide risk assessment take?

There is no set format. Firms can complete their assessment as a spreadsheet, or a Word document, or maybe a table. The SRA has produced a template risk assessment that firms may wish to use as a starting point (**www.sra.org.uk/globalassets/documents/solicitors/firm-wide-risk-assessment-template.docx?version=4a4d74**). However, be aware that any template must be amended to suit the firm, and the SRA has been critical in the past of firms it has audited who have used a template and not tailored it to the firm.

What are the compliance challenges?

- The risk assessment must be in a format that is understood by those who need to consider it (MLRO, MLCO, board, risk team, etc.). Risk assessments can become complicated if the firm has many practice areas, clients from many geographical areas and so on and as such a summary version for firm-wide circulation should be considered.
- The risk assessment must feed into the PCPs set by the firm to address the AML risk that the assessment highlights.
- Firms should consider what format would suit the firm.

What resources will help?

- The SRA has produced guidance on the requirement for a firm-wide AML risk assessment guidance entitled 'Firm risk assessments' (updated 25 November 2019, **www.sra.org.uk/solicitors/guidance/firm-risk-assessments/**); and they have also produced a template (**www.sra.org.uk/globalassets/documents/solicitors/firm-wide-risk-assessment-template.docx?version=4a4d74**).
- The LSAG guidance, 'Anti-money laundering guidance for the legal sector' (20 January 2021, **www.lawsociety.org.uk/topics/anti-money-laundering/anti-money-laundering-guidance**) has a very useful guide outlining what a firm's AML risk assessment should cover and how that might be approached.
- The Law Society has a wealth of guidance, such as:
  - 'Anti-money laundering (AML) compliance for small firms' (16 January 2020, **www.lawsociety.org.uk/topics/anti-money-laundering/aml-compliance-for-small-firms**) covering conducting an AML risk assessment; PCPs; and CDD and warning signs;
  - 'Risk assessments: anti-money laundering' (20 January 2020, **www.lawsociety.org.uk/en/topics/anti-money-laundering/anti-money-laundering-risk-assessments**).

Compliance tips – how to mitigate the risk of getting it wrong

- The firm-wide risk assessment may seem daunting at first. It is important to start with something and build on what is being assessed over a period of time.
- The format of the assessment must be accessible and understood. It is important for each firm to do what is right for them whilst assessing the AML risk as per the regulations. A template is, of course, a good start – but it must be tailored.

2.3 What should be included in the practice-wide risk assessment?

AML Regulations 2017, reg.18 sets out that firms must take appropriate steps to identify and assess the risks of money laundering and terrorist financing in their practice. The regulation further sets out that the firm must consider information available from their supervisory body, in the case of most firms the SRA, and risk factors relating to:

- its clients;
- the countries and geographic areas in which the firm operates;
- the firm's products or services;
- the firm's transactions; and
- the delivery channels of that service.

Below are suggestions on how these risk factors could be considered.

- **The firm's clients**:
  - What kind of clients instruct the firm (individuals, companies, trusts, etc.)?
  - Where are they based?
  - Are they based in high risk jurisdictions?
  - Where do their assets come from?
  - Do fee earners know what is usual behaviour for the firm's clients?
  - Are fee earners good at collating and understanding source of funds and wealth information?
  - Do the clients operate in high risk sectors; are they politically exposed persons (PEPs); are they sanctioned or is there adverse media about the client (that is, media stories that suggest criminal activity and possible proceeds of crime being present); are they large cash businesses? And so on.
- **Countries and geographical areas which the firm operates or receives funds from**:
  - Does the firm operate in jurisdictions with equivalent AML regulations as the UK?
  - Is the firm referred work from persons/entities based in jurisdictions that are high risk?
  - Do funds come from high-risk jurisdictions?
- **The services the firm provides and the transactions the firm is involved with** – Examples might be:
  - company formation;
  - conveyancing;
  - trust formation;
  - sham litigation;
  - tax havens; and
  - how risky those activities are.

- **Transactions:**
  - Does the firm ever receive unsolicited payments and if so, what is the process to resolve those?
  - Does the firm deal with complex transactions or transactions that facilitate anonymity?
- **How the firm delivers its services, i.e. face-to-face or remotely:**
  - What safeguards does the firm deploy to mitigate any risk when the client is not met physically or remotely (via video for example)?
  - Does the firm accept payments from non-clients, and if so what steps are taken?

Further, the firm needs to consider how the firm's people are screened to mitigate AML risk. See **5.1–5.5**.

What are the compliance challenges?

- It is important to ensure that all areas of practice as outlined above are carefully considered, their risk assessed and PCPs implemented. The challenge is to ensure that the assessment is meaningful and carried forward with appropriate mitigating steps.

What resources will help?

- SRA materials:
  - The SRA has produced guidance on the requirement for a firm-wide AML risk assessment entitled 'Firm risk assessments' (updated 25 November 2019, **www.sra.org.uk/solicitors/guidance/firm-risk-assessments/**); and they have also produced a template (**www.sra.org.uk/globalassets/documents/solicitors/firm-wide-risk-assessment-template.docx?version=4a4d74**).
  - SRA warning notice: 'Compliance with the money laundering regulations – firm risk assessment' (updated 25 November 2019, **www.sra.org.uk/solicitors/guidance/compliance-money-laundering-regulations-firm-risk-assessment/**).
- The LSAG guidance, 'Anti-money laundering guidance for the legal sector' (20 January 2021, **www.lawsociety.org.uk/topics/anti-money-laundering/anti-money-laundering-guidance**) has a very useful guide outlining what a firm's AML risk assessment should cover and how that might be approached.
- The Law Society has a wealth of guidance, such as:
  - 'Anti-money laundering (AML) compliance for small firms' (16 January 2020, **www.lawsociety.org.uk/topics/anti-money-laundering/aml-compliance-for-small-firms**) covering conducting an AML risk assessment; PCPs; and CDD and warning signs.
  - 'Risk assessments: anti-money laundering' (20 January 2020, **www.lawsociety.org.uk/en/topics/anti-money-laundering/anti-money-laundering-risk-assessments**).

Compliance tips – how to mitigate the risk of getting it wrong

- The risk assessment must cover the risks outlined above. To do this, it is likely that the person conducting the risk assessment needs to engage with others in the firm. These people could be fee earners, department heads/team leaders, MLRO, MLCO, compliance officer for legal practice (COLP), compliance officer for finance and administration (COFA) and so on.
- Ensuring proper engagement across the firm will ensure that all areas of AML risk are understood and assessed and also understanding and buy-in to the risk assessment process should be more easily achieved.

2.4 Once the risk assessment is done, what should happen to it?

Once the risk assessment is done, what steps can you take to make PCPs integrate with it? How can you make sure other people understand it?

Once a risk assessment is completed, the firm should undertake the following:

1. Implement the PCPs required to mitigate the risks assessed in the risk assessment.
2. Consider making the risk assessment available to everyone in the firm. Consider providing a summary of it if it is particularly large/lengthy.
3. Communicate about the risk assessment and summary and the resulting PCPs (it is a good idea to communicate in writing and also to attend meetings such as team meetings to explain verbally).
4. Test the effectiveness of the PCPs by way of independent audit (see **5.10**);
5. Regularly revisit the risk assessment when, for example, new work streams are undertaken, clients are coming from different jurisdictions or new delivery channels for the work is being undertaken. The risk assessment should also be revisited when new regulatory changes take place. Further, the risk assessment should be periodically reviewed at least once a year. It is important to record on the assessment when the review took place and keep prior copies in case the SRA want to see the evolution of the risk assessment.

What are the compliance challenges?

- It is important to make sure that people in the firm understand the risk assessment and what it is designed to do. Communication is key here – but also important is putting the information into an easily accessible format that can be understood.
- If people in the firm do not understand the purpose of the risk assessment and therefore the PCPs, they will not understand why they need to abide by the PCPs and this could lead to non-compliance.

What resources will help?

- The SRA has produced guidance on the requirement for a firm-wide AML risk assessment entitled 'Firm risk assessments' (updated 25 November 2019, **www.sra.org.uk/solicitors/guidance/firm-risk-assessments/**). They have also produced a template (**www.sra.org.uk/globalassets/documents/solicitors/firm-wide-risk-assessment-template.docx?version=4a4d74**).
- The LSAG guidance 'Anti-money laundering guidance for the legal sector' (20 January 2021, **www.lawsociety.org.uk/topics/anti-money-laundering/anti-money-laundering-guidance**) has a very useful guide outlining what a firm's AML risk assessment should cover and how that might be approached.

Compliance tips – how to mitigate the risk of getting it wrong

- Ensure that the risk assessment is in a format that is easily accessible and easy to understand, or provide a summary of it.
- Ensure that resulting PCPs are implemented, communicated and then audited.
- Make sure that the risk assessment is regularly reviewed, especially when there is a change to work streams, jurisdictions of clients, delivery channels and so on, or a change in the regulations.

CLIENT AND MATTER RISK ASSESSMENTS

2.5 What is the requirement to undertake a client and matter risk assessment?

Relevant persons must record their assessment of risk when acting for clients and on their matters. This assessment forms the basis of the due diligence that is required.

AML Regulations 2017, reg.28(13) sets out that in assessing risk in a matter, the relevant person must take into account, amongst other things:

- the purpose of an account, transaction or business relationship;
- the level of assets to be deposited by the client or the size of the transaction; and
- the regularity and duration of the business relationship.

There should be a connection between the firm-wide AML risk assessment (see above) and the client and matter risk assessment – with the latter reflecting the firm's assessment in the former. For example, if the firm-wide risk assessment sets out the firm's stance that a certain type of work or method in which transactions occur (for example, not face-to-face) were high risk meaning that enhanced due diligence (EDD) needed to be undertaken, then this should be reflected in the client and matter risk assessment by way of asking the reviewer a question about the work type or the method of the service being provided, with instructions on what to do if the answer is positive/negative.

The purpose of writing the assessment down is to evidence that it took place. It will be very hard to show that the regulatory requirements have been met if there is no written evidence of it. The SRA expect to see fully completed client and matter risk assessments when it audits firms for AML compliance.

What are the compliance challenges?

- Some solicitors may be fearful of getting their assessment wrong and therefore are reluctant to come to a conclusion when it comes to assessing the AML risk in transactions. It is important to understand that it is far better to make an assessment and get that wrong than not make an assessment at all. The latter is a breach of the AML Regulations, and the former can provide mitigation.

What resources will help?

- The LSAG guidance 'Anti-money laundering guidance for the legal sector' (20 January 2021, **www.lawsociety.org.uk/topics/anti-money-laundering/anti-money-laundering-guidance**) provides very useful guidance in this area.
- Further, the firm's own resources will help those within the firm.

Compliance tips – how to mitigate the risk of getting it wrong

- The firm should have a template client and matter risk assessment. This assessment could be generic across all work streams, or could be bespoke for each type of work. The more relevant the questions are to the work, the more likely solicitors are to engage with it.
- The client and matter risk assessment should reflect the firm's findings in the firm-wide AML risk assessment and instructions on how and when to undertake the client and matter risk assessment set out in separate guidance and if possible, the firm's AML policy.
- Further training should be provided.

2.6 What should a client and matter risk assessment cover?

AML Regulations 2017, reg.28(13) sets out that in assessing risk in a matter, the relevant person must take into account, amongst other things:

- the purpose of an account, transaction or business relationship
- the level of assets to be deposited by the client or the size of the transaction; and
- the regularity and duration of the business relationship.

This list is not exhaustive, and a client and matter risk assessment is a wonderful opportunity to ask far wider questions that focus on AML risk or other types of risk in addition.

When designing a firm's client and matter risk assessment, the firm must take into account the SRA 'Sectoral Risk Assessment – Anti-money laundering and terrorist financing' (28 January 2021, **www.sra.org.uk/sra/how-we-work/reports/aml-risk-assessment/**), as well as the money laundering warning signs as outlined in the LSAG guidance 'Anti-money laundering guidance for the legal sector', 20 January 2021, **www.lawsociety.org.uk/en/topics/anti-money-laundering/anti-money-laundering-guidance**).

The AML Regulations require relevant persons to take into account guidance produced by those who regulate them. The SRA's risk assessment as well as LSAG guidance, must therefore be taken into account when complying with the regulatory requirements.

Below are some questions that could be asked when assessing the risk relating to the client or the matter. Those questions denoted with an * require EDD to be undertaken as set out by the AML Regulations (see **3.9**).

Client risk assessment questions

- Is the client a regulated person or entity, or is the client listed on a regulated market? This will help decide if simplified due diligence can be adopted.
- Is the client resident in, operating from or controlled from a high-risk jurisdiction?* To assist those who complete the assessment, it is best to set out a list of high-risk jurisdictions that relevant persons are most likely to come across, as well as share a link to the Corruptions Perception Index (**www.transparency.org/en/cpi/2020/index/nzl**) and guide those in the firm on what is and is not an acceptable level/score.
- Does the client operate in any of the following sectors which are regarded as potentially high-risk?:
  - high-end art/goods;
  - cultural artefacts;
  - public works contracts and construction;
  - real estate and property development;
  - oil and gas;
  - nuclear industry;
  - mining (of any sort);
  - tobacco products
  - arms manufacturing/supply and the defence industry.
- Is the client, director or beneficial owner a PEP?* This includes UK and foreign PEPs, their family members and known close associates.
- Is the client, director or beneficial owner sanctioned?*
- Is the client, director or beneficial owner resident in or a national of a country which is the subject of UK financial sanctions?* Here a schedule of countries should be provided to those completing the assessment.
- Is the firm aware of any adverse media about the client, a director or beneficial owner that gives rise to suspicion of criminal activity and/or money laun-

dering? This question also provides an opportunity for the assessor and firm to consider reputational risk to the firm.

- Have any of the client's shares been issued in the form of bearer shares (corporates only)?
- Has the client been evasive or obstructive in relation to your AML checks especially regarding beneficial ownership or source of funds or wealth?
- Has the individual acting met the client (for companies this could be a director, beneficial owner or person with authority such as a general counsel)?
- Has the firm previously had to file a suspicious activity report (SAR) about the client? This may be difficult for a fee earner who is making an assessment to answer and so instead of this question being a part of the risk assessment a system flag of some kind could be placed on the client so that the MLRO is aware as soon as a new matter is opened for the client so further steps, if needed, can be considered.
- If the client is unregulated does the client's ownership structure seem unusual or unnecessarily complex/opaque?* This must be viewed in the context of the client, the work/transactions they undertake and whether what is in place is normal or unusual. What might be usual for one client may be unusual for another.
- Does the fee earner have satisfactory client due diligence documentation?
- Does the information provided by the client match the people with significant control register (**www.gov.uk/government/publications/guidance-to-the-people-with-significant-control-requirements-for-companies-and-limited-liability-partnerships**)? If not, consider obligation to report under the AML Regulations.

Matter risk assessment questions

- Are instructions for this matter being given by a third party? If so, ensure you have identified and verified that third party as appropriate.
- Does it make sense for the firm to be instructed? Is there an underlying legal transaction?*
- Does the client's business involve dealing with large amounts of cash?
- Is the client asking the firm to create a corporate structure or trust structure that is unnecessarily complex and/or could lead to tax evasion?*
- Is the transaction unusually large or is there an unusual pattern of transactions?*
- Does the transaction carry with it additional risk, e.g. it is handling high-value items such as art for which ownership is not clear, or does it create or facilitate anonymity of ownership, or is the transaction unnecessarily complex?
- Is the transaction consistent with what you know about the client's business or level of wealth generally?
- What is the source of funds for this transaction? Do you understand the client's source of wealth? Does the information you are being given tally with

what you know? This analysis needs to be documented, and the client and matter risk assessment is a great place to do this.

- Will funds for the transaction be sent from a sanctioned jurisdiction OR high-risk country?* These should be listed for the person completing the assessment and/or a link provided to where this jurisdictions/countries can be found.
- If funds are coming from a third party, are you satisfied that you know who the third party is and why they are funding? Consider if you need to undertake due diligence.
- Is the client insisting that you proceed on an urgent basis without a reasonable explanation, and this is unusual for this client?
- Is there anything else of concern to you? (Remember, if you suspect money laundering, please speak to the MLRO straight away.)

Other questions (not AML-related) which could be added

- As far as you are aware, has another law firm refused to accept the client or terminated their retainer? This could indicate suspicion, but is more likely to indicate a relationship issue with prior solicitors which may be repeated.
- Does the value of the transaction exceed your professional indemnity cover of £*[insert]*? Ensure that liability is capped to £*[insert]*.

The possibilities as to what questions can be posed on a client and matter risk assessment are not endless, but can be extensive.

Finally, the risk assessment must reach a rational conclusion as to the risk assessed, whether that be low, medium or high. Firms may wish to assess risk as either low or high and dispense with medium, and this will depend on the nature of the work that the firm does, its client base and how the firm considers its risk as set out in the firm-wide risk assessment (see **2.1**).

Against each risk assessment question or in accompanying guidance, there could be an explanation of what a positive or negative answer might mean, what steps should be taken to mitigate any AML risk and whether ongoing monitoring is required.

What are the compliance challenges?

- The client and matter risk assessment must reflect the firm-wide risk assessment, be meaningful and be engaged with by solicitors in the firm.
- Non-completion is taken very seriously by the SRA.

What resources will help?

- LSAG guidance 'Anti-money laundering guidance for the legal sector' (20 January 2021, **www.lawsociety.org.uk/topics/anti-money-laundering/anti-money-laundering-guidance**) provides very useful guidance and should be consulted.

Compliance tips – how to mitigate the risk of getting it wrong

- Firms should ensure that the client and matter risk assessment takes its cue from the risks found in the firm-wide risk assessment.
- If possible, firms may wish to design a client and matter risk assessment depending on the type of work undertaken so that the questions are tailored. This may increase a solicitor's desire to complete it.
- Firms should also provide guidance and training on the client and matter risk assessment.

2.7 What is the crossover between the practice-wide risk assessment and the client and matter risk assessment?

The purpose of the firm-wide risk assessment is to assess AML risk across the firm and then implement PCPs to mitigate those risks as far as possible. One of these PCPs are client and matter risk assessments.

In other words, the client and matter risk assessment is a *measure* taken to highlight and address the risks assessed in the firm-wide risk assessment.

For example, if the firm has determined in its firm-wide risk assessment that not meeting a client physically face-to-face carries high risk and mitigating steps are to conduct a video meeting, then the firm's client and matter risk assessment could ask the question, 'Have you met the client physically face-to-face? If not, have you met the client via video? If you have not met the client physically or via video, we consider this to be high risk and the following steps should be taken *[set out steps]*'.

As and when the firm's firm-wide risk assessment changes, consideration needs to be given to amending the firm's client and matter risk assessment to address any new or changing AML risks that have been identified.

What are the compliance challenges?

- The client and matter risk assessment must reflect the firm-wide risk assessment, be meaningful and be engaged with by solicitors in the firm. The challenge is incorporating the risks found in the firm-wide risk assessment into the client and matter risk assessment template that solicitors need to complete.

What resources will help?

- LSAG provides very useful guidance which should be consulted: 'Anti-money laundering guidance for the legal sector' (20 January 2021, **www.lawsociety.org.uk/topics/anti-money-laundering/anti-money-laundering-guidance**).

Compliance tips – how to mitigate the risk of getting it wrong

- Firms should ensure that the client and matter risk assessment takes its cue from the risks found in the firm-wide risk assessment and as and when the firm-wide risk assessment is updated, the client and matter risk assessment may need to be also.

2.8 Do I need to repeat my risk assessment for a new matter or during a matter?

Each new matter for an existing client should have a fresh risk assessment. The risk assessment on the client should be periodically reviewed and amended if there is a change – for example, if the client changes how they generate income, what country that income comes from or the client's ownership structure changes.

There is also much merit in reviewing the client and matter risk assessment at key milestones in a transaction, such as in a property transaction before monies are receipted, before exchange and before completion.

The firm may wish to build in triggers for the fee earner to review the risk assessment, either by way of workflow within the case management system or by placing questions on any forms or processes when requesting payments to be allocated to the file or pay out.

Reviewing the risk assessment at regular intervals or at key milestones will serve to assist in monitoring the risk on an ongoing basis.

What are the compliance challenges?

- Solicitors need to continue to assess the risk in transactions and at the beginning of each new matter.
- It is important that this is not seen as a tick box exercise.

What resources will help?

- LSAG provides very useful guidance which should be consulted: 'Anti-money laundering guidance for the legal sector' (20 January 2021, **www.lawsociety.org.uk/topics/anti-money-laundering/anti-money-laundering-guidance**).
- Law Society Practice Advice Service Q&As, e.g.: 'Should I carry out an AML risk assessment on every new regulated matter?' (**www.lawsociety.org.uk/contact-or-visit-us/helplines/practice-advice-service/q-and-as** and under 'Topic' choose 'Anti-money laundering').

Compliance tips – how to mitigate the risk of getting it wrong

- The firm should have a process whereby new matter risk assessment and risk assessment reviews during the transaction take place.

2.9 What are the consequences of not completing the client and matter risk assessment?

Failure to undertake a client and matter risk assessment means failing to follow the requirements of the AML Regulations. This is a criminal offence punishable by up to two years in prison, or a fine, or both. Not only can this offence be prosecuted by the relevant authorities, it can lead to SRA disciplinary action where the sanctions can be severe such as strike off or suspension for solicitors, order prohibiting non-solicitors working for law firms without SRA approval and firms being fined as well as resulting reputational damage. When the SRA audits firms for their AML compliance, it expects to see completed client and matter risk assessments and take non-completion very seriously.

Failure to undertake a client and matter risk assessment means the relevant person is less likely to spot money laundering risk which could lead to becoming unwittingly involved in money laundering, and again this can lead to prosecution.

What are the compliance challenges?

- Law firms must ensure that their fee earners are completing the client and matter risk assessments.

What resources will help?

- LSAG provides useful guidance: 'Anti-money laundering guidance for the legal sector' (20 January 2021, **www.lawsociety.org.uk/topics/anti-money-laundering/anti-money-laundering-guidance**).

Compliance tips – how to mitigate the risk of getting it wrong

- Firms must ensure that relevant people in the firm understand the importance of the client and matter risk assessment, why it must be completed and the consequences of not completing it.
- Firms should audit compliance on a frequent basis.
- When firms or solicitors are prosecuted or disciplined, these stories could be shared by the MCLO to those in the firm as part of the firm's training strategy.

CHAPTER 3

Client due diligence

CLIENT DUE DILIGENCE

Note on terminology: The AML Regulations refer to 'customers' in relation to due diligence requirements. We have generally changed that term to 'client', which is the terminology commonly used in law firms, unless where quoting from the regulations.

3.1 What is the requirement to undertake client due diligence and why do we need to undertake it?

Money Laundering, Terrorist Financing and Transfer of Funds (Information on the Payer) Regulations 2017, SI 2017/692 (AML Regulations), reg.27 requires relevant persons (individuals and firms) to undertake client due diligence (CDD) if a business relationship is to be established, an occasional transaction is taking place, there is a suspicion of money laundering or there is doubt as to the veracity or adequacy of documentation provided for the purposes of identification and verification of that information.

Regulation 28 sets out the actual measures that need to be undertaken and, in a nutshell, these are to identify the client and verify that identity, unless they are already known to the relevant person. Further, the regulation requires the relevant person to obtain information on the purpose and nature of the business relationship.

It is helpful to think of CDD as more than ID gathering, and it most certainly should not be seen as a tick-box exercise. Each firm's CDD process should cover the following five steps:

1. Identification and verification of the client.
2. Client and matter risk assessment.
3. Understanding purpose and nature of the work.
4. Understanding source of funds and wealth.

5. Ongoing monitoring of the work and client.

The purpose of undertaking CDD is ultimately to make sure that firms and individuals understand who they are acting for and to satisfy themselves as far as possible that they are not involved in money laundering.

What are the compliance challenges?

- Ensuring that relevant persons understand what CDD is and why it needs to be done is key to the successful completion of CDD. ID requirements for corporates or trusts, for example, can be complicated and so a clear policy on what the firm requires as well as clear instructions should be given.
- Another challenge is proportionality. If the work is high-risk but the value of the work in terms of fees is low, this can lead to the perception that as the fee value is low the risk should also be low and less CDD is needed. This is a slippery slope to go down. What is important is that the CDD processes in the firm are proportionate to the money laundering risk.

What resources will help?

- The Legal Sector Affinity Group (LSAG) guidance 'Anti-money laundering guidance for the legal sector' (20 January 2021, **www.lawsociety.org.uk/topics/anti-money-laundering/anti-money-laundering-guidance**) has very useful and detailed guidance on CDD.
- Law Society guidance: 'Customer due diligence' (20 January 2020, **www.lawsociety.org.uk/en/topics/anti-money-laundering/customer-due-diligence**).
- Further extensive guidance can be found in *Financial Crime: A Compliance Manual* (Rebecca Atkinson, Law Society Publishing, 2021).

Compliance tips – how to mitigate the risk of getting it wrong

- Make it clear what CDD is required for each type of client and work in the firm by way of policy, procedures and training.
- Create client-facing documentation to explain to clients what is needed for fee earners to send to clients.
- Make sure that CDD measures are proportionate to the money laundering risk.
- Consider centralising (for example, into a risk team) the checking of ID obtained and possibly the gathering of it.

3.2 What ID do I need to obtain on my clients, and can it differ depending on work type?

Documentation required to show and verify the identity of a client will differ depending on the type of client. Firms have a choice to implement a 'one size fits all' approach to ID requirements, or to alter what is asked for depending on work type, whether that be for non-regulated work vs regulated work or low vs high money laundering risk (this could be because the work is transactional and not merely advisory).

Below is a high-level outline of the ID documentation that firms may wish to gather for each client type: individuals; companies; partnerships; trusts and estate administration; charities; clubs and associations; churches and places of worship; schools, colleges and universities; government agencies and councils; pension funds; and well-known entities.

Individuals

Evidence of identity can include passports and photocard driving licences or other forms of confirmation including assurances from persons within the regulated sector or those in the firm who have dealt with the person for some time. Caution should be exercised, however, on relying on the confirmation of others as they may not have conducted appropriate checks themselves, or they may have accepted confirmation from others who may not have conducted appropriate checks or taken documentation which may not be deemed appropriate. It is always recommended that firms conduct their own due diligence and not rely on the assessment of others (see **3.32–3.35** below on reliance).

It is good practice to have either:

(a) one government document which verifies either name and address, or name and date of birth; or
(b) one government document which verifies the client's full name and another document which verifies their name and either their address or date of birth.

Companies

AML Regulations 2017, reg.28(3) sets out that where the client is a body corporate, the relevant person must obtain and verify:

- the name of the body corporate;
- its company number and registration number;
- the address of its registered office; and
- if relevant, its principal place of business.

Further, the relevant person must take steps to determine and verify the law to which the company is subject and its constitution and the full names of the board of directors (or if there is no board, the members of the equivalent management body) and other senior persons responsible for the operations of the body corporate.

Regulation 28(4) goes on to set out that where a client is beneficially owned by another person, the relevant person must:

- identify the beneficial owner (defined as someone who exercises ultimate control or owns or controls more than 25 per cent of shares);
- take reasonable steps to verify the identity of the beneficial owner so that the relevant person is satisfied that they know who the beneficial owner is; and

- if the beneficial owner is a legal person, trust, company, foundation or similar legal arrangement, to take reasonable measures to understand the ownership and control structure of that entity.

What the above means in practice is that the relevant person must secure documentation which provides the information needed in regulation 28(3) including the information needed to determine if there is a beneficial owner. Most firms will do this by obtaining relevant documentation from Companies House, such as the certificate of incorporation; details of the company's registration number; articles of association; and registered office and filed audited accounts. The relevant person will also need to consult the Persons of Significant Control Register held at Companies House (**www.gov.uk/government/publications/guidance-to-the-people-with-significant-control-requirements-for-companies-and-limited-liability-partnerships**), though this cannot be relied upon to confirm beneficial ownership.

Where the company is not in the UK, overseas registers (where possible) can be consulted – otherwise the client itself will need to be asked to provide the information needed.

For large companies, overseas or not, a good starting point is to ask the company to provide a structure chart showing how it is beneficially owned. By starting with a structure chart, the relevant person can determine what is needed in one go rather than asking for information in a piecemeal fashion which tends to frustrate clients.

For listed companies, regulation 28(5) sets out that the relevant person must obtain the name of the body corporate, company number of registration and address of its registered office and if different its principal place of business.

Partnerships

Partnerships (unless in Scotland) are not a separate legal entity and so relevant persons need to obtain identity information on its partners. This means identifying those partners as individuals as described above.

If the partnership is a limited liability partnership (LLP) then the relevant person can obtain information as if the LLP was a company.

Where the partnership or unincorporated business is well-known, reputable, has a long history and there is a substantial amount of public information about the partnership, their principles and controllers, then obtaining the name, registered address if any, trading address and nature of the business should be enough to identify it.

If the partnership is made up of regulated professionals (for example, solicitors or accountants) it is sufficient to confirm the existence of the partnership through a professional directory or search facility.

Trusts and estate administration

The first step is to identify who the client is. A trust is not a legal personality and therefore it cannot be a firm's client. When advising in relation to a trust, the relevant person may be advising the settlor, the trustee(s), the protector(s) or one or more of the beneficiaries.

If the relevant person is advising on the set up of the trust, then the settlor will usually be the client and their identity should be verified. The sources of funds and wealth being used to set up the trust will need to be considered. If the settlor is not a natural person but instead an entity, then the appropriate identification measures need to be undertaken in relation to that entity.

If the relevant person is advising the settlor or trustee on the trust once the trust has been set up, the beneficial owner of the trust will need to be identified and their identity verified. In order to understand who the beneficial owner is, the trust deed is often needed.

AML Regulations 2017, reg.6(1) sets out that beneficial owner in relation to a trust means the settlor, the trustees and beneficiaries and where the individuals benefitting from the trust have not been determined, the class of persons in whose main interest the trust was set up and anyone who has control over the trust ('control' meaning power to dispose, vary, add or remove a beneficiary or appoint or remove a trustee).

Beneficiaries whose interest has vested need to be identified. If the beneficiaries are a class of which individuals are not yet identified, i.e. to grandchildren not yet born, then no identification documentation can be obtained and it will be enough for the relevant person to note the class of beneficiaries. Note, however, that in the case of a discretionary trust if the relevant person does not note the names of the beneficiaries who are named in the trust deed or any associated document on the basis that their interest has not yet vested, the relevant person will need to seek regular updates on this aspect. It therefore may be better to obtain the names of the beneficiaries where possible and note the same.

Note that regulation 30(7) requires the relevant person to establish and verify the identity of any beneficiary before payment is made to the beneficiary or the beneficiary exercises it vested rights in the trust, legal entity or legal arrangement.

In relation to acting in an estate administration the client will be the personal representative of the deceased and often therefore the executor. Identification and verification of that person(s) identity will be required. The relevant person may also want to obtain a copy of the death certificate and the grant of probate or letters of administration.

Charities

Charities may be registered or unregistered, excepted such as churches or exempt such as museums. What due diligence is required will depend on what type of charity the client is.

If a charity is registered, then it is generally enough (in the absence of suspicion) to note the name, registration number and place of business of the charity from the registration directory. In England and Wales this would mean consideration of the Charity Commission's website. Other countries may have a similar registration process and register. As with all categories of client, a charity should be checked for PEP status, sanctions and adverse media (see **3.6–3.7**).

If the charity is not registered, then what the relevant person requests in terms of identification and verification will depend on the business structure of the charity. If the charity is very well known, then the relevant person may decide that it does not need as much information as a small unknown charity.

Clubs and associations

In order to carry out due diligence on these entities, the relevant person needs to verify that the club or association exists, and this could be done via the entity's articles of association, recent audited accounts, statement from a bank and so on. The relevant person should have enough information to obtain and verify the full name; legal status; purpose; registered address; and names of all office holders.

Churches and places of worship

The entity may have registered as a charity, in which case follow the guidance above. The entity can also apply for registration as a certified building of worship with the General Register Office, which will issue the entity a certificate. Also, charitable status will be registered with HM Revenue and Customs (HMRC).

If the entity is not a registered charity, identification may therefore take place with reference to their General Register Officer certificate or by enquiry with HMRC. Again, proportionality is key, and if the entity instructing the relevant person is well known, a note to that effect on the file, together with the gathering of open-source information may be enough.

Schools, colleges and universities

These entities can be a number of different legal formations and depending on what they are will depend on what identification measures are needed. The Department for Education maintains a list of approved educational establishments, which should be consulted to assist in verifying the identity of an educational establishment. Again, if the establishment is very well known and there is enough open-source information about the entity, this may be enough to identify it.

Government agencies and councils

Steps need to be taken to verify that the entity exists, and how far a relevant person needs to go in doing so will depend on the risk of money laundering. Public domain information which confirms name of the entity; nature and status; address; names of key personnel such as directors or equivalent; name of the instructing person and their authority to do so; and an extract from the official government website will be enough. PEP, sanction and adverse media may highlight some information which means that the relevant person should ask for more information from the client (see **3.6–3.7**).

Pension funds

Under regulation 37(3)(b)(iii) it is possible for pension, superannuation or similar schemes which satisfy certain conditions to qualify for simplified due diligence. That simplified due diligence may be seeing a copy of the page showing the name of the pension scheme, or seeing the deed for the scheme.

Well-known entities

Where any entity is a well-known brand or enterprise (such as 'household' names or institutions such as the NHS) firms may decide that they do not need to undertake as much ID gathering. This will depend on how much information can be gathered from open sources. If it is decided that less ID should be gathered, then this needs to be documented with what the firm knows and why it was considered ok not to ask for certain pieces of information.

What are the compliance challenges?

ID requirement can become complicated for complex structures and a challenge for people to understand.

What resources will help?

- The LSAG guidance 'Anti-money laundering guidance for the legal sector' (20 January 2021, **www.lawsociety.org.uk/topics/anti-money-laundering/anti-money-laundering-guidance**) has very useful and detailed guidance on ID and CDD.
- Further extensive guidance can be found in *Financial Crime: A Compliance Manual* (Rebecca Atkinson, Law Society Publishing, 2021).

Compliance tips – how to mitigate the risk of getting it wrong

- Firms should set out their ID requirement for each client type in the firm's AML policy, and also consider creating client-facing information that can be shared with clients outlining what ID is needed. This will also aid fee earners.

- Firms may also wish to consider centralising the ID gathering process into a risk team.

3.3 What is meant by independent verification of ID?

The identification of clients as outlined above is the first step of identifying who a client is. The next step is to independently verify the information that is being given. Essentially, relevant persons should not take what they are being told at face value and should seek verification to prove what is being said.

Verification should come from a source that is independent of the client. Ordinarily for individuals this means obtaining ID documentation such as passport, photo driving licence or ID card (with the option of requesting that it is certified by a regulated professional as either being a 'true likeness' of the individual or a true copy of the original). Where ID is not possible to obtain (for example, the ID is out-of-date and up-to-date ID cannot be obtained in time) then an alternative is confirmation from a regulated professional of the client's identity.

It is possible to use electronic identification and verification tools (see **3.4**). These tools require name, address and DOB of a person and will match that against electoral roll information and other sources. There are also options for the client to upload their passport/driving licence into an app and then take a photo of themselves for biometric scanning. There is also the option of biometric video scanning where the individual is guided through an app to turn their face left and right and directed to say a few words. This is then compared to the photo ID they have uploaded. Clever stuff!

For non-individuals, proof of identity should be obtained from documentation which shows the client and its structure. This could be for example information from Companies House as outlined above. However, note that firms are unable to rely on the people with significant control register (**www.gov.uk/government/publications/guidance-to-the-people-with-significant-control-requirements-for-companies-and-limited-liability-partnerships**) at Companies House (see regulation 28(9)).

Where independent verification is proving challenging, the relevant person needs to consider if this does or ought to raise suspicion of money laundering. 'Out of the box' thinking may need to be deployed where clients are unable to produce normal documentation (see **3.11**). One alternative method is to rely on the CDD undertaken by others (see **3.35**) or seek confirmation of identity from a regulated professional without seeking reliance. Careful thought needs to be given, though, to how that regulated professional was able to identify the client when the relevant person is unable to.

What are the compliance challenges?

- Generally speaking, individuals can provide enough documentation to verify their identity. However beneficial owners of complex corporate structures may not be willing to do so, especially if they are removed from the business activity.

What resources will help?

- LSAG provides useful guidance on what verification can be sought: 'Anti-money laundering guidance for the legal sector' (20 January 2021, **www.lawsociety.org.uk/topics/anti-money-laundering/anti-money-laundering-guidance**).

Compliance tips – how to mitigate the risk of getting it wrong

- Firms should set out their verification of ID requirements for each client type in the firm's AML policy and also consider creating client-facing information that can be shared with clients outlining what ID and verification evidence is needed. This will also aid fee earners.
- Firms may also wish to consider centralising the ID gathering process into a risk team.
- When faced with an inability to provide normal documentary evidence, 'out of the box' thinking needs to be deployed and a puzzle-solving, solution-finding mindset adopted.
- Electronic methods to verify should be considered.

3.4 What is electronic identification and verification, and can I use it? What needs to be considered?

The AML Regulations specifically allow for the use of electronic identification processes to meet the requirement of obtaining information as to identity from an independent reliable source (reg.28(19)). To enable the use of such methods, the user needs to be sure that the process is secure from fraud and misuse, and capable of providing assurance that the person claiming to be a particular identity is in fact that person and not simply confirmation that the identity exists.

There are numerous legal technology tools in the space of electronic identification and verification and they range at one end from the inputting of name, address and date of birth and that data being checked against open-source information such as electoral role and other resources, all the way to biometric applications where the client takes a photo of their ID and then a photo or video of themselves which is then matched as well as the use of open sources to verify that information.

Firms may wish to use such tools on a risk-based approach. So, for example, they could use such applications for lower risk work and request physical documents for higher risk work. If different standards are adopted for different work streams, then due diligence documents may be needed once a client passports from a lower risk to higher risk work.

What are the compliance challenges?

- When using such technology, firms must understand how the technology works and determine if the technology used needs to be supplemented by additional checks.
- The money laundering compliance officer (MLCO) in particular must vet and understand how the technology works and be able to explain it to the Solicitors Regulation Authority (SRA).

What resources will help?

- The technology provider should be able to easily explain their piece of kit. If they cannot, and the MLCO cannot therefore understand it, it should not be used.

Compliance tips – how to mitigate the risk of getting it wrong

- The MLCO must understand the technology and therefore must adequately vet it and be able to explain it to a third party.
- Technology that is not understood should not be used.

3.5 What are the consequences of not undertaking CDD on clients?

Undertaking CDD on clients is a requirement of the AML Regulations (see regs.27 and 28). Failure to complete CDD is a breach of the regulations, a criminal offence (see reg.86) and would leave the relevant person (practitioner acting and the firm and possibly the MLCO) open to prosecution by the SRA and authorities together with serious long-lasting reputational damage.

What are the compliance challenges?

- It is vital that relevant persons understand what is expected of them under the AML Regulations, the firm's policies, controls and procedures (PCPs) and the consequences of failure to adhere to the regulations or PCPs.

What resources will help?

- The firm's own PCPs should make it clear what is expected of everyone in the firm.
- LSAG's guidance is also very useful: 'Anti-money laundering guidance for the legal sector' (20 January 2021, **www.lawsociety.org.uk/topics/anti-money-laundering/anti-money-laundering-guidance**).

Compliance tips – how to mitigate the risk of getting it wrong

- Everyone in the firm must understand the content of the firm's PCPs and the consequences of their breach or the breach of the AML Regulations.
- Further, all relevant persons must receive AML training on a regular basis.

3.6 What is a politically exposed person, and how can I check if my client is one?

When onboarding clients, relevant persons need to understand whether they are acting for a politically exposed person (PEP). PEPs are considered to carry an increased risk of money laundering due to the position they hold.

A PEP is defined as someone who was entrusted in the last year with a prominent public function such as head of state, ministers, members of parliament, judges, members of boards of certain organisations. Further, family members or known close associates of PEPs are also considered to be PEPs.

AML Regulations 2017, reg.35 should be consulted for further information on who can be classed as PEPs.

Where a PEP is present, enhanced due diligence (EDD) must be undertaken (see **3.9**) and therefore it is vital for firms to have a process by which a client is checked for PEP status.

There are a number of online platforms that can be utilised to check if a person is a PEP. These come at cost, however, and so may not be affordable to all firms. If the client's PEP status is not clear (i.e. they are not a government minister, for example) then an alternative method to understand PEP status is to simply explain to a client what a PEP is and ask if they are one. Further, an internet search should be undertaken to verify as far as possible what the client is informing the firm and further the outcome of that search should be recorded.

Note that it is not sufficient for firms to take the view that they are unlikely to act for a PEP and therefore they do not need to check. The definition of a PEP is wider than most people realise.

Thought needs to be given by the firm on who to conduct PEP checks on for non-individual clients such as companies. It is recommended that a PEP check is undertaken on directors and beneficial owners.

Remember also that the regulations require 'senior management' approval of the firm acting for a PEP. Senior management in the context of a law firm is likely to be the money laundering reporting officer (MLRO) or MLCO or managing partner or someone of equivalent senior management standing.

What are the compliance challenges?

- Ascertaining if the client is a PEP needs to be built into the firm's onboarding process. Further guidance needs to be provided to all relevant personnel in the firm so that they can explain what a PEP is to a client if asked.
- When a client is a PEP, EDD must be undertaken and this needs to be understood by relevant persons in the firm. Failure to follow the requirements of the AML Regulations is a criminal offence.

What resources will help?

- The firm's AML policy should have within it a section dedicated to PEPs for relevant persons to read/reference.
- LSAG provide good guidance on PEPs: 'Anti-money laundering guidance for the legal sector' (20 January 2021, **www.lawsociety.org.uk/topics/anti-money-laundering/anti-money-laundering-guidance**).
- The AML Regulations 2017 themselves set out the requirements clearly.
- Law Society guidance: 'Politically exposed persons' (19 December 2019, **www.lawsociety.org.uk/en/topics/anti-money-laundering/peps**).

Compliance tips – how to mitigate the risk of getting it wrong

- Ensure that the firm's AML policy explains what a PEP is, how the firm ascertains whether a client is a PEP (i.e. the process) and what needs to be done if a PEP is present (i.e. senior management approval, EDD and recording this in the firm's client risk assessment process).
- Ensure that all relevant persons receive regular AML training to include PEPs.
- Audit compliance with the firm's PCPs to ensure that processes are being followed.

3.7 What other checks might I want to take on clients?

Firms may also wish to undertake sanctions and adverse media checks whilst checking for PEP status. Again, there are platforms that can do this but if that is not an option for firms then an internet search would suffice. It is not likely to be desirable to ask a client if they are sanctioned (and they are very unlikely to know what that means and may mistake it for something else) or whether they have adverse media about them. Therefore, these are checks that should be done in the background when onboarding the client. For Q & As on sanctions, see **Chapter 8**.

In terms of adverse media, this is important to know of any media reports that confirm or suggest criminal activity that would give rise to suspicion of money laundering. This is also a good opportunity to consider whether the firm wants to act for the client given any adverse media as although the media found may not suggest criminal activity, it may show that the client conducts themselves in a way which is not in keeping with the ethos, principles and values of the firm.

What are the compliance challenges?

- Firms may unwittingly act for clients who are sanctioned or have adverse media about them which gives rise to suspicion of money laundering.
- Acting in contravention of some sanctions is a criminal offence, as too is the failure to report suspicious activity under the Proceeds of Crime Act 2002 (POCA 2002).

What resources will help?

- There are some books that can help, such as *Financial Crime: A Compliance Manual* (Rebecca Atkinson, Law Society Publishing, 2021). (LSAG provides little advice in this area.)

Compliance tips – how to mitigate the risk of getting it wrong

- Ensure that the firm's AML policy explains how the firm ascertains whether a client is a sanctioned or has adverse media about them (i.e. the process and who does this check) and what needs to be done if a result is found (i.e. speak to the MLRO, possible EDD and recording this in the firm's client risk assessment process).
- Ensure that all relevant persons receive regular AML training to include sanctions and adverse media.
- Audit compliance with the firm's PCPs to ensure that processes are being followed.

3.8 What is simplified due diligence?

The regulations allow what is called simplified due diligence (SDD) in certain circumstances such as where there is considered to be a low risk of money laundering. This assessment outcome might be because the client is a public body, an institution which has to comply with the AML Regulations such as a bank or any other regulated entity or individual or a company listed on a regulated market.

When considering whether SDD can be undertaken instead of standard CDD, the work undertaken needs to also be considered. So if, for example, a regulated entity is instructing the firm in relation to a high-risk piece of work (e.g. an investment in art) thought needs to be given to what additional information needs to be obtained.

What actually is SDD? Both the AML Regulations and LSAG do set out what information can be obtained to satisfy the due diligence requirements once a firm has decided it can accept SDD. Dependant on the client, SDD might encompass checking the client's entry on a regulator's registry or the stock market to evidence the client's identity when applying SDD.

The analysis which leads to the decision to undertake SDD must be documented, and a good place to do this is in the client and matter risk assessment.

Firms must also keep under review the decision to apply SDD and if the client's regulatory or position on the stock market, for example, changes then the ability to apply SDD ceases. Further, if the firm suspects money laundering, EDD needs to be undertaken.

What are the compliance challenges?

- SDD cannot be automatically applied and should only be applied where there is a low risk of money laundering.

What resources will help?

- The AML Regulations and LSAG provide little guidance on what SDD could entail. Firms need to therefore determine on a case-by-case basis what SDD might look like in certain circumstances.

Compliance tips – how to mitigate the risk of getting it wrong

- The firm's AML policy should set out what SDD is and when it is appropriate to undertake SDD in place of standard due diligence.
- The firm should also factor SDD into any onboarding process and provide questions in the firm's standard client and matter risk assessment which will help ascertain if SDD is appropriate.

3.9 What is enhanced due diligence? Under what circumstances must enhanced due diligence be done?

EDD is better described as 'additional' or 'extra' diligence. It is about doing more than standard due diligence.

EDD must be conducted under certain circumstances, as follows:

- The case has been identified as one where there is a high risk of money laundering or terrorist financing in the firm's risk assessment or in the information made available by the SRA (this is why it is a good idea to consider the SRA's risk assessment and LSAG's guidance and factor those into the firm-wide risk assessment so that it is only your firm risk assessment that you need to consider).
- If the firm is carrying out an occasional transaction and either party to the transaction is established in a high-risk third country. Note here that high-risk third countries are listed under the Money Laundering and Terrorist Financing (High-Risk Countries) (Amendment) Regulations 2022 SI 2022/393, and is subject to change. Further, an occasional transaction is defined as 'a transaction which is not carried out as part of a business relationship' (AML Regulations, reg.3, 'General interpretation') and therefore is very unlikely that a law firm would carry out an occasional transaction. However, the firm needs to understand if the client is established in a high-risk country, and this should be checked as a matter of course.
- The client is a PEP, or a family member or known close associate of a PEP.
- The client is established in a high-risk third country (see above).
- The client has provided false or stolen identification documentation or information on establishing the relationship and the firm has decided to continue

dealing with the client (though serious thought needs to be given as to whether to continue acting and whether to submit a suspicious activity report (SAR) (see **Chapter 4**)).
- The firm has assessed and considers that there is higher risk of money laundering or terrorist financing.

In circumstances set out above, the regulations helpfully provide a list of what EDD measures should be undertaken.

Regulation 33 sets out that for non-PEP and non-high-risk third country scenarios, EDD could take the following form:

- seeking additional independent, reliable sources to verify information provided or made available to the relevant person;
- taking additional measures to understand better the background, ownership and financial situation of the customer, and other parties to the transaction;
- taking further steps to be satisfied that the transaction is consistent with the purpose and intended nature of the business relationship;
- increasing the monitoring of the business relationship, including greater scrutiny of transactions.

As part of the above, understanding source of funds and wealth for transactional work should occur. See **3.20**.

If the firm is acting for a PEP, then the above EDD needs to occur, as well as the following:

- approval from senior management for establishing or continuing the business relationship with that person (see **3.6**);
- take adequate measures to establish the source of wealth and source of funds which are involved in the proposed business relationship or transactions with that person; and
- where the business relationship is entered into, conduct enhanced ongoing monitoring of the business relationship with that person.

If the firm is establishing a relationship with a client from a high-risk third country or undertaking an occasional transaction where any party is from a high-risk third country (see above for comments), then EDD must take the following form:

- obtaining additional information on the client and on the client's beneficial owner;
- obtaining additional information on the intended nature of the business relationship;
- obtaining information on the source of funds and the source of wealth of the client and the client's beneficial owner;
- obtaining information on the reasons for the transactions;
- obtaining the approval of senior management for establishing or continuing the business relationship; and

- conducting enhanced monitoring of the business relationship including increasing the frequency and number of checks or other controls applied; and selecting patterns of transactions that trigger a requirement of further explanation to your practice.

Once EDD has been undertaken, enhanced ongoing monitoring of the client and the work must take place. Essentially this means more frequently checking that the due diligence and understanding of the client and transaction has not changed.

EDD should be completed before any substantial work has been undertaken, transactional monies receipted or transaction completed. The earlier the better – and if a client is not prepared to provide the information needed which means the firm cannot act, then it is better to know this early on rather than mid-way through or towards the end of a transaction. Never leave EDD to the last minute, unless that cannot possibly be helped.

What are the compliance challenges?

- Understanding when EDD is needed is crucial and the criteria must not be missed.

What resources will help?

- The AML Regulations 2017 should be consulted, and in particular regs.33 and 35.
- LSAG also provides good guidance in this area: 'Anti-money laundering guidance for the legal sector' (20 January 2021, **www.lawsociety.org.uk/topics/anti-money-laundering/anti-money-laundering-guidance**).

Compliance tips – how to mitigate the risk of getting it wrong

- The firm's AML policy should set out what EDD is and when EDD must be undertaken in place of standard due diligence.
- The firm should also factor EDD into any onboarding process and provide questions in the firm's standard client and matter risk assessment which will help ascertain if EDD is required.

3.10 What is ongoing monitoring? When should it be done, and what methods could be used to undertake it?

The AML Regulations require ongoing monitoring to take place. This is defined under regulation 28(11) as:

(a) scrutiny of transactions undertaken throughout the course of the relationship (including, where necessary, the source of funds) to ensure that the transactions are consistent with the relevant person's knowledge of the customer, the customer's business and risk profile;

(b) undertaking reviews of existing records and keeping the documents or information obtained for the purpose of applying customer due diligence measures up-to-date.

Essentially, ongoing monitoring is about regularly and/or at pivotal points reconsidering the position whether that be rechecking what is known, re-evaluating the risk or rerunning checks.

When EDD has been applied, then ongoing monitoring should occur throughout the transaction at hand.

Below are some practical ways in which implementation of ongoing monitoring might occur:

- if the client or matter is considered to be higher risk, then a supervisor and the conducting fee earner could agree to meet regularly to discuss whether the risk has changed and whether any further information is needed;
- if the client or matter is considered to be higher risk, then the client could be placed on a high-risk register from which PEP, sanction and adverse media checks are rerun;
- CDD could be reviewed on each new matter and PEP, sanction and adverse media checks rerun;
- PEP, sanction and adverse media checks could be rerun prior to the receipt of monies or transaction completing;
- a flag could be placed on the firm's payment request form/process to ask the fee earner to consider and confirm that the risk assessment has not changed and it is ok to proceed, etc. (the aim of this flag is to trigger analysis).

This list is not exhaustive.

What are the compliance challenges?

- Understanding when ongoing monitoring is needed and at what level is crucial and must not be missed.
- Fee earners need to understand how to conduct ongoing monitoring.

What resources will help?

- The AML Regulations 2017 should be consulted, and in particular regulation 28.
- LSAG also provides guidance in this area: 'Anti-money laundering guidance for the legal sector' (20 January 2021, **www.lawsociety.org.uk/topics/anti-money-laundering/anti-money-laundering-guidance**).

Compliance tips – how to mitigate the risk of getting it wrong

- The firm's AML policy should set out what ongoing monitoring is, when it must be undertaken and how.
- Firms should regularly check that it is being undertaken.

3.11 My client cannot provide the 'normal' ID documents – what can I ask for?

Sometimes clients cannot provide the usual ID documents such as photo ID and proof of address. The first thought needs to be whether this inability to provide ID documents rings true. If it does not, then relevant persons may need to speak to their MLRO about whether suspicions should arise that money laundering is occurring.

If the inability to provide standard ID documents appears legitimate (this might be because the Home Office has the client's ID documents and the firm is being instructed in an immigration case or the client is elderly and has no photo ID) then some 'out of the box' thinking needs to be undertaken. The first step is always to remember *why* you need to obtain ID in the first place. Yes, the regulations require you to identify a client – but why? Generally speaking, providing ID documentation mitigates the chances of money laundering occurring, but it does not mean that those who provide ID documents are not money launderers. What is important is to obtain what the client is able to give, and consider whether that is proportionate to the AML risk. In an immigration case, for example, the AML risk is low and therefore a letter from the Home Office confirming status would suffice. Where the client is unable to prove their home address because they live in a care home or hostel, then a letter from the care home or hostel manager confirming their residency could be taken.

It is important to be proportionate in approach to align with the assessment of risk.

What are the compliance challenges?

- Being able to adapt to the client's inability to produce usual ID documentation.

What resources will help?

- LSAG provides guidance in this area: 'Anti-money laundering guidance for the legal sector' (20 January 2021, **www.lawsociety.org.uk/topics/anti-money-laundering/anti-money-laundering-guidance**).

Compliance tips – how to mitigate the risk of getting it wrong

- ID documentation taken should be proportionate to the AML risk.
- In most cases, clients that are unable to provide usual identification documentation can provide something and something is far better than nothing (a view can often be taken on something but rarely on nothing at all). 'Out of the box' thinking is needed.
- The AML Regulations are not there to deny client access to justice and should not be a barrier to obtaining legal advice.

3.12 I cannot verify my client's identity – can I still act?

AML Regulations, reg.31(1) sets out that if a firm is unable to fulfil CDD measures as required by regulation 28 then the relevant person:

(a) must not carry out any transaction through a bank account with the [client] or on behalf of the [client];
(b) must not establish a business relationship or carry out a transaction with the [client] otherwise than through a bank account;
(c) must terminate any existing business relationship with the [client];
(d) must consider whether the relevant person is required to make a disclosure [of suspicious of money laundering and a disclosure made to the National Crime Agency (NCA)].

It is clear, therefore, that where CDD cannot be obtained, the firm and fee earner should not act.

However, note that regulation 28(6)–(8) sets out that when acting for a body corporate if the relevant person has exhausted all possible means of identifying the beneficial owner but has not been able to do so or is not satisfied that the individual identified is in fact the beneficial owner, then the relevant person may treat the senior person who is responsible for management of the body corporate as its beneficial owner. This decision must be documented as well as all steps taken to verify the beneficial owner.

Even though the regulations allow relevant persons to continue to act in these circumstances, significant thought needs to be had as to whether to continue to act and if the inability to identify the beneficial owner gives cause for suspicion then the firm's MLRO should be consulted for further guidance.

What are the compliance challenges?

- It is possible that fee earners may still want to act and it is important that they understand that verification of ID is a requirement of the AML Regulations.

What resources will help?

- LSAG provides some guidance in this area: 'Anti-money laundering guidance for the legal sector' (20 January 2021, **www.lawsociety.org.uk/topics/anti-money-laundering/anti-money-laundering-guidance**).

Compliance tips – how to mitigate the risk of getting it wrong

- If due diligence gathering is not centralised, then it is more vital for fee earners to understand that if they are unable to verify identity then they need to stop work (if it has begun) and speak to the MLRO.
- This should be set out in the firm's AML policy and regular checks on the ID and verification of that ID undertaken.

3.13 What work can I do whilst I am in the process of obtaining CDD?

AML Regulations 2017, reg.30 sets out that provided that the verification of ID is completed as soon as practicable after contact is first established, verification may be completed during the establishment of a business relationship if this is necessary not to interrupt the normal conduct of business and there is little risk of money laundering and terrorist financing. In all other cases, a relevant person must comply with the requirement to verify the identity of the client, any person purporting to act on behalf of the client and any beneficial owner of the client before the establishment of a business relationship or the carrying out of the transaction.

It should be noted, however, that regulation 31 allows the relevant person to continue acting in the absence of due diligence if the relevant person is in the course of ascertaining the legal position for a client or performing the task of defending or representing that client in, or concerning, legal proceedings, including giving advice on the institution or avoidance of proceedings.

Practically speaking, unless there are concerns of money laundering, it is permissible to begin preliminary work on a transaction (for example, writing to parties to confirm that the firm has been instructed and putting in hand property searches) or advising a client. However, no monies should be receipted unless for fees and disbursements, no substantive work should be delivered and no transactions completed.

What are the compliance challenges?

- Naturally fee earners are keen to get on with the work as soon as possible. It is important that fee earners understand what they can and cannot do before the CDD process is complete. The risk is that monies are taken in or substantive work done before the CDD process has been completed.

What resources will help?

- The firm's AML risk policy should make clear what is and is not permissible before CDD is completed.

Compliance tips – how to mitigate the risk of getting it wrong

- Ensure that the firm's AML policy is clear, and provide clear guidance and training.
- Ensure that the AML policy is clear that no transactional monies should be taken before CDD is complete.
- The AML policy should set out the steps to be taken if transactional monies are sent to the firm before the CDD process completed.

3.14 What is a high-risk third country and what do I have to do if I am dealing with someone in such a country?

When establishing a business relationship with a client who is established in a high-risk third country, EDD must be undertaken. See **3.9**.

Further, the AML Regulations require that if either party in a relevant transaction are established in a high-risk third country, then EDD must be undertaken. Note, however, that the requirement for EDD when the other party is from a high-risk third country applies only to relevant transactions as defined under regulation 27. This means that further due diligence must be undertaken in the event that the other party is established in a high-risk third country where there is a suspicion of money laundering or the firm is engaging in an occasional transaction. Law firms do not enter into occasional transactions and therefore unless there is concern of money laundering relating to the other party to a matter, no further due diligence will be required as far as the other party being established in a high-risk country is concerned. Please see **3.15**.

Being 'established in' is defined in regulation 33(3)(c) as:

(i) in the case of a legal person, being incorporated in or having its principal place of business in that country, or, in the case of a financial institution or a credit institution, having its principal regulatory authority in that country; and

(ii) in the case of an individual, being resident in that country, but not merely having been born in that country.

A list of high-risk third countries can be found in the Money Laundering and Terrorist Financing (High-Risk Countries) (Amendment) Regulations 2022, SI 2022/393. Regular consultation with this list should occur, as it is subject to change.

High-risk countries (as opposed to high-risk third countries defined by the above regulations) are not confined to this list, and when considering where a client is from, a separate list should be consulted also. A good starting point is the Corruption Perception Index (**www.transparency.org/en/cpi/2020/index/nzl**).

What are the compliance challenges?

- The concept of a high-risk third country is relatively new. It is important that fee earners are made aware of the regulatory requirements and that they are required to check where their clients are established.

What resources will help?

- Money Laundering and Terrorist Financing (High-Risk Countries) (Amendment) Regulations 2022, SI 2022/393.
- LSAG guidance: 'Anti-money laundering guidance for the legal sector' (20 January 2021, **www.lawsociety.org.uk/topics/anti-money-laundering/anti-money-laundering-guidance**).

Compliance tips – how to mitigate the risk of getting it wrong

- Ensure that high-risk third country requirements are set out in the firm's AML policy and are also included in the firm's client risk assessment to be undertaken and revisited on each new matter.
- This could be in the form of a question such as 'Is your client established in a high-risk country?' and then a list provided of the most likely encountered high-risk countries to include high risk third countries and a link to the above named regulations and perhaps the Corruption Perception Index (**www.transparency.org/en/cpi/2020/index/nzl**).

3.15 What is an occasional transaction and am I undertaking one?

An occasion transaction is defined as 'a transaction which is not carried out as part of a business relationship' (AML Regulations, reg.3, 'General interpretation') and therefore is very unlikely that a law firm would carry out an occasional transaction.

If a firm considers that it is undertaking an occasional transaction, then it needs to consider whether it is appropriate to do so.

What are the compliance challenges?

- It is important for firms to know under what circumstances the AML Regulations apply.

What resources will help?

- The LSAG guidance will help here: 'Anti-money laundering guidance for the legal sector' (20 January 2021, **www.lawsociety.org.uk/topics/anti-money-laundering/anti-money-laundering-guidance**).

Compliance tips – how to mitigate the risk of getting it wrong

- The firm's AML policy should set out under what circumstances the AML Regulations apply and what an occasional transaction means.

3.16 Do I need to identify an intermediary, agent or representative of the client?

AML Regulations 2017, reg.28(10) requires relevant persons to identify and verify the identity of intermediaries, agents or representatives of clients. Further evidence of the person's authority to provide instructions on behalf of the client should be obtained to mitigate the possibility of fraud (also note that the SRA

Code of Conduct for Solicitors, rule 8.1 requires solicitors to identify who they are acting for).

A proportionate approach needs to be taken. Employees of a client would not generally be seen to be purporting to act on behalf of a client, because they are, in effect, the client. Therefore, if acting for a bank and an employee who has the correct role within the bank to be providing instructions does provide instructions, there is no requirement to identify and verify the identity of that individual (and trying to do so will no doubt upset the client). Where it will be necessary is where, for example, a family member is giving instructions on behalf of the client or is some other independent third party separate from the client.

What are the compliance challenges?

- The requirement to identify an intermediary, agent or representative of a client is relatively new and may have taken firms and solicitors time to get to grips with.
- It is important to be proportionate and not seek to identify and verify the identity of people who are clearly employees of the client.

What resources will help?

- LSAG provides useful guidance: 'Anti-money laundering guidance for the legal sector' (20 January 2021, **www.lawsociety.org.uk/topics/anti-money-laundering/anti-money-laundering-guidance**).

Compliance tips – how to mitigate the risk of getting it wrong

- Firms should ensure that their AML policy includes what should be done, when and how.
- It would also be prudent to place a question about intermediaries in the client and matter risk assessment as an aide memoire to the rule and the steps that need to be taken.

3.17 I am being referred a matter from another law firm and that law firm wants to be my client instead of the underlying client of theirs – can the law firm be the client?

A law firm may refer work to another where they do not have the specific expertise to provide advice to a client. Sometimes that referring law firm will ask to be the client of the law firm who is conducting the work and ask that they rather than the underlying client is billed.

Whether it is appropriate for the referring law firm to be the client or the underlying client to be the client of record will depend on the facts. If the work is of a sub-contracting nature – for example, where one small aspect of a large transaction is being referred to the other law firm – then the referring law firm could be the client and the bill addressed to it. However, whether the law firm or the underlying client is the client of record does not circumnavigate the need for due diligence to be undertaken on the underlying client. This is because the money laundering regulations require relevant persons to identify beneficial owners and this extends to the underlying client on whose behalf the work is being conducted.

LSAG provides a useful table setting out the position:

Intermediaries, agents or representatives	Referrals
If you are instructed by a law firm or other professional intermediary the law firm/professional intermediary are your client, and you will need to undertake CDD on them. If the effective beneficial owner of the advice is the law firm's/professional intermediary's client, you should consider the risks and identify/verify their client as you would any other ultimate beneficial owner. This could include understanding the checks the intermediary has carried out.	Where a legal practice or other intermediary refers a client to you and you have the direct relationship with the client, you should treat the referred entity as the client and carry out CDD in the usual way. You may wish to consider, having regard to the risks (and regulated status of the referring entity), whether a reliance agreement with the referring entity is appropriate in the circumstances.

LSAG, 'Anti-money laundering guidance for the legal sector' 2021, p.58.

Care must also be taken not to be a party to the referring law firm passing off the work as their own. The underlying client should be made aware who is providing advice, and their choice of legal representation must not be fettered in any way.

Further considerations for the firm undertaking the referred work are:

- conflict checking before work begins;
- how the client is set up in the firm's systems so as to ensure conflict checking in the future works;
- who will benefit from the firm's terms of business and insurance;
- who does the file belong to;
- who should the engagement letter be addressed to;
- who will be responsible for paying fees; and so on.

Relevant persons must also remember the AML Regulations do not have a fee *de minimis*, i.e. if the work will only pay a small fee, the regulations apply all the same, and therefore it may not be cost-effective to onboard clients where the fee is small (although the referring law firm may be able to provide what CDD they have which should cut down the time needed).

What are the compliance challenges?

- Often a challenge is managing the expectations of the referring law firm, particularly when they are overseas. Overseas firms, even when in Europe, sometimes do not undertake the same level of due diligence that UK law firms do, and therefore very careful thought needs to be given on the use of reliance (see **3.33–3.36**). If the work is of low value, the CDD burden will seem to outweigh the benefit.

What resources will help?

- LSAG provides very useful guidance: 'Anti-money laundering guidance for the legal sector' (20 January 2021, **www.lawsociety.org.uk/topics/anti-money-laundering/anti-money-laundering-guidance**).

Compliance tips – how to mitigate the risk of getting it wrong

- Firms should ensure that their AML policy is clear on who is the client and the level of CDD needed. Separate guidance and training may be needed.
- A question could be included in the client and matter risk assessment as an aide memoire to the requirements.

3.18 A partner in the firm is saying that he or she knows the client and therefore we do not need to obtain ID documentation or undertake any form of risk assessment – is this correct?

There is no provision in the AML Regulations for waiving any aspect of the CDD process for long-standing relationships. It is that simple. When referring family members, those family members must also be onboarded in the same way as non-family member clients.

It is important that at any stage, relevant persons can show regulators and authorities the CDD they have on a client. If no CDD is undertaken, the regulations will not be met – and further, if the partner or other relevant person is no longer at the firm, then the CDD knowledge is likely lost. Lastly, confirmation requests from third parties in transactional work that CDD has been undertaken on clients is widespread and this confirmation cannot be given if reliance is placed on a relevant person (partner or otherwise) knowing the client in place of CDD.

Firms must therefore adopt a policy not to accept such confirmation. That having been said, the fact the client is well-known to the relevant person can form part of the client and matter risk assessment.

What are the compliance challenges?

- If this is a change of policy for firms, it may be challenged by internal persons. Generally speaking, in the writer's experience, family members of firm staff or partners do not mind providing their ID documents.
- It is always helpful to explain that law firms are regulated just like banks, and if you know the bank branch manager it doesn't mean you can have an account

opened without providing ID documents. There may, however, be some upset amongst certain people which will need to be carefully managed.

What resources will help?

- LSAG provides helpful guidance: 'Anti-money laundering guidance for the legal sector' (20 January 2021, **www.lawsociety.org.uk/topics/anti-money-laundering/anti-money-laundering-guidance**).

Compliance tips – how to mitigate the risk of getting it wrong

- The firm's stance should be clearly set out in the firm's AML policy.
- A system should also be in place for checking CDD on files, whether that be through a centralised process or file reviews.

3.19 What the client is telling me does not match the people with significant control register – what do I need to do?

AML Regulations 2017, reg.30A states that before establishing a business relationship with a company, limited liability partnership (LLP) or Scottish Partnership, the relevant person must collect proof of registration or an excerpt of the relevant register for that corporate body (this will often be the people with significant control (PSC) register).

If the register is at odds with the information provided by the body, the relevant person will need to report the same to Companies House. Law firms do not need to hunt out discrepancies or seek to ensure that there are none, and legal professional privilege will apply. Reports should be made as soon as possible.

In practice, if discrepancies are found, the firm or relevant person may well wish to raise them with the client and ask that they correct the anomaly and provide an explanation for it. To report without giving a client a chance to put the position right will undoubtedly damage client relationships. Should the client not put the register right, then the firm or relevant person has no choice but to report the matter to Companies House via their portal. It is recommended that a question is asked about discrepancies with the PSC Register on the client and matter risk assessment.

What are the compliance challenges?

- If the PSC Register is not checked, meaning the discrepancy is not picked up and reported, this will be a breach of the AML Regulations.

What resources will help?

- LSAG's guidance is helpful: 'Anti-money laundering guidance for the legal sector' (20 January 2021, **www.lawsociety.org.uk/topics/anti-money-laundering/anti-money-laundering-guidance**).

Compliance tips – how to mitigate the risk of getting it wrong

- Firms should ensure that this is covered in the firm's AML policy and also a question about it asked in the client risk assessment.

FUNDS

3.20 What are source of funds and source of wealth?

As part of due diligence on a transaction, relevant persons need to consider whether they should investigate the client's *source of funds* to be used in the transaction and also the client's *source of wealth*.

Understanding the source of funds for a transaction is about understanding what monies will be used and where the monies are coming from.

Source of someone's wealth is about how they accumulated the monies that they have, and understanding the client's body of wealth.

It is not enough to ask to see the monies in a bank account statement. The question that must be asked is – how did it get there?

Source of funds and wealth investigations do not need to be undertaken if the only monies being receipted are for fees and disbursements. The caveat to that is if the relevant person becomes aware of something that gives cause for suspicion, then that should be investigated despite the monies only being for fees and disbursements.

What are the compliance challenges?

- The most challenging aspect of this area of compliance is knowing how far to go and when to be comfortable. Solicitors are not detectives, and their job is not to prove the monies are clean. Their job is to ask about the funds and wealth, verify what is being said and consider if this makes sense in the context of what the solicitor knows about the client and the transaction (it is for this reason that in the writers' opinion this cannot be delegated to anyone else, including a centralised risk team).

What resources will help?

- LSAG provides some guidance: 'Anti-money laundering guidance for the legal sector' (20 January 2021, **www.lawsociety.org.uk/topics/anti-money-laundering/anti-money-laundering-guidance**).

Compliance tips – how to mitigate the risk of getting it wrong

- Firms should ensure that this is covered in the firm's AML policy.
- Further guidance and training should be given, with the training being as practical as possible.

- A dedicated question should be placed in the client and matter risk assessment with enough space for the conducting fee earner to set out their source of funds and wealth investigations, outcome and views.

3.21 Why do I need to be concerned with source of funds and source of wealth?

The purchase of assets is a way to convert proceeds of crime for on-selling later, thereby 'cleaning' monies. Law firms, with client accounts to pay monies into and lawyers to provide an air of legitimacy, provide an opportunity to launder money.

Relevant persons who investigate and understand source of funds and wealth are far less likely to be involved in a transaction using proceeds of crime and therefore money laundering.

It is vital, therefore, that on matters which carry money laundering risk, source of funds and wealth questions and investigations take place.

What are the compliance challenges?

- As above, the most challenging aspect of this area of compliance is knowing how far to go and when to be comfortable. Solicitors are not detectives, and their job is not to prove the monies are clean. Their job is to ask about the funds and wealth, verify what is being said and consider if this makes sense in the context of what the solicitor knows about the client and the transaction (it is for this reason that in the writers' opinion this cannot be delegated to anyone else, including a centralised risk team).

What resources will help?

- LSAG provides some guidance: 'Anti-money laundering guidance for the legal sector' (20 January 2021, **www.lawsociety.org.uk/topics/anti-money-laundering/anti-money-laundering-guidance**).

Compliance tips – how to mitigate the risk of getting it wrong

- Firms should ensure that this is covered in the firm's AML policy.
- Further guidance and training should be given, with the training being as practical as possible.
- A dedicated question should be placed in the client and matter risk assessment with enough space for the conducting fee earner to set out their source of funds and wealth investigations, outcome and views.

3.22 How can I investigate source of funds and wealth, and what do I need to obtain?

Firstly, the key to understanding the source of funds and wealth of a client in the absence of open-source information (for example, if the client is a well-known individual where their source of funds is well-known publicly) is to ask the client about it. Some firms may choose to ask the client to complete a short form setting out the source of the funds and wealth, together with the information that is required from the client to evidence it. The answers given by a client must be evidenced, and firms should not accept what the client is saying at face value.

Below is a table outlining possible source of funds and wealth, and information that firms might want to obtain to evidence it.

Source of funds/source of wealth	Information/documentation that may be required
Employment income	• Nature of employer's business • Name and address of employer • Annual salary and bonuses for the last couple of years • Last three months' pay slips • Confirmation from employer of annual salary • Latest accounts or tax declaration if self employed
Savings/deposit	• Bank statements showing monies and bank statements showing where monies come from
Property sale	• Details of the property sold (i.e. address, date of sale, value of property sold) • Copy of contract of sale • Title deed from land registry
Sale of shares or other investment	• Copy of contract • Sale value of shares sold and how they were sold • Statement of account from agent • Transaction receipt/confirmation • Shareholder's certificate • Date of sale
Loan	• Loan agreement • Amount, date and purpose of loan • Name and address of lender • Details of any security
Company sale	• Copy of the contract of sale • Internet research of company registry • Name and address of company • Total sales price • Clients' share participation • Nature of business

Source of funds/source of wealth	Information/documentation that may be required
	• Date of sale and receipt of funds • Media coverage
Company profits/dividends	• Copy of latest audited financial statements • Copy of latest management accounts • Board of Directors approval • Dividend distribution • Tax declaration form
Inheritance	• Name of deceased • Date of death • Relationship to client • Date received • Total amount • Solicitor's details so facts can be checked
Gift	• Date received • Total amount • Relationship to client • Letter from donor explaining the reason for the gift and the source of donor's wealth • Certified identification documents of donor
Maturity/surrender of life policy	• Amount received • Policy provider • Policy number/reference • Date of surrender
Other income sources	• Nature of income, amount, date received and from who • Appropriate supporting documentation

What are the compliance challenges?

- As above, the most challenging aspect of this area of compliance is knowing how far to go and when to be comfortable. Solicitors are not detectives, and their job is not to prove the monies are clean. Their job is to ask about the funds and wealth, verify what is being said and consider if this makes sense in the context of what the solicitor knows about the client and the transaction (it is for this reason that in the writers' opinion this cannot be delegated to anyone else including a centralised risk team).

What resources will help?

- LSAG now provides some guidance: 'Anti-money laundering guidance for the legal sector' (20 January 2021, **www.lawsociety.org.uk/topics/anti-money-laundering/anti-money-laundering-guidance**).

Compliance tips – how to mitigate the risk of getting it wrong

- Firms should ensure that this is covered in the firm's AML policy (with the above table possibly included).
- Further guidance and training should be given with the training being as practical as possible.
- A dedicated question should be placed in the client and matter risk assessment with enough space for the conducting fee earner to set out their source of funds and wealth investigations, outcome and views.

3.23 I cannot get clarity on my client's source of funds and wealth – should I be suspicious? Can I proceed?

If a firm/individual cannot get clarity on a client's source of funds and wealth, then careful thought needs to be given as to whether this should raise suspicions and whether a SAR needs to be made to the NCA. See **Chapter 4**.

The individual acting should raise the matter with their MLRO and take further instruction from them. Whether the matter can proceed or not will depend on whether a defence against money laundering is needed. Certainly, most law firms would not seek to act in a matter where they cannot adequately understand and verify the source of funds and wealth of a client.

What are the compliance challenges?

- Some sources of funds and wealth may be challenging to unravel and understand (for example, see below for guidance on cryptocurrencies).

What resources will help?

- The firm's own AML policy should set out what is required and whom to speak to if there are concerns.

Compliance tips – how to mitigate the risk of getting it wrong

- Firms should ensure that this is covered in the firm's AML policy and that it is made clear that if there are concerns about the client's source of funds and wealth or it is proving challenging to get clarity on it, the MLRO should be consulted.

3.24 My client's source of funds and wealth is cryptocurrency – what do I need to consider?

There is very little guidance on how to understand a client's source of funds and wealth when it is made up of cryptocurrency/cryptoassets. As more people invest and make money from cryptocurrencies, law firms will come across clients wishing to spend those funds by, for example, purchasing real estate.

If faced with crypto as a source of funds and wealth, the law firm needs to analyse the risk at hand and independent legal advice may need to be taken.

Below are some questions that firms may wish to ask clients and themselves in relation to this source of funds/wealth:

- What are the cryptoasset(s) to be used in the transaction – e.g. Bitcoin, Ethereum?
- What is the value of the monies coming from cryptoassets?
- How the cryptoassets that are to be used are held or stored by the client, i.e. hosted wallet (which are regulated in the UK and parts of Western Europe) or unhosted wallet (self-hosted, or controlled by another individual)?
- If the cryptoasset is stored in a hosted wallet, is a reputable provider used and are they regulated?
- How will the cryptoassets be applied to the transaction, i.e. will a reputable exchange be used, which one and in which jurisdictions are they regulated?
- How the cryptoassets came to be acquired in the first place – e.g. was government-issued currency exchanged for cryptoassets via a centralised exchange? Was it through crypto mining or an Initial Coin Offering?
- How long has the client had the cryptoasset, when was it first acquired and over what time period has it performed? What was the source of those funds?

If the client has a cryptoasset that attracts a high degree of privacy or anonymity or holds/stores the cryptoasset in a way that is not regulated, then the firm will be a need to ask the client questions about why they choose to use that type of cryptoasset/store in this manner and considering whether this fits in with what the firm knows about the client.

If the cryptoassets proposed to be used were acquired with government-issued currency, then the firm needs to understand the source of those funds in the normal way.

Assistance in the form of a letter and/or evidence could be sought from a client's accountant or other regulated entity to help with the client's explanation of the funds.

What are the compliance challenges?

- Understanding cryptocurrency/assets is very challenging, and independent legal advice may need to be sought.

What resources will help?

- There is little guidance out there for the legal profession on this subject, sadly.

Compliance tips – how to mitigate the risk of getting it wrong

- Everyone in the firm needs to be aware that if their client is intending to buy assets with monies made by cryptocurrencies/assets, they need to ask the questions above and speak to the MLRO for guidance (who then may take independent legal advice).

3.25 What happens if I undertake source of funds and wealth enquiries and I am satisfied, but it later turns out that the monies used were proceeds of crime?

If the relevant person has asked all appropriate questions, carefully analysed the responses, determined that the responses made sense in the context of what the relevant person knew about the client and matter and documented this analysis – then in the event that the monies used were proceeds of crime but there was nothing the relevant person could have done to uncover it, prosecution is unlikely.

The role of the relevant person here is not to prove that the monies are clean nor be a detective. Their role is to investigate the source of funds and wealth on a proportionate basis.

What are the compliance challenges?

- Solicitors are sometimes wary of coming to a conclusion when it comes to assessing the AML risk in transactions, either asking others to make that judgment or not making an assessment at all for fear that it will be incorrect and be something they will regret later.
- It is important to understand that it is far better to make an assessment and get it wrong than not make an assessment at all. The latter is a breach of the AML Regulations and the former can provide mitigation.

What resources will help?

- The firm's own AML policy and guidance should assist solicitors in their analysis.

Compliance tips – how to mitigate the risk of getting it wrong

- The firm's AML policy should make clear that an assessment as to AML risk including source of funds and wealth must take place and from whom guidance can be sought.
- Fee earners should also be assured that assessments properly made but where money laundering still occurs is unlikely to lead to prosecution.
- Failures to adhere to the AML Regulations can and are prosecuted.

3.26 Can my central onboarding team deal with source of funds and wealth investigations?

When considering source of funds and wealth, the assessor needs to consider whether what is being said by the client or other party makes sense in the context of what is known about the client and matter.

A central onboarding team will not meet the client and will not be undertaking the work. It is very difficult for a central onboarding team to analyse whether the information being presented tallies with what the relevant person knows. Further, if the central team is to undertake this analysis, the relevant person will not be as able to spot when the analysis should change due to change in funding or suspicious behaviour.

Relevant persons may be keen to pass over the analysis and sign off to a central team, but this could be a dangerous move as it distances the relevant person from the analysis. Because of this, it is not recommended. That said, a central team could *assist* the relevant person with their analysis, but just not do it for them.

What are the compliance challenges?

- Solicitors are sometimes wary of coming to a conclusion when it comes to assessing the AML risk in transactions either asking others to make that judgment or not making an assessment at all for fear that it will be incorrect and be something they will regret later.
- Delegating that analysis to a central onboarding/risk team does not alleviate that burden on the solicitor, could lead to incorrect conclusions and an inability on behalf of the solicitor to understand when the analysis should change or when suspicious behaviour is occurring.

What resources will help?

- The firm should set out what is required in its AML policy.
- LSAG also provides useful guidance: 'Anti-money laundering guidance for the legal sector' (20 January 2021, **www.lawsociety.org.uk/topics/anti-money-laundering/anti-money-laundering-guidance**).

Compliance tips – how to mitigate the risk of getting it wrong

- The firm's AML policy should make clear that an assessment as to AML risk including source of funds and wealth must take place and from whom guidance can be sought.
- Fee earners should also be assured that where assessments are properly made but where money laundering still occurs this is unlikely to lead to prosecution. However, failure to adhere to the AML Regulations can be and is prosecuted.
- Solicitors need to be clear also that a firm's onboarding team can assist with the analysis but not undertake it on behalf of the solicitor.

3.27 A deposit of monies has been made unsolicited and now the sender wants the monies back – what steps should we take?

The first step is to understand why the payment has been made, by whom and what their connection is to any client. Sometimes the other party to a transaction will make a payment directly to their opposite number's solicitor thinking that this will be more convenient. The reasons could well be innocent – however, the reasons could also be suspicious. Making an unsolicited payment and then requesting it back is a good way of giving monies a legitimate-looking audit trail, especially if the monies are being asked to be sent to a different account from where they came.

Once an understanding of why any payment has been made and by whom is ascertained, thought needs to be given as to whether due diligence ID documents of the sender should be gathered and what comfort that might give. Further still, if the sending of the monies and request for return is suspicious then the MLRO needs to consider if a defence to a money laundering offence request (in the form of a SAR) to the NCA should be made. See **Chapter 4**.

If the opposing party has sent the money directly rather than through their own solicitor, then their solicitor can confirm that they have undertaken all due diligence checks to include source of funds and wealth and are satisfied as to the same. Whether the firm requests reliance on this assessment is a judgement call and such a request may be declined. If the solicitor refuses to provide such confirmation again the MLRO need to consider if a defence against money laundering from the NCA should be sought before the monies are returned or used.

Finally, it is important for firms to have a policy process around payments that are made unsolicited.

What are the compliance challenges?

- Returning funds can provide monies a legitimate-looking audit trail and therefore careful analysis and thought needs to be given to returning funds.

What resources will help?

- LSAG guidance should be consulted: 'Anti-money laundering guidance for the legal sector' (20 January 2021, **www.lawsociety.org.uk/topics/anti-money-laundering/anti-money-laundering-guidance**).

Compliance tips – how to mitigate the risk of getting it wrong

- The firm's AML policy should set out the process when payments are received from non-clients or clients unsolicited before the monies are used, returned or sent elsewhere.

3.28 Our client wants to pay us in cash – should we accept?

The first thing to understand is that cash is not automatically bad. However, cash can be proceeds of crime and therefore be used to launder money. It is perfectly fine for firms to accept a little cash. That said, the days of being paid in suitcases full of cash in a solicitor's office are well and truly gone, and it is important that the firm has a policy about whether it will accept cash; and if so, up to what amount. This should also feature in the firm's terms of business and be understood by all in the firm including reception and accounts, who are likely to be the recipient of cash requests.

What are the compliance challenges?

- Accepting cash increases the risk of being involved in money laundering.

What resources will help?

- LSAG guidance should be consulted: 'Anti-money laundering guidance for the legal sector' (20 January 2021, **www.lawsociety.org.uk/topics/anti-money-laundering/anti-money-laundering-guidance**).

Compliance tips – how to mitigate the risk of getting it wrong

- The firm should set out in its AML policy and terms of business its policy on the acceptance of cash.
- Further, it is a good idea to set out in the firm's terms that the firm are able to charge for time spent in investigating the source of cash if this policy is breached (because sadly it is generally not possible to instruct the firm's bank to not accept cash or only cash up to a certain amount, and so it is possible for people to put any amount of cash in to the client account. It is worth checking that this is the case with the firm's bank and whether a restriction can be put on).

3.29 Just before completion our client informs us that funds are to come from a separate corporate entity – what do we need to do?

First of all, you need to understand why the funds are coming from this source and what connection the corporate entity (or any other third party) has to the client. If the corporate entity is a company within the client's group structure and the source of funds and wealth is understood, then this may well not give rise to suspicion of money laundering. Further, if the client is an individual and monies are to come from a company that the individual owns 100 per cent and is their source of income, this again might not give rise to any suspicion.

The explanation given for monies coming from a separate entity should not be taken at face value. It must be questioned, checked out and evidenced. So, for example, if the firm is told that monies will come from a separate unconnected entity because that entity owes money to the client, then evidence to prove this should be sought.

You might think that asking the third party entity to pay the monies to the client and the client paying the monies to the firm will resolve the issue but it really doesn't as the firm knows that the monies have come from the third party.

Further, it is part of the firm's due diligence to understand source of funds and wealth and so they would need to take steps to understand where the monies have come from and why.

If the entity is not connected and the explanation does not seem to stack up then there might be suspicion of money laundering and the MLRO should be consulted so that any future defence to a money laundering offence from the NCA can be considered.

What are the compliance challenges?

- Monies from an unexpected party can come at the very last minute – just before exchange or completion, for example.
- This can place immense pressure on solicitors to utilise the monies without further investigation. *This must not happen.*

What resources will help?

- LSAG guidance should be consulted: 'Anti-money laundering guidance for the legal sector' (20 January 2021, **www.lawsociety.org.uk/topics/anti-money-laundering/anti-money-laundering-guidance**).

Compliance tips – how to mitigate the risk of getting it wrong

- The firm's AML policy should set out the steps to take when monies are sent from an unexpected source.
- Further, the firm may wish to place in its terms of business that the firm are able to charge for time spent in investigating the source of funds if it is sent from an unexpected party.
- The firm may decide not to charge, but at least the warning is in the terms nonetheless.

3.30 My client's family member/friend wants to pay our fees – what do I need to do?

Any payment that is to be made must be understood in terms of who it is coming from and why.

Monies sent for the payment of fees and disbursements are by their nature non-transactional, and there is no requirement to undertake due diligence on the sender of such funds. However, some firms may decide to implement a policy whereby the sender of funds is required to provide their ID documentation, checks are undertaken on them (such as PEP, sanction and adverse media checks) and an explanation of their source of funds and wealth. If the firm decides not to implement such a policy, the firm and those within it must still have their eyes open to anything suspicious when it comes to the person or entity making the payment and the monies themselves (for example, there might be a news story about the money sender or that the funds are coming from a high-risk jurisdiction).

What are the compliance challenges?

- It can be misunderstood that persons who pay monies to firms must be onboarded as a client. This is not correct, and in fact to open the person as a client when the firm is not acting for them will skew the firm's conflict checking in the future.
- What must happen, though, is an investigation around why the person is paying money, whether there are any suspicions and whether to undertake any form of CDD.

What resources will help?

- LSAG guidance should be consulted: 'Anti-money laundering guidance for the legal sector' (20 January 2021, **www.lawsociety.org.uk/topics/anti-money-laundering/anti-money-laundering-guidance**).

Compliance tips – how to mitigate the risk of getting it wrong

- The firm's AML policy should set out the firm's process when a third party pays the fees of the client.
- Further, the firm may wish to place in its terms of business that the firm are able to charge for time spent in conducting CDD on the third party if it is the firm's policy to do so.
- The firm may decide not to charge but at least the warning is in the terms nonetheless.

3.31 My client's family/friend wants to pay all/part of the transaction monies – what do I need to do?

Unlike monies for fees and disbursements, monies for the transaction itself require due diligence to be undertaken on the individual or entity sending the monies. This should be undertaking ID checks; PEP, sanction and adverse media checking; as well as understanding why the person or entity is paying and their source of funds and wealth.

What are the compliance challenges?

- It can be misunderstood that persons who pay monies to firms must be onboarded as a client. This is not correct, and in fact to open the person as a client when the firm is not acting for them will skew the firm's conflict checking in the future.
- What must happen, though, is CDD on the individual and consideration as to whether there are any suspicions.

What resources will help?

- LSAG guidance should be consulted: 'Anti-money laundering guidance for the legal sector' (20 January 2021, **www.lawsociety.org.uk/topics/anti-money-laundering/anti-money-laundering-guidance**).

Compliance tips – how to mitigate the risk of getting it wrong

- The firm's AML policy should set out the firm's process when a third party pays transactional monies to the firm.
- Further, the firm may wish to place in its terms of business that the firm are able to charge for time spent in conducting CDD on the third party.
- The firm may decide not to charge but at least the warning is in the terms nonetheless.

RELIANCE

3.32 What does reliance mean under the AML Regulations? What should be obtained?

AML Regulations 2017, reg.39 allows a relevant person to rely on the CDD conducted by a person who is required to undertake CDD under the regulations. However, the regulation is explicit that the relevant person who is seeking to rely remains liable for any failure in that CDD undertaken.

Regulation 39(2) goes on to state:

> When a relevant person relies on the third party to apply customer due diligence measures or carry out any of the measures required by regulation 30A under paragraph (1) it —
>
> (a) must immediately obtain from the third party all the information needed to satisfy the requirements of regulation 28(2) to (6) and (10) and regulation 30A in relation to the customer, customer's beneficial owner, or any person acting on behalf of the customer;
>
> (b) must enter into arrangements with the third party which —
>
> (i) enable the relevant person to obtain from the third party immediately on request copies of any identification and verification data and any other relevant documentation on the identity of the customer, customer's beneficial owner, or any person acting on behalf of the customer;
>
> (ii) require the third party to retain copies of the data and documents referred to in paragraph (i) for the period referred to in regulation 40.

Therefore, the relevant person must obtain from the third party the name of the client and how their identity was verified (regulation 28(2)), the name of the senior person if the third party was unable to identify the beneficial owner and how that person's identity was verified (regulation 28(6)) and where a third party is acting on behalf of the client, the name of that third party and how their identity was verified by the third party upon whom reliance is to be placed (regulation 28(10).

To use reliance under the regulations, the person relying must therefore obtain CDD information and not simply ask if they can rely. The information obtained from the relevant person being relied upon must be in writing.

What are the compliance challenges?

- Those relying remain liable if the CDD has not been completed properly.
- Those who rely need to understand that CDD information as outlined above must be sought and given.

What resources will help?

- LSAG provides useful guidance: 'Anti-money laundering guidance for the legal sector' (20 January 2021, **www.lawsociety.org.uk/topics/anti-money-laundering/anti-money-laundering-guidance**).
- AML Regulations 2017, reg.39 should also be consulted.

Compliance tips – how to mitigate the risk of getting it wrong

- The firm must set out its stance on reliance in its AML policy.
- This must be communicated and understood by those in the firm.

3.33 What is the problem with reliance?

From the perspective of those seeking to rely, they remain liable should the CDD gathering and analysis they are relying is wrong in some way. It can therefore be quite dangerous to rely, especially when the client and/or the matter is anything other than low risk.

Not all relevant persons and firms will be as thorough, or indeed view the AML risk in the same way, and this can lead to the risk that insufficient CDD was obtained on the client.

From the perspective of those granting reliance, there is some concern that some liability will stick to those being relied on if the CDD is insufficient. Because of this, the relevant person being relied upon may wish to adopt an exclusion of liability.

What are the compliance challenges?

- Those relying remain liable if the CDD has not been completed properly.

What resources will help?

- LSAG provides useful guidance: 'Anti-money laundering guidance for the legal sector' (20 January 2021, **www.lawsociety.org.uk/topics/anti-money-laundering/anti-money-laundering-guidance**).
- AML Regulations 2017, reg.39 should also be consulted.

Compliance tips – how to mitigate the risk of getting it wrong

- The firm must set out its stance on reliance in its AML policy, and this must be communicated and understood by those in the firm.
- If the firm is allowing others to rely on it, it may wish to include an exclusion of liability.

3.34 A regulated entity has asked to rely on our assessment of the CDD – should we agree?

Each firm should have a policy on whether they will allow others to rely on their due diligence assessment at all, and if they will allow it, under what circumstances. For example, a firm may decide that they will allow reliance where the risk is low and the firm is instructing another regulated professional such as counsel or an accountant. Where the risk is considered to be higher, the firm may not wish to allow others to rely as the concern is that some liability will attach. As set out above, an exclusion of liability could overcome this concern.

If the firm does not wish to allow reliance as a matter of policy (and many firms take this stance), then they may wish, with client consent, to provide the due diligence ID documentation to the person or entity seeking to rely with the following wording:

> Subject to obtaining our client's consent, we will provide you with a copy of the due diligence we hold on our file to assist your due diligence requirements under the Money Laundering Regulations. However, it is for you to form your own opinion of these documents.
>
> For the avoidance of doubt, [*name of firm*] does not consent to the application of Regulation 39 of the Money Laundering, Terrorist Financing and Transfer of Funds (Information on the Payer) Regulations 2017 amended by the Money Laundering and Terrorist Financing (Amendment) Regulations 2019 and you cannot place reliance on this firm's assessment.

What are the compliance challenges?

- Although technically no liability should attach to those providing reliance, this is not tested and as such a limitation of liable could be included.

What resources will help?

- LSAG provides useful guidance: 'Anti-money laundering guidance for the legal sector' (20 January 2021, **www.lawsociety.org.uk/topics/anti-money-laundering/anti-money-laundering-guidance**).
- AML Regulations 2017, reg.39 should also be consulted.

Compliance tips – how to mitigate the risk of getting it wrong

- The firm must set out its stance on reliance in its AML policy and this must be communicated and understood by those in the firm.
- If the firm is allowing others to rely on it, it may wish to include an exclusion of liability.

3.35 We want to rely on the CDD assessment of another regulated entity – what do we need to think about?

A relevant person can only rely on the assessment of another if that other person or entity is subject to AML Regulations of an equivalent standard. Those in the European Economic Area (EEA) can therefore be relied upon. Other countries may also have equivalent standards and that would need to be researched before reliance is sought (the Commission de Surveillance du Secteur Financier have published a list which may be of use: **www.cssf.lu/en/2020/12/publication-of-cssf-regulation-no-20-09-on-the-equivalence-of-the-united-kingdom-for-the-purpose-of-the-mifir-third-country-national-regime/**). However, not all firms in all countries with the equivalent AML standards apply the same due diligence measures in practice, and therefore it is very important to get a full explanation of what due diligence has been undertaken and it is not enough to simply ask to rely without any detail on what due diligence has been undertaken.

It may be convenient to rely, but the relevant person relying remains liable, and therefore careful thought needs to be given as to whether reliance is appropriate in the context of the client and matter. The alternative is to ask for a copy of the CDD undertaken so that the relevant person can form their own view.

What are the compliance challenges?

- Those who seek to rely remain liable for the CDD undertaken and could be prosecuted if it is inadequate.
- Further information on the CDD undertaken needs to be obtained and not just a blanket request and agreement to allow reliance.

What resources will help?

- LSAG provides useful guidance: 'Anti-money laundering guidance for the legal sector' (20 January 2021, **www.lawsociety.org.uk/topics/anti-money-laundering/anti-money-laundering-guidance**).
- AML Regulations 2017, reg.39 should also be consulted.

Compliance tips – how to mitigate the risk of getting it wrong

- The firm must set out its stance on reliance in its AML policy and this must be communicated and understood by those in the firm.

RECORDS

3.36 What is the requirement to maintain records under the AML Regulations?

AML Regulations 2017, reg.40(3) requires documents and information obtained by the relevant person to satisfy CDD requirements and supporting records in respect of the transaction which was subject to ongoing monitoring, to be kept for five years beginning on the date on which the relevant person knows or has reasonable grounds to believe:

(a) that the transaction is complete, for records relating to an occasional transaction; or

(b) that the business relationship has come to an end for records relating to —

 (i) any transaction which occurs as part of a business relationship, or

 (ii) customer due diligence measures taken in connection with that relationship.

The regulation goes on further to state that the relevant person will not be required to keep records relating to the transaction for more than 10 years.

Under regulation 40(5), once the relevant period has expired (five years for CDD records and 10 years for records relating to the transaction) the personal data obtained for the purposes of the regulations must be destroyed save for in the following circumstances:

(a) the relevant person is required to retain records containing personal data —

 (i) by or under any enactment, or

 (ii) for the purposes of any court proceedings;

(b) the data subject has given consent to the retention of that data; or

(c) the relevant person has reasonable grounds for believing that records containing the personal data need to be retained for the purpose of legal proceedings.

It must be remembered that regulation 40 is not simply about destruction. It is about retention of relevant records to be called upon to show compliance with the regulations, and also to assist enforcement agencies in their investigations. Law firms should consider creating a designated file space for due diligence gathering and analysis such as the client and matter risk assessment (see **2.5–2.9**) and also a place for filing due diligence for easy future access (such as a sub-folder within the electronic file structure).

What are the compliance challenges?

- Firms must make sure they retain and destroy documentation at the right times to stay in line with the AML Regulations and also the Data Protection Act 2018.

What resources will help?

- LSAG provides useful guidance: 'Anti-money laundering guidance for the legal sector' (20 January 2021, **www.lawsociety.org.uk/topics/anti-money-laundering/anti-money-laundering-guidance**).
- AML Regulations 2017, reg.40 should also be consulted.

Compliance tips – how to mitigate the risk of getting it wrong

- Systems need to be put in place to ensure that records are kept then destroyed in line with legislation and the firm's policy/terms. See **3.37** below.

3.37 How can we vary the timescale by which we maintain records? Why would we want to?

As set out above, records must be retained for a minimum of five years after the end of a business relationship and should be destroyed after five years for CDD records and 10 years for transaction records unless certain conditions apply. Further, data protection laws require data to be destroyed when there is no legal basis to retain it.

Firms must therefore have sufficient processes and procedures in place to delete the data at the relevant time and may decide to seek the consent of the data subject to retain the data for longer than the regulations allow. This consent could be placed in the firm's engagement letter or terms of business. Note, however, that consent to data retention for longer periods will likely need a positive confirmation, and so this needs to be factored in and may be achieved by the client signing the engagement letter.

If the relevant person does not seek such consent or consent is denied then in all likelihood the firm will need to have a mechanism in place which seeks to destroy the CDD material potentially before the file (physical and electronic) is destroyed which is likely to be retained for longer. This is because in the event that the client instructed the relevant person for one piece of work, say a house purchase and then the relationship ended, the CDD material gathered under the regulations will need to be destroyed five years after but the firm will want to keep the file for at least six years and until the possibility of a negligence claim has elapsed. As such, the timescales are at odds with each other, and so it is likely to be far simpler to seek the client's consent for a longer retention period.

What are the compliance challenges?

- The timescale for which CDD material should be destroyed is likely to be at odds with the timescale for file destruction, meaning that the CDD material must be separately destroyed. This will be challenging to practically carry out.

What resources will help?

- LSAG provides useful guidance: 'Anti-money laundering guidance for the legal sector' (20 January 2021, **www.lawsociety.org.uk/topics/anti-money-laundering/anti-money-laundering-guidance**).
- AML Regulations 2017, reg.40 should also be consulted.

Compliance tips – how to mitigate the risk of getting it wrong

- Firms may wish to amend their terms of business or engagement letter to confirm that the client consents to retention of the CDD material to be in line with that of the time limit for destruction of the file.

CHAPTER 4

Suspicion and suspicious activity reports

4.1 What is suspicion?

Under the Proceeds of Crime Act 2002 (POCA 2002), relevant persons are required to disclose their suspicions of money laundering to the National Crime Agency (NCA) and seek a defence to what might be a money laundering offence (called a Defence Against Money Laundering – DAML).

POCA 2002 not only creates principal money laundering offences, but also creates the offence of failing to report suspicious activity and tipping off. See **1.3**.

Save for failing to report and tipping off, POCA 2002 applies to everyone and not just regulated persons.

To be convicted of an offence of failure to report under POCA 2002, the prosecution must prove knowledge, suspicion or reasonable ground for suspicion. Further, the prosecution must prove that the property involved was criminal property, i.e. that it was obtained through criminal conduct and that at the time of the alleged offence the individual knew or suspected it was criminal property. Updated guidance has been provided by the Crown Prosecution Service (CPS) to prosecutors setting out that money laundering does not need to have actually occurred to prosecute a defendant for a failure to report suspicious activity ('Money laundering offences', updated: 2 June 2021, **www.cps.gov.uk/legal-guidance/money-laundering-offences**).

It is vital, therefore, that everyone in a firm understands what suspicion means and what to do when it has arisen.

Case law guidance on what constitutes suspicion can be found in *R* v. *Da Silva* [2007] 1 WLR 303. Here the judge commented that suspicion is where a defendant must think that there is a possibility which is more than fanciful that the relevant facts exist, i.e. facts leading to a possibility of money laundering, and that 'a vague feeling of unease would not suffice' (para.16).

LSAG comments that: 'There is no requirement for the suspicion to be clear or firmly grounded on specific facts, but there must be a degree of satisfaction, not necessarily amounting to belief, but at least extending beyond speculation' ('Anti-money laundering guidance for the legal sector', p.184).

A person does not need to be clear that money laundering or some crime is occurring, but if they suspect a crime might be occurring, they should discuss this with the firm's money laundering reporting officer (MLRO). Suspicion does not extend only to a firm's client and may arise due to suspicion about another party involved in a transaction. If this is the case, then the relevant person should discuss this with the MLRO.

What are the compliance challenges?

- The threshold for suspicion is low and everyone in the firm must understand this and know whom to speak to when the test for suspicion is met.

What resources will help?

- The Legal Sector Affinity Group (LSAG) provides useful guidance: 'Anti-money laundering guidance for the legal sector' (20 January 2021, **www.lawsociety.org.uk/topics/anti-money-laundering/anti-money-laundering-guidance**).

Compliance tips – how to mitigate the risk of getting it wrong

- The firm's anti-money laundering (AML) policy must make it clear what suspicion is and whom to report it to.
- Further, the policy must set out what can and cannot be said or done vis-a-vis the client.
- All relevant persons in the firm must be provided with AML training which covers suspicion and what to do.

4.2 When I am suspicious, what should I do?

The first thing anyone who is suspicious that money laundering is occurring must do is speak to the firm's MLRO. Their role is outlined at **1.7**. The MLRO will provide further guidance on what can be said to the client, if anything, what work can be done and whether a suspicious activity report (SAR) needs to be made.

No further steps should be made until the MLRO advises. The relevant person reporting their suspicions to the MLRO will be protected if he or she follows this procedure, and risks committing an offence if he or she does not.

What are the compliance challenges?

- Relevant persons need to understand what should give rise to suspicion, and what to do if that occurs.

What resources will help?

- LSAG provides useful guidance, and also warning flags which could give rise to suspicion: 'Anti-money laundering guidance for the legal sector', sections 16.7

and 18 (20 January 2021, **www.lawsociety.org.uk/topics/anti-money-laundering/anti-money-laundering-guidance**).

Compliance tips – how to mitigate the risk of getting it wrong

- The firm's AML policy must make it clear what suspicion is and who to report it to.
- Further, the policy must set out what can and cannot be said or done vis-a-vis the client.
- All relevant persons in the firm must be provided with AML training which covers suspicion and what to do.
- Finally, it is a good idea to place the LSAG warning flags into the firm's AML policy.

4.3 What is the role of the MLRO?

Money Laundering, Terrorist Financing and Transfer of Funds (Information on the Payer) Regulations 2017, SI 2017/692 (AML Regulations), reg.21(3) requires that firms have a nominated officer who is tasked with receiving disclosures of suspicious activity from those within the firm and to then subsequently make disclosures to the NCA and seek an appropriate defence to money laundering. This officer is also known as the MLRO.

If a firm does not provide services within the regulated sector, they do not have to appoint a nominated officer – but should consider doing so as good practice. Note, however, that the definition of 'tax adviser' is wide and so firms who consider that they are not caught under the regulations may find that they in fact are (see **1.10**).

The MLRO needs to be someone who has sufficient seniority and access to client files and business information to enable him or her to make decisions on reporting.

In larger firms, it is a good idea for the MLRO to appoint a deputy to provide cover in the MLRO's absence and assist if SARs are a regular occurrence.

Naturally the MLRO will also liaise with the NCA and/or police and respond to any queries that he or she may have, taking into consideration privilege (see **4.6**).

It is important that firms view the role of an MLRO as a job and not just a job title. Sufficient time should be dedicated to being the MLRO and therefore careful thought needs to be given as to whether the role holder is a full-time fee earner or a business services person dedicated to being the MLRO (and possibly other things).

What are the compliance challenges?

- The MLRO needs to be of sufficient seniority, have access to all information that he or she needs to fulfil their role and be given the appropriate amount of time to undertake MLRO tasks.

What resources will help?

- LSAG's guidance is an MLRO's 'bible' and should be consulted: 'Anti-money laundering guidance for the legal sector' (20 January 2021, **www.lawsociety.org.uk/topics/anti-money-laundering/anti-money-laundering-guidance**).
- Further, the MLRO would do well to read the AML Regulations 2017.
- Lastly, the Solicitors Regulation Authority's (SRA's) *Money Laundering Governance: Three Pillars of Success* provides very useful guidance (22 November 2021, **www.sra.org.uk/sra/how-we-work/reports/money-laundering-governance-three-pillars-of-success/**).

Compliance tips – how to mitigate the risk of getting it wrong

- Firms need to make sure that they select an MLRO who has sufficient seniority, access to information and time to undertake MLRO tasks.

4.4 What is a SAR, what does it do and what is the timescale for a response?

A SAR is a method by which a relevant person (normally via the MLRO) can report to the NCA suspicious activity and where appropriate seek a defence against a money laundering offence for an act that will take place.

Once submitted, the NCA have seven working days starting the day after the submission (provided it was submitted before 5pm) to either provide or refuse the defence sought.

A SAR should be submitted even if no defence is needed so as to impart suspicious activity information on the NCA.

What are the compliance challenges?

- The threshold for suspicion is low and everyone in the firm must understand this and know whom to speak to when the test for suspicion is met.
- The firm's MLRO must understand the SAR regime.

What resources will help?

- LSAG provides useful guidance in this area: 'Anti-money laundering guidance for the legal sector' (20 January 2021, **www.lawsociety.org.uk/topics/anti-money-laundering/anti-money-laundering-guidance**).
- The NCA also provides useful guidance: 'Guidance on submitting better quality Suspicious Activity Reports (SARs)' (September 2021, V6.0, **www.nationalcrimeagency.gov.uk/who-we-are/publications/446-guidance-on-submitting-better-quality-sars-1/file**).

- Law Society guidance: 'Suspicious activity reports' (3 June 2021, **www.lawsociety.org.uk/en/topics/anti-money-laundering/suspicious-activity-reports**).
- SRA warning notice: 'Money laundering and terrorist financing suspicious activity reports' (updated 25 November 2019, **www.sra.org.uk/solicitors/guidance/money-laundering-terrorist-financing-suspicious-activity-reports/**).

Compliance tips – how to mitigate the risk of getting it wrong

- MLROs need to understand when to make a SAR, and training should be provided.

4.5 What is the best way to draft a SAR? What should it cover?

Providing a well-written and clear SAR is essential to obtaining a defence.

The SAR needs to be submitted using the NCA online reporting system (**www.ukciu.gov.uk/(pcn1tt55qhxnur55arehtp45)/saronline.aspx**). Those who report need to register with the NCA website and log on to enable a SAR to be filed.

The online SAR system is outdated and clunky. A good portion of the form does not feel applicable to law firms and there may be some information that the reporter does not have (and if that is the case the SAR should say this to ensure the NCA do not ask the law firm for what they consider to be missing information).

There is within the form a text box to set out the detail of matter and suspicion. It is a good idea to draft this in Word, save it then copy-and-paste the text into the online form, in case there are any issues with the NCA website.

The structure of the text of the SAR needs to be logical and contain certain elements. SARs should be written from the point of view of telling a story, and on the basis that the person reading it is coming to the story cold. It needs to be a standalone document where any person at the NCA can pick it up, understand what is happening and what is being asked of the NCA. Below is a suggested structure to follow:

1. Outline of the reporter, i.e. name of the firm, where it is located and what it does. Do not assume that the NCA will know this from a firm's name.
2. Confirmation that the report is made pursuant to POCA 2002, s.330.
3. The proposed activity for which a defence is sought, i.e. set out the act to which the firm is seeking a defence in a succinct way, for example to receipt monies from XYZ account and send to XYZ account on exchange of contracts.
4. Set out that there is suspicion that there may be proceeds of crime and what offences under POCA 2002 (s.327 and/or s.328 and/or s.329) may be committed.
5. Outline of the matter, including whom the firm acts for, details of the retainer, what monies have been received and from where, what the proposed

activity is, when it will take place (the NCA want to have a timescale) and what the suspicion is (firms are encouraged to use the NCA Glossary Codes to speed up the SAR (*Suspicious Activity Report (SAR): Glossary Codes and Reporting Routes*, June 2022 **www.nationalcrimeagency.gov.uk/who-we-are/publications/597-sar-glossary-codes-and-reporting-routes-june-2022/file**)).

6. Summarise again what the defence is sought for.

Here are some things *not* to do:

- When making a SAR, a reporter should not ask for 'consent' to proceed. The NCA will not give this, and it may lead to the SAR being rejected or a defence refused.
- Do not give no timescale for the act. Even if the firm is not sure precisely when monies will pass or an act will happen, firms should give a timescale such as six months. The NCA are likely to reject a SAR without a timescale.
- Do not ask for a blanket defence to act. The NCA will not provide a blanket defence to acting in a matter. They need to have a specific act put to them, such as an exchange and completion of a property purchase.
- Do not ask a hypothetical question, e.g. 'if the firm were to do XYZ, would the NCA provide a defence?' The NCA will reject this.
- Do not be vague, illogical in structure or not set out what the suspicion is – this is a SAR after all.

If the firm does not have certain information – for example, the bank account to where monies will be sent at the time of the making of a SAR – the SAR needs to set this out and confirm when information will become available.

In complicated matters, SARs can be tricky and legal advice should be considered.

What are the compliance challenges?

- The SAR needs to logical and easy for the NCA to follow.

What resources will help?

- LSAG provides useful guidance in this area: 'Anti-money laundering guidance for the legal sector' (20 January 2021, **www.lawsociety.org.uk/topics/anti-money-laundering/anti-money-laundering-guidance**).
- NCA guidance: 'Guidance on submitting better quality Suspicious Activity Reports (SARs)' (September 2021, V6.0, **www.nationalcrimeagency.gov.uk/who-we-are/publications/446-guidance-on-submitting-better-quality-sars-1/file**).
- Law Society guidance: 'Suspicious activity reports' (3 June 2021, **www.lawsociety.org.uk/en/topics/anti-money-laundering/suspicious-activity-reports**).

Compliance tips – how to mitigate the risk of getting it wrong

- MLROs who have little experience in drafting a SAR should consult the NCA's guidance above.
- It would be wise to practise mock drafting a SAR.

4.6 How does privilege come into play when it comes to SARs?

Privilege is a fundamental right enabling clients to be open and frank with their legal advisers without concern the information will be disclosed later. This is an absolute right that only statute or waiver can override.

When deciding whether to make a SAR, relevant persons need to consider whether (a) legal advice privilege, (b) litigation privilege or (c) information obtained in privileged circumstances apply, and whether any exceptions bite.

Very briefly, *legal advice privilege* relates to communications between a legal professional acting in his or her capacity as a legal professional and a client if that communication is confidential and for the purpose of seeking legal advice or providing it. Communications are not privileged purely by being made between a legal professional and a client nor because they are labelled 'privileged'.

Communications between a client and a legal professional will attract privilege even if the document itself contains no advice, as long as the documents relate to the underlying transaction.

The LSAG guidance should be consulted – the 2021 version has been comprehensively re-written in this area, and contains a useful decision template ('Anti-money laundering guidance for the legal sector', 20 January 2021, **www.lawsociety.org.uk/topics/anti-money-laundering/anti-money-laundering-guidance**). Further, the Law Society has a Practice Note on Legal Professional Privilege which is useful (12 August 2021, **www.lawsociety.org.uk/en/topics/client-care/legal-professional-privilege**).

Litigation privilege relates to confidential communications made after litigation has started or is reasonably in prospect between a legal professional and a client, agent or third party, and that communication is for seeking or giving advice, obtaining evidence to be used in relation to the advice or obtaining information leading to obtaining such evidence. Litigation privilege is wider than legal advice privilege.

Information being provided in privileged circumstances is not the same as legal professional privilege and is a design of POCA 2002 to comply with the exemptions from reporting set out in the European directives.

Privileged circumstances means information communicated:

- by a client, or a representative of a client, in connection with the giving of legal advice to the client; or

- by a client, or by a representative of a client, seeking legal advice from the professional adviser; or
- by a person in connection with legal proceedings or contemplated legal proceedings.

If a legal professional forms a genuine but mistaken belief that the privileged information exemption applies, then the legal professional will be able to rely on the reasonable excuse defence.

Information that is subject to legal professional privilege cannot be disclosed. There is an exception to this, and that is the crime/fraud or otherwise called the iniquity exception.

Information gathered with the intention of furthering a criminal purpose is not privileged. However, advice given to a client to avoid them committing a crime or warning them about their proposed actions is subject to privilege.

If the relevant person knows that the transaction he or she is instructed to advise on is a principal criminal offence, then the relevant person may be committing an offence themselves and such communications are not privileged.

If a relevant person has a suspicion that money laundering is occurring, then privilege will not attach if that conclusion is correct – but if it is incorrect, privilege remains.

Privilege can be a difficult area to navigate and a law firm faced with a challenging privilege question may wish to take legal advice. If using this exemption as a reason not to report a suspicion, that analysis and decision should be recorded.

What are the compliance challenges?

- Privilege can be a complicated area to navigate and firms may wish to seek independent legal advice.

What resources will help?

- LSAG provides very useful guidance: 'Anti-money laundering guidance for the legal sector' (20 January 2021, **www.lawsociety.org.uk/topics/anti-money-laundering/anti-money-laundering-guidance**).
- The Law Society's Practice Note on Legal Professional Privilege is useful (12 August 2021, **www.lawsociety.org.uk/en/topics/client-care/legal-professional-privilege**).

Compliance tips – how to mitigate the risk of getting it wrong

- MLROs need to understand the principles of privilege, and to that end should read the relevant section of the LSAG guidance and seek advice where needed.

4.7 I have made a SAR – what can I tell the client?

It is a criminal offence to 'tip off'. Tipping off can occur if a person is informed that a SAR (internal, or external to the NCA) has been made, and the person informing the party knows or suspects that by disclosing the information any subsequent investigation will likely be prejudiced.

Although a person may not know or suspect that disclosing that a SAR has been made will prejudice an investigation, it is far safer to have a blanket policy in the firm not to inform any external person that a SAR has been made unless speaking to a legal adviser.

The challenge can sometimes be what to inform the client during the seven working days that the NCA has to provide or refuse a defence if you cannot disclose the fact a SAR has been made. If the SAR is stalling the transaction, then the client will naturally want to know why their matter has ground to a halt.

Sadly, there is no magic answer. Those who are acting for the client must find a way of stalling the transaction whilst maintaining integrity, being honest and acting in the best interests of the client. This can at times feel impossible to do, and the MLRO should provide guidance. It is, however, for this reason why matters such as source of funds and wealth (see **3.20**) should be investigated at the beginning of a retainer and not just before exchange or completion for example.

When responding to a client's queries about why their matter has stalled or slowed, care must be taken *not* to use language that could give a hint of a SAR – examples of language *not* to use might be telling the client that the compliance team are undertaking checks, or worse still, that the person in charge of money laundering compliance or the MLRO is undertaking checks. This type of language is bound to open up the possibility of tipping off.

What are the compliance challenges?

- It can be very challenging to know what to say to a client whilst waiting for the outcome of a SAR without tipping off or opening up the possibility of tipping off.

What resources will help?

- The LSAG guidance should be consulted: 'Anti-money laundering guidance for the legal sector' (20 January 2021, **www.lawsociety.org.uk/topics/anti-money-laundering/anti-money-laundering-guidance**).

Compliance tips – how to mitigate the risk of getting it wrong

- Those in the firm must understand the concept of tipping off, that they must not inform the client when a SAR has been made (either internally to the MLRO or externally to the NCA) and be provided with assistance by the MLRO where needed.

- The firm's AML policy must be clear on these aspects and be supplemented with training for all relevant staff.

4.8 The NCA haven't come back to me on my SAR – can I act?

If the NCA have not retuned with a response to a DAML SAR after the seven working days allowed, then the reporter has what is called a 'deemed defence' (sometimes called a 'deemed consent') and can proceed with the acts set out in the SAR.

What are the compliance challenges?

- MLROs must wait for the seven days to pass before determining that they have a deemed defence.

What resources will help?

- LSAG provides useful guidance: 'Anti-money laundering guidance for the legal sector' (20 January 2021, **www.lawsociety.org.uk/topics/anti-money-laundering/anti-money-laundering-guidance**).
- The NCA have also provided guidance: *SARs Regime Good Practice: Frequently Asked Questions: Defence Against Money Laundering (DAML)* (May 2019, V2.0, **www.nationalcrimeagency.gov.uk/who-we-are/publications/167-defence-against-money-laundering-daml-faq-may-2018/file**).

Compliance tips – how to mitigate the risk of getting it wrong

- MLROs must understand the reporting regime and therefore should consult POCA 2002 and the LSAG guidance, and receive training.

4.9 The NCA have refused to provide a defence – what does this mean?

Where a defence is refused, a moratorium period of 31 calendar days begins from the date of refusal. During this moratorium period (and the seven working-day period for the SAR itself), the firm must not undertake the prohibited act. The purpose of the moratorium period is to allow the enforcement agencies to investigate further and potentially injunct the firm from taking steps.

If no NCA/enforcement action comes, the firm is able to proceed – however, careful thought needs to be taken as to whether the firm should. Note that the moratorium period can be increased by court order.

There is a possibility that the NCA provide a reply which is neither a defence nor a refusal to provide one. These are rare, and again legal advice should be sought should this occur.

What are the compliance challenges?

- MLROs must understand the SAR regime and seek advice in the event of a refusal to provide a defence if needed.

What resources will help?

- LSAG provides useful guidance: 'Anti-money laundering guidance for the legal sector' (20 January 2021, **www.lawsociety.org.uk/topics/anti-money-laundering/anti-money-laundering-guidance**).
- The NCA have also provided guidance: *SARs Regime Good Practice: Frequently Asked Questions: Defence Against Money Laundering (DAML)* (May 2019, V2.0, **www.nationalcrimeagency.gov.uk/who-we-are/publications/167-defence-against-money-laundering-daml-faq-may-2018/file**).

Compliance tips – how to mitigate the risk of getting it wrong

- MLROs must understand the reporting regime and therefore should consult POCA 2002 and the LSAG guidance, and receive training.

4.10 I have made a SAR but the facts or proposed activity has changed – what do I need to do?

This will depend on whether the defence has been granted or not.

If the defence has already been granted, then a fresh 'standalone' SAR needs to be made, repeating all relevant detail. The SAR must not expect the NCA to pull up the prior SAR for any detail because they will not do this, and this could lead to the second SAR being rejected.

If the defence has not yet been provided and the seven working-day period is still running, then it is possible to email the NCA at DAML@nca.gov.uk and amend the SAR by quoting the reference provided when the SAR was submitted. Submitting a new SAR in these circumstances can lead to SAR rejection as the NCA try to rationalise what has been submitted.

Any defence given is only valid for the facts submitted and so if details have changed, such as bank account details or parties' names, a fresh SAR or amendment to the SAR must be submitted.

What are the compliance challenges?

- It is important to understand when a fresh SAR or an amendment to the SAR can be made, if the facts have changed. Failure to obtain a defence on the correct facts could lead to an offence being committed.

What resources will help?

- LSAG provides useful guidance: 'Anti-money laundering guidance for the legal sector' (20 January 2021, **www.lawsociety.org.uk/topics/anti-money-laundering/anti-money-laundering-guidance**).

- The NCA have also provided guidance: *SARs Regime Good Practice: Frequently Asked Questions: Defence Against Money Laundering (DAML)* (May 2019, V2.0, **www.nationalcrimeagency.gov.uk/who-we-are/publications/167-defence-against-money-laundering-daml-faq-may-2018/file**).

Compliance tips – how to mitigate the risk of getting it wrong

- MLROs must understand the reporting regime and therefore should consult POCA 2002 and the LSAG guidance, and receive training.

4.11 My client is sending money from China in contravention of the local laws there – is this a problem?

China has placed on its citizens a limit on the amount of cash that can be transferred out of the country and the purpose for that transfer. Currently this limit is $50k per individual each year via a Chinese bank. Note that Chinese companies do not have these restrictions, and so an individual can set up a Chinese company and invest that way.

Individuals are able to transfer more if the relevant authorities agree. Individuals cannot transfer money for certain purposes (e.g. gambling) but they can move money for trips, living costs and studying. However, other investments – including property – are prohibited. Acting in contravention of these rules is a criminal offence in China.

In order to transfer the monies, the bank will issue a SAFE certificate setting out the amount of the transfer and permitted purpose.

It is not a criminal offence in the UK for monies to be sent overseas, nor for anyone in the UK to receipt monies sent in contravention of the rules in China.

For a money laundering offence to occur – whether it be concealing, disguising, transferring or removing from the jurisdiction (POCA 2002, s.327), becoming concerned in an arrangement which facilities the acquisition or, retention of, criminal property (POCA 2002, s.328) or acquiring, use of or having possession of 'criminal property' (POCA 2002, s.329) – the following needs to have happened:

- criminal conduct has been committed;
- a benefit has been obtained from this conduct;
- the benefit has resulted in criminal property.

Criminal conduct can occur overseas if that conduct would be an offence in the UK.

Sending or receipting monies in contravention of the Chinese rules is not an offence in the UK, and so no criminal conduct has taken place. This means, therefore, that the monies received cannot be proceeds of crime, and no money laundering in this way can be taking place.

However, firms should investigate the source of funds and wealth (see **3.20**) and in doing so seek to understand how the Chinese national took more than the allowed sum out of China. If the national lied to the authorities or bank in China about the purpose for which the monies were to be used, then there is an argument that fraud in China may have been committed. Fraud is an offence in the UK too, and this is where POCA 2002 will bite.

Firms also need to consider if any tax evasion has taken place. If there is concern about a fraud or tax evasion, then the firm and MLRO needs to consider whether to file a SAR and seek a defence.

Firms also need to consider their obligations under the SRA Principles (for example, Principle 1 – rule of law/proper administration of justice; Principle 2 – public trust and confidence; and Principle 5 – integrity) and Codes of Conduct (**www.sra.org.uk/solicitors/standards-regulations/**).

Finally, firms need to be aware of the use of 'underground banking' to launder proceeds of crime, and therefore must conduct enhanced due diligence (EDD – see **3.9**) on such transactions and thoroughly investigate source of funds and wealth.

What are the compliance challenges?

- Firms and people within them need to understand that there may be POCA 2002 issues when receipting and using monies sent in contravention of the Chinese banking rules.

What resources will help?

- Independent legal advice may be sought.
- Further, the NCA has produced some guidance which may prove useful: *Chinese Underground Banking and "Daigou"* (October 2019, **www.nationalcrimeagency.gov.uk/who-we-are/publications/445-chinese-underground-banking/file**).

Compliance tips – how to mitigate the risk of getting it wrong

- The issues should be communicated across the firm and should be placed in the firm's AML policy and the firm-wide risk assessment.

4.12 My client's source of funds is investment in cannabis growing abroad where it is legal – is this a problem?

For a money laundering offence to occur – whether it be concealing, disguising, transferring or removing from the jurisdiction (POCA 2002, s.327), becoming concerned in an arrangement which facilities the acquisition or, retention of, criminal property (POCA 2002, s.328) or acquiring, use of or having possession of 'criminal property' (POCA 2002, s.329) – the following needs to have happened:

- criminal conduct has been committed;
- a benefit has been obtained from this conduct;
- the benefit has resulted in criminal property.

Criminal conduct can occur overseas if that conduct would be an offence in the UK.

The monies that emanate from cannabis growing companies could pose a POCA 2002 issue. In the UK, cultivating, producing, supplying, importing or exporting cannabis without a Home Office licence is a criminal offence.

If the 'cannabis activity' abroad was without a licence of equivalent Home Office standard, this could equate to a criminal offence when viewed from the UK, and the proceeds generated 'criminal property'.

Whether there is in fact a criminal offence and criminal property will depend on the facts and would need to be determined on its own merits.

If analysis leads to the conclusion that criminal activity has taken place and criminal property is to be used, then the firm and MLRO need to consider the reporting requirements under POCA 2002 to the NCA. Note that no offence of failing to report can be committed if the activity takes place entirely outside of the UK and is legal in the country in which it takes place (POCA 2002, s.330(7A)).

What are the compliance challenges?

- The issue of funds generated from overseas cannabis activity is complicated to navigate, and firms may wish to take independent legal advice in relation to it.

What resources will help?

- There is little guidance and for this reason, firms may wish to take independent legal advice in relation to it.

Compliance tips – how to mitigate the risk of getting it wrong

- If a client is providing funds for a transaction that have been generated from overseas cannabis activity, then the solicitor acting needs to report this to the MLRO as soon as possible for further consideration.
- Firms may wish to highlight this issue in their AML policy and provide guidance.

4.13 My client has breached a legal requirement which is a criminal offence and the proceeds they have gained from this activity is £500. Do I still need to make a SAR? Can I act?

In theory, the proceeds of crime here are the £500 gained from the criminal activity. When considering obligations to report suspicions of money laundering, there is no *de minimis* sum. What must be considered is whether a criminal offence may have taken place producing proceeds of crime (the criminal property) and that proceeds of crime are being laundered. Depending on the facts, the £500 criminal property could be within a pool of money held by the client and to be used for the purchase of an asset. Maybe also the £500 was gained some time ago and has since been invested and is 10 times that amount now.

Whether to suspect money laundering and whether to report suspicious activity to the NCA (taking into account privilege) is dependent on the facts in each situation. However, the point is that there is no *de minimis* sum.

What are the compliance challenges?

- Solicitors may decide to turn a blind eye to such small sums, but this would be incorrect and a dangerous thing to do.

What resources will help?

- LSAG guidance generally: 'Anti-money laundering guidance for the legal sector' (20 January 2021, **www.lawsociety.org.uk/topics/anti-money-laundering/anti-money-laundering-guidance**).

Compliance tips – how to mitigate the risk of getting it wrong

- This issue should be highlighted to relevant persons in the firm, and also set out in the firm's AML policy.

CHAPTER 5

Practice management and HR

EMPLOYEE SCREENING

5.1 What do the regulations say?

Money Laundering, Terrorist Financing and Transfer of Funds (Information on the Payer) Regulations 2017, SI 2017/692 (AML Regulations), reg.21(1)(b) requires firms to carry out screening of relevant employees both before the appointment is made and during the course of their appointment.

The regulations go on to further set out that screening means an assessment of skills, knowledge and expertise of an individual to carry out their functions effectively and also an assessment of the person's conduct and integrity.

As per the regulations, a relevant employee is someone whose work is connected to any requirement that the firm has in the regulations or whose role means they are capable of contributing to identifying, mitigating, preventing or detecting money laundering or terrorist financing.

Note that ensuring screening is undertaken is the responsibility of the money laundering compliance officer (MLCO).

What are the compliance challenges?

- Firms must ensure that they have the proper processes in place for screening at appointment stage and during appointment.

What resources will help?

- The Legal Sector Affinity Group (LSAG) offers useful guidance: 'Anti-money laundering guidance for the legal sector' (20 January 2021, **www.lawsociety.org.uk/topics/anti-money-laundering/anti-money-laundering-guidance**).

Compliance tips – how to mitigate the risk of getting it wrong

- The firm needs to put in place screening processes at the appointment stage and during appointment. Firms may need to review current screening procedures and make sure they are robust enough.

5.2 What steps could I take to screen my firm's people?

The AML Regulations 2017 require that steps are taken to assess the person's skills, knowledge, expertise, conduct and integrity.

The LSAG guidance sets out that (at para.9.4) the following screening options ('Anti-money laundering guidance for the legal sector', 20 January 2021, **www.lawsociety.org.uk/topics/anti-money-laundering/anti-money-laundering-guidance**):

On appointment	**Skills, knowledge and expertise**	• Qualification checks (seeing original certificates or verified copies) particularly in relation to AML/risk management • Test of knowledge/skills as pertaining to role, particularly in relation to AML/risk management • Validating practising status via the relevant register applicable regulator.
	Conduct and integrity	• Taking up references. • Checking criminal history via Disclosure and Barring Service, Disclosure Scotland, Access Northern Ireland or equivalent • Finance or credit check • Checking disciplinary history via their regulator. • Adverse media checks via search engines. • E-verification, if available.
During employment (annually)	**Skills, knowledge and expertise**	• Annual competence declaration. • Appraisal procedure with recorded outcome recorded. • Review of any AML related training or qualifications undertaken through the course of the preceding year.
	Conduct and integrity	• Adverse checks via search engines. • Checking disciplinary history via the relevant register applicable regulator. • Electronic identification and verification, if available.

LSAG, 'Anti-money laundering guidance for the legal sector', 2021, p.122.

It is not mandatory to undertake criminal history checks, and firms may decide to do so on a risk basis (i.e. higher areas of risk such as transactional work or those in the accounts team).

For ongoing screening this could be undertaken by either a firm's HR team or risk team on an annual basis and reported to the board or other senior management group.

What are the compliance challenges?

- Firms must ensure that they have the proper processes in place for screening at the appointment stage and during appointment.

What resources will help?

- LSAG offers useful guidance: 'Anti-money laundering guidance for the legal sector' (20 January 2021, **www.lawsociety.org.uk/topics/anti-money-laundering/anti-money-laundering-guidance**).

Compliance tips – how to mitigate the risk of getting it wrong

- The firm needs to put in place screening processes at the appointment stage and during appointment.
- Firms may need to review current screening procedures and make sure that they are robust enough. Compliance with the firm's screening processes should be audited.

5.3 Should everyone be screened, including consultants and suppliers?

Firms need to consider how extensive they need to make their screening. The AML Regulations use the language of 'employee', and firms could legitimately limit their screening to those individuals who are employees. However, if, for example, a solicitor were to be employed via an agency as a locum or as a self-employed consultant solicitor, then it would seem absurd to screen those in the firm who are employed directly and not those who are not but may have roles which means they are capable of contributing to identifying, mitigating, preventing or detecting money laundering or terrorist financing.

Agencies may conduct their own screening, and firms may wish to consider if that screening meets their requirements negating the need to undertake their own screening.

In relation to other forms of supplier, each firm should consider what role that supplier plays in the firm's identification, mitigation, prevention or detection of money laundering or terrorist financing.

Firms should consider putting into a written policy the minimum checks and balances required before a person can begin working with the firm. This is especially important when the recruitment market is very buoyant and demand is high, leading to the need for people to start working as soon as possible and before certain checks are complete. Below are suggested minimum checks that could be undertaken before a role-holder begins working at a firm – these need to be tailored for each firm.

Lawyer to include consultants

- Confirmation of complaints, claims and any conduct investigations with the Solicitors Regulation Authority (SRA) or other regulatory body.
- Practising certificate check – i.e. that the individual holds one and there are no conditions on it (to include where the certificate is held in another jurisdiction or non-solicitor, e.g. barrister).
- Regulatory check via the SRA website to ensure that there are no orders against the individual or restrictions on his or her certificate.
- References to ensure there are no issues around dishonesty or misconduct.
- Adverse media check and social media check.

Business services support staff/PA/secretarial support staff

- Confirmation of any conduct investigations with the SRA or other regulatory body.
- Regulatory check via the SRA website to ensure no orders against the individual.
- References to ensure that there are no issues around dishonesty or misconduct.
- Adverse media check and social media check.

Business services consultants and contractors

- Confirmation of any conduct investigations with the SRA or other regulatory body.
- Regulatory check via the SRA website to ensure no orders against the individual or restrictions on his or her certificate.
- Adverse media check and social media check.

What are the compliance challenges?

- Firms must ensure that relevant persons providing services within the firm but who are not directly employed are not missed out when it comes to screening.

What resources will help?

- LSAG offers useful guidance: 'Anti-money laundering guidance for the legal sector' (20 January 2021, **www.lawsociety.org.uk/topics/anti-money-laundering/anti-money-laundering-guidance**).

Compliance tips – how to mitigate the risk of getting it wrong

- The firm needs to put in place screening processes at the appointment stage and during appointment.
- Firms may need to review current screening procedures and make sure they are robust enough.
- Compliance with the firm's screening should be audited.

5.4 Can I outsource screening? Who remains responsible?

Screening can be outsourced, and there are a number of third party suppliers who will undertake this task for a fee. The screening company should report their findings against pre-agreed checks and balances for the firm to consider prior to the person starting work with the firm.

The firm will always remain liable for the screening undertaken by a third party because neither the firm nor the firm's MLCO can abdicate their responsibilities under the AML Regulations. It is therefore important that where a third party supplier is being used to outsource screening, the firm and its MLCO are completely satisfied with the veracity of the screening undertaken by the supplier.

What are the compliance challenges?

- Outsourcing screening can be cost-effective. However, firms must make sure that it is robust and meets the regulatory requirements.

What resources will help?

- LSAG offers useful guidance: 'Anti-money laundering guidance for the legal sector' (20 January 2021, **www.lawsociety.org.uk/topics/anti-money-laundering/anti-money-laundering-guidance**).

Compliance tips – how to mitigate the risk of getting it wrong

- Any third party screening supplier must be properly vetted to ensure that the regulatory requirements are met.

5.5 Our screening has shown an adverse result – what now?

If an adverse result has been found, the result needs to be analysed carefully and the following points need to be considered depending on the nature of the result found:

- How severe is the result? For example, is it a conviction?

- What is the impact of the result? If appropriate, consider the vulnerability of any victim.
- When did the facts which gave rise to the result take place? Was it many years ago and does this make a difference? Does this in any way lessen the impact of the result?
- How old was the person at the time? Were they young/immature? Does this make a difference?
- Was the person a qualified solicitor or other professional at the time?

Whilst firms must never unfairly or illegally discriminate, firms are not obligated to employ someone for whom a screening result is found which causes concern. If the result is found during employment, then appropriate HR processes should be followed, e.g. disciplinary procedure if appropriate.

What are the compliance challenges?

- Knowing what to do when an adverse result is found can be a challenge.

What resources will help?

- LSAG should be consulted: 'Anti-money laundering guidance for the legal sector' (20 January 2021, **www.lawsociety.org.uk/topics/anti-money-laundering/anti-money-laundering-guidance**).
- The MLCO should be consulted.

Compliance tips – how to mitigate the risk of getting it wrong

- A discussion should take place between the MLCO and HR team who are likely to be handling the screening results, with the understanding that adverse results are referred to the MLCO for input.

TRAINING

5.6 What do the AML Regulations say in relation to training? Who should undertake training?

AML Regulations 2017, reg.24 sets out the requirements to train. The firm and MLCO must ensure that relevant employees are made aware of the law relating to money laundering, terrorist financing and data protection and are regularly given training on how to recognise and deal with transactions and other activities or situations which may be related to money laundering or terrorist financing.

The regulations set out that a relevant employee is someone whose work is connected to any requirement that the firm has in the regulations or whose role means that he or she is capable of contributing to identifying, mitigating, preventing or detecting money laundering or terrorist financing. Firms may wish to implement training across the entire firm regardless of role. On the other hand, firms may want to implement different training for higher risk practice areas.

A record of the training must be made, and will need to be produced at short notice should the SRA request it. There is no set frequency for training to take place, and generally speaking formal training ought to take place every one to two years.

What are the compliance challenges?

- Ensuring that relevant persons undertake their training can be a challenge.

What resources will help?

- Some online training providers are able to provide built in 'nag ware' which reminds people about their outstanding training.
- For guidance on the training itself, LSAG guidance should be conducted: 'Anti-money laundering guidance for the legal sector' (20 January 2021, **www.lawsociety.org.uk/topics/anti-money-laundering/anti-money-laundering-guidance**).

Compliance tips – how to mitigate the risk of getting it wrong

- The MLCO should have a robust training plan. See below for different methods of training.

5.7 What methods of training are appropriate? How can we train our people most effectively?

The AML Regulations set out that when deciding what training should be given, the firm needs to consider the nature and size of its business and the nature and extent of the risks of money laundering and terrorist financing which could occur in its business.

There is no 'one size to fit all' approach to training, and each firm must decide its own training programme. Below are some training ideas:

- **Online training modules** are a good way to train consistently and provide a method of recording the training undertaken. Further, they are useful if there are many people to train at any one time.
- **In-person (physical or virtual) training** is by far the most effective method of training, especially where interaction with the trainer through questions and answers is possible.
- **Attendance at team meetings** on a regular basis to discuss a latest issue or trend in AML compliance or to remind people of the firm's AML policies can also form part of the firm's training strategy.

- **Regularly written guidance pieces or short articles** on AML news stories are also a useful way to train.
- **Regular newsletters or bulletins**, perhaps providing additional news and guidance and/or incorporating the items described above, can also be useful.

Variety is key when training, as not everyone will learn in the same way.

What are the compliance challenges?

- Ensuring that relevant persons undertake their training can be a challenge.

What resources will help?

- LSAG provides guidance: 'Anti-money laundering guidance for the legal sector' (20 January 2021, **www.lawsociety.org.uk/topics/anti-money-laundering/anti-money-laundering-guidance**).

Compliance tips – how to mitigate the risk of getting it wrong

- Variety in training methods will help ensure that fatigue doesn't take place.
- Further, the MLCO should create a training plan to include some of the methods set out above.

5.8 Should the MLRO and MLCO receive additional training?

It is not a requirement under the AML Regulations for the money laundering reporting officer (MLRO) and MLCO to receive additional training. However, given the importance and personal responsibility these roles carry, it is good practice to provide extra training for these role-holders.

There are many free resources for new MLROs and MLCOs provided by the Law Society and the SRA, and these should be the firm's starting-point before seeking external training.

What are the compliance challenges?

- The roles of MLRO and MLCO are serious and carry personal consequences.
- In the case of the MLCO, the breadth of what needs to be understood is wide.

What resources will help?

- The AML Regulations provide good overall guidance.
- LSAG also provides good overall guidance: 'Anti-money laundering guidance for the legal sector' (20 January 2021, **www.lawsociety.org.uk/topics/anti-money-laundering/anti-money-laundering-guidance**).
- The SRA also provides relevant guidance (see 'Money laundering' resources at **www.sra.org.uk/solicitors/resources/money-laundering/**).

Compliance tips – how to mitigate the risk of getting it wrong

- MLROs and MLCOs should receive adequate training and be given sufficient time to fulfil their roles.

AUDITING – INTERNAL AND EXTERNAL

5.9 What do the AML Regulations say in relation to audits?

AML Regulations 2017, reg.21 sets out that firms should have (taking into account the size and nature of the firm), as part of their internal controls, an independent audit function. The purpose of this function is to examine and evaluate the adequacy and effectiveness of the policies, controls and procedures (PCPs) adopted by the firm to meet the regulatory requirements. The function should also make recommendations in relation to those PCPs and monitor compliance with those recommendations.

LSAG's guidance sets out that the independent audit must be carried out by someone who is removed from the setting of and ensuring compliance with the firm's AML compliance regime. The audit cannot, therefore, be carried out by the firm's MLRO, MLCO and possibly the risk team. The person who conducts the audit must have the necessary skills and knowledge in auditing and AML compliance in order to be able to audit the firm against the requirements. The auditor must have access to all the necessary documentation.

There is no set frequency for an independent audit to take place, and undoubtedly frequency should be determined based on risk. If the firm has a number of high-risk practice areas or an audit has highlighted a certain degree of noncompliance, then higher frequency of auditing should be considered, perhaps every 18 months to two years. Further, any substantial changes in the AML Regulations should prompt an audit or compliance post implementation of those changes (or indeed to assist with the changes needed).

The LSAG guidance sets out that practices should keep a record of all audits and make this available to their supervisors as requested – this should include:

- the scope of the audit and sampling basis used;
- the records audited, what was checked and by whom;
- the findings and recommended actions of the audit;
- records of senior management/board discussions regarding the findings of the audit; and
- the practice's response and implementation of actions (and any reasoning for not implementing those recommendations).

What are the compliance challenges?

- The audit can feel burdensome and it needs to be determined who will be able to conduct the audit.

What resources will help?

- Independent consultants can help.
- LSAG guidance should be consulted: 'Anti-money laundering guidance for the legal sector' (20 January 2021, **www.lawsociety.org.uk/topics/anti-money-laundering/anti-money-laundering-guidance**).

Compliance tips – how to mitigate the risk of getting it wrong

- Firms should ascertain who in their firm is able to undertake the audit – and if there is no one, consider instructing someone externally. See below.

5.10 Should the independent audit be done by an external person? What should it include?

As outlined above, the auditor should be sufficiently independent from the firm's setting of and ensuring compliance with the firm's AML compliance regime and also have the required skills and knowledge to be able to audit. As the MLRO, MLCO and quite probably the risk team are unable to conduct the independent audit, this often leaves no one in the firm to conduct the audit. Because of this, some firms chose to engage an external consultant to conduct the audit. Alternatively, firms could enter into a reciprocal arrangement with each other if that is deemed appropriate and there are the right confidentiality agreements in place. Whoever is the chosen auditor, the firm must be sure as to the capability of that auditor.

The audit should review the firm's compliance with the regulatory requirements to include the following:

- firm-wide risk assessment compliance (reg.18);
- PCPs (reg.19) to include:
  - risk management practices;
  - internal controls (see below);
  - client due diligence (CDD) (regs.27, 28, 30, 33, 35, 37) (see **Chapter 3**);
  - reliance (reg.39) (see **3.32–3.35**) and record-keeping (reg.40);
  - monitoring and management of compliance with and the internal communication of such PCPs.
- internal controls (reg.21) to include:

  - appointment of MLCO and MLRO and if both are approved by the SRA;
  - screening of employees;
  - independent audit function in the past;

- training (reg.24) (see **5.6–5.8**).

What are the compliance challenges?

- Firms need to determine who will be able to conduct the audit.

What resources will help?

- Independent consultants can help.
- LSAG guidance should be consulted: 'Anti-money laundering guidance for the legal sector' (20 January 2021, **www.lawsociety.org.uk/topics/anti-money-laundering/anti-money-laundering-guidance**).

Compliance tips – how to mitigate the risk of getting it wrong

- Firms should ascertain who in their firm is able to undertake the audit – and if there is no one, consider instructing someone externally.

RED FLAGS AND WARNING SIGNS

5.11 What are the red flags/warning signs of money laundering?

The LSAG guidance sets out a series of red flags/warning signs of money laundering having taken account of the FATF report on *Money Laundering and Terrorist Financing Vulnerabilities of Legal Professionals* (2013) and the FATF guidance on *Concealment of Beneficial Ownership* (2018) (LSAG, 'Anti-money laundering guidance for the legal sector', at chapter 18, pp.194–204, 20 January 2021, **www.lawsociety.org.uk/topics/anti-money-laundering/anti-money-laundering-guidance**). This list is too lengthy to reproduce here, and it should be consulted by all law firms.

When firms are considering what should constitute a warning sign of money laundering, the firm should take into account the ' National risk assessment of money laundering and terrorist financing 2020' as amended from time to time (HM Treasury and Home Office, **www.gov.uk/government/publications/national-risk-assessment-of-money-laundering-and-terrorist-financing-2020**) and the SRA's guidance 'Sectoral Risk Assessment – Anti-money laundering and terrorist financing' (28 January 2021, **www.sra.org.uk/sra/how-we-work/**

reports/aml-risk-assessment/) which sets out what are emerging money laundering risks in their view.

What are the compliance challenges?

- Firms and those within the firm need to understand the red flags/warning signs of money laundering so that they can spot when suspicion of money laundering should arise.
- Criminals will always seek to find new ways of laundering money, and as such firms need to stay on top of trends.

What resources will help?

- LSAG provides an excellent overview of red flags/warning signs, and this should be consulted: 'Anti-money laundering guidance for the legal sector', chapter 18 (20 January 2021, **www.lawsociety.org.uk/topics/anti-money-laundering/anti-money-laundering-guidance**).
- Law Society guidance: 'Warning signs of money laundering' (20 January 2020, **www.lawsociety.org.uk/en/topics/anti-money-laundering/money-laundering-warning-signs**).

Compliance tips – how to mitigate the risk of getting it wrong

- Firms may wish to place the LSAG content in their AML policy and direct persons in the firm to it.
- All relevant persons should receive training that covers red flags/warning signs of money laundering.

5.12 How can I make sure that those in the firm understand these red flags/ warning signs?

So that people in a firm can spot possible money laundering, they need to be aware of what to look out for, and to do this they need to understand the warning signs of money laundering, sometimes called red flags.

As set out above, the LSAG guidance has a comprehensive list of possible warning signs. Below are a few suggestions on steps that could be taken to ensure that these are understood in the firm:

- ensure that the warning signs are set out in the firm's AML policy, and that the policy is shared and that a request made to read it (if possible, make the reading of the policy mandatory, with a positive confirmation when done),
- as and when new emerging trends arise, circulate a note about them and update the firm's AML policy;
- provide training on the warning signs – in-person is better if possible; and
- embed the warning signs into the firm's client and matter risk assessment in the format of questions – for example: Does it make sense for the firm to be

instructed? Is the client instructing us to create a complicated corporate structure without legitimate reason? Is the purpose of the trust clear? Does the source of funds and wealth make sense (please document)?

What are the compliance challenges?

- Ensuring that relevant persons in the firm understand when to spot a red flag/warning sign is challenging.

What resources will help?

- LSAG provides an excellent overview of red flags/warning signs, and this should be consulted: 'Anti-money laundering guidance for the legal sector', chapter 18 (20 January 2021, **www.lawsociety.org.uk/topics/anti-money-laundering/anti-money-laundering-guidance**).

Compliance tips – how to mitigate the risk of getting it wrong

- Follow the steps above at **5.11**.

SRA AML VISITS

5.13 The SRA is visiting to review our AML compliance – what is it likely to ask?

The SRA has a dedicated team tasked with supervising AML compliance in law firms. It can visit and conduct a review at any time. If a firm is to be visited, it may be asked to provide the following before a visit:

- any policies and information held by the firm demonstrating its approach to AML/countering the financing of terrorism (CFT);
- either physical or electronic access to the CDD, time recording and risk assessment records for two of each fee earner's selected files;
- your firm's AML/CFT training records;
- records of any internal suspicious activity reports (SARs) made by staff to the firm's MLRO and the MLRO's decision, in each case, during the past two years;
- records relating to any SARs made to the National Crime Agency (NCA) by the MLRO during the past two years.

During the visit, the firm may be asked the following (normally by interviewing the MLRO and MLCO):

- Have the AML/CTF policies and procedures been communicated across the firm? And if so, how?
- How does the firm screen new and existing employees?
- When did the firm last audit its PCPs? Did the firm have an internal or external audit? The SRA does not normally request to see the audit. The MLCO may decide, however, to share this with the SRA to show the controls the firm has implemented to tackle AML compliance.
- Does the firm have an AML risk assessment covering the areas it should, such as (i) areas identified by the SRA risk assessment; (ii) clients; (iii) products and services; (iv) types of transactions; (v) delivery channels?
- Has the firm turned work away in the light of the AML risk?
- Is the firm's AML policy based on the firm's risk assessment, and does it take the LSAG guidance into account?
- Does the firm's AML policy set out how to identify and scrutinise complex or unusual transactions, or transactions that have no apparent legal economic reason?
- Does the firm use simplified CDD, and if so when?
- How are sanctions lists checked?
- How long does the firm keep CDD records for?
- Is there a written policy on politically exposed people (PEPs) and does this include senior management approval to act for PEPs? How are PEPs identified?
- Who has received training in the firm? Are relevant people trained on AML, terrorist financing, data protection and recognising and reporting suspicious activities?
- When was training last delivered? Have those people completed it?
- How many internal SARs have been made to the MLRO and how many of those have been reported to the NCA? What is the conversion rate?
- Has consent been refused by the NCA?

Of the fee earners, the SRA may ask the following:

- Do the fee earners know who the MLRO is? Who is it?
- Do they know how to identify suspicious activity? What would they do if they suspected money laundering?
- Do they understand their responsibilities under the AML Regulations?
- In relation to each file, the fee earner may be asked to explain:
  - what the retainer is about;
  - who the client is;
  - what does the fee earner know about the client;
  - any suspicious activity;
  - produce the risk assessment;
  - produce documentary evidence of ID, source of funds and wealth and any analysis.

What are the compliance challenges?

- Firms must be ready for an SRA visit at any time, and so must ensure that their compliance with the AML Regulations is in a good place.

What resources will help?

- An independent audit will greatly assist.
- LSAG guidance: 'Anti-money laundering guidance for the legal sector' (20 January 2021, **www.lawsociety.org.uk/topics/anti-money-laundering/anti-money-laundering-guidance**).

Compliance tips – how to mitigate the risk of getting it wrong

- Having regard to the size and nature of the firm's business, firms should undertake an independent audit of their compliance with the AML Regulations and implement any suggested outcomes. Doing so will ensure that the firm is ready for an SRA visit.

5.14 What steps can I take to prepare for an SRA visit?

Below are a series of steps that firms can take to ensure readiness for an SRA AML visit:

1. Make sure that the firm-wide AML risk assessment is complete, covers all the areas it needs to and is up-to-date. When it is reviewed, the firm should document that it has done so.
2. Ensure that screening of new and existing employees is undertaken, and document this in the firm's AML policy.
3. Make sure the AML policy is up-to-date, taking into account the LSAG guidance, and that the policy states this.
4. Remind all fee earners of the regulatory requirement that each client and matter must have a documented risk assessment and ask they ensure that all their risk assessments are up-to-date. Note that the SRA takes this aspect very seriously.
5. Make sure that fee earners appreciate the requirement to understand and obtain evidence of source of funds and wealth (see **3.20**) and that this must be documented on the file.
6. If the firm's internal and external SARs are not up-to-date, update them. If the firm does not have a method of recording such reports internal or external, it should devise one as soon as possible and start using it. The firm must be ready to provide the numbers of internal and external reports to the SRA, and also what the conversion rate of internal to external reports is.
7. Make sure that if the firm has a central onboarding team, fee earners understand that their overall AML obligations are not delegated to that team. The

SRA is keen to make sure that this is understood, and the firm does not want fee earners saying otherwise.

8. If the firm has not trained in a while, it should get some training out. That could be via an online module, face-to-face sessions (in-person or virtual), attendance at team meetings, guidance notes, the use of stories that have happened in the firm or outside of the firm (such as Solicitors Disciplinary Tribunal (SDT) cases) to illustrate compliance. There are many ways to train, and not all people take information in in the same way.
9. If it has not done so already, the firm should undertake an independent audit of the firm's AML PCPs.
10. The firm should make sure it is up-to-date on its implementation of any money laundering legislation requirements.

What are the compliance challenges?

- Firms must be ready for an SRA visit at any time, and so must ensure that their compliance with the AML Regulations is in a good place.

What resources will help?

- An independent audit will greatly assist.
- LSAG guidance: 'Anti-money laundering guidance for the legal sector' (20 January 2021, **www.lawsociety.org.uk/topics/anti-money-laundering/anti-money-laundering-guidance**).

Compliance tips – how to mitigate the risk of getting it wrong

- See suggested steps above at **5.13**.

5.15 What are the possible outcomes for an SRA visit?

After an SRA AML visit has taken place, the SRA will write a letter confirming the outcome of the visit, any corrective action and recommendations.

They will also inform the firm whether any further action is going to be taken. This action could be a further formal investigation and possible disciplinary procedures.

The SRA's letter with the outcome should come around six to eight weeks after the visit, but it may depend on the issues found as to when the outcome is known. If the SRA considers serious breaches are occurring, presumably it will act quickly.

What are the compliance challenges?

- Firms must be ready for an SRA visit at any time, and so must ensure that their compliance with the AML Regulations is in a good place. That way the possibility of action being taken by the SRA will be minimal.

What resources will help?

- An independent audit will greatly assist.
- 'Anti-money laundering guidance for the legal sector' (20 January 2021, **www.lawsociety.org.uk/topics/anti-money-laundering/anti-money-laundering-guidance**).

Compliance tips – how to mitigate the risk of getting it wrong

- The steps as outlined in **5.14** above will help mitigate the risk of any SRA action.

PART II

Financial crime

CHAPTER 6

Anti-bribery and corruption

6.1 What offences does the Bribery Act 2010 create?

The Bribery Act 2010 (BA 2010) came into force 1 July 2011 and created the following offences:

- **Bribing a person to induce or reward them to perform a relevant function.** 'Relevant function' is defined a function of a public nature, activity connected with a business, trade or profession, activity carried out in the course of employment or activity carried out on behalf of a body of persons (corporate or unincorporated).
- **Improperly requesting, accepting or receiving a bribe as a reward for performing a relevant function.**
- **Improperly using a bribe to influence a foreign public official to gain a business advantage.** A 'foreign public official' is a person who holds a legislative, administrative or judicial position of any kind, whether appointed or elected, of a country or territory outside the UK or someone who exercises a public function for or on behalf of a country or territory outside the UK or any public agency or public enterprise of that country or territory (or subdivision) or someone who is an official or agent of a public international organisation (an example could be the World Health Organization).

What are the compliance challenges?

- It is important that everyone in the firm understands the above bribery offences.

What resources will help?

- BA 2010 itself.
- Law Society Practice Note: Bribery Act 2010 (25 November 2019, **www.lawsociety.org.uk/en/topics/regulation/bribery-act-2010**).

Compliance tips – how to mitigate the risk of getting it wrong

- Firms need to ensure that everyone in the firm understands the offences created by BA 2010, and this should be communicated through training and an anti-bribery and corruption policy.

6.2 Is there a corporate offence?

Yes. In essence BA 2010 creates a 'failure to prevent' offence.

Under BA 2010, s.7, if one of the offences is committed by an associated person with the intention of gaining or retaining a business advantage for a law firm, then that firm will also be guilty of a corporate offence if it failed to prevent bribery it its firm.

An 'associated person' is a person who performs services for or on behalf of the firm, whether that be an employee, agent or subsidiary. Whether the person performed services on behalf of the firm will be determined on the facts (this is a rebuttable presumption) and not purely by reference to the relationship between the person and the firm.

Associated person may also include contractors and therefore it is important to vet contractors to a firm carefully.

Where a firm has committed an offence and a senior officer has consented to or conspired in the commission of the offence, then the senior officer can also be held liable for the offence. In the context of a law firm, this could be the compliance officer for legal practice (COLP), compliance officer for finance and administration (COFA), money laundering reporting officer (MLRO), money laundering compliance officer (MLCO) or perhaps the chief executive or managing partner who gave their blessing to the act. It could also in theory be a person within a firm's business development team who sanctioned the act.

A law firm will have a defence to a corporate offence if they took all reasonable steps to prevent an act of bribery in their organisation – e.g. undertook a risk assessment, had a policy and communicated it and provided training.

What are the compliance challenges?

- It is important that everyone in the firm understands the offences created by BA 2010 and the firm's policy and procedures.

What resources will help?

- BA 2010 itself.
- Law Society Practice Note: Bribery Act 2010 (25 November 2019, **www.lawsociety.org.uk/en/topics/regulation/bribery-act-2010**).

Compliance tips – how to mitigate the risk of getting it wrong

- Firms should:
  - undertake a risk assessment;
  - implement an anti-bribery and corruption policy;
  - communicate that policy; and
  - provide training.

6.3 What are the penalties for a BA 2010 offence?

Under BA 2010, bribery by individuals is punishable by up to 10 years' imprisonment and/or an unlimited fine. If a law firm is found to have taken part in bribery or to lack adequate procedures to prevent bribery, it too could face an unlimited fine.

A conviction for a bribery or corruption related offence would of course have severe reputational and financial consequences for a firm and is likely to bring on a Solicitors Regulation Authority (SRA) investigation with resulting consequences.

What are the compliance challenges?

- It is important that everyone in the firm understands the offences created by BA 2010 and the firm's policy and procedures.

What resources will help?

- BA 2010 itself.
- Law Society Practice Note: Bribery Act 2010 (25 November 2019, **www.lawsociety.org.uk/en/topics/regulation/bribery-act-2010**).

Compliance tips – how to mitigate the risk of getting it wrong

- Firms should:
  - undertake a risk assessment;
  - implement an anti-bribery and corruption policy;
  - communicate that policy; and
  - provide training.

6.4 What is the best way to assess a firm's bribery risk?

As BA 2010 creates a corporate 'failure to prevent' offence, it is important to assess the bribery risk and put in place mitigation measures. The first step is to conduct a risk assessment to assess the extent and nature of the firm's activities and the bribery risk they may create.

This assessment should record the risk identified and the means by which the firm prevents or mitigates exposure to such risk. The assessment should be reviewed each year, and firms may wish to combine it into their firm-wide risk assessment.

The firm should then implement an anti-bribery and corruption policy which sets out:

- the firm's stance on bribery and corruption (that it is not tolerated);
- the offences created under BA 2010;
- what steps people should take to prevent bribery and corruption; and
- whom to report concerns to (and to that end, appoint an anti-bribery officer (ABO)).

Firms should also provide regular training.

What are the compliance challenges?

- The consequences of not getting compliance with BA 2010 right can be severe to include penalties and reputational damage.

What resources will help?

- BA 2010 itself.
- Law Society Practice Note: Bribery Act 2010 (25 November 2019, **www.lawsociety.org.uk/en/topics/regulation/bribery-act-2010**).

Compliance tips – how to mitigate the risk of getting it wrong

- Firms must ensure that they take steps to adequately assess the bribery risk in their business and put appropriate policies and procedures in place to mitigate it, including training.

6.5 Should my firm have an anti-bribery and corruption policy? How could that policy be implemented and its implementation checked?

Undoubtedly yes, firms should have an anti-bribery and corruption policy. The reasons are twofold. Firstly, so that everyone understands what BA 2010 says, what bribery is, how to avoid it and what to do if it is suspected; and secondly, to partly demonstrate that the firm has done all that it can to prevent bribery in its business, thereby providing it with a defence to a corporate offence allegation.

The policy (like all policies) should be communicated across the firm, and if possible positive confirmation sought from those in the firm that they have read it and understand the contents.

The policy should be periodically brought to people's attention so that it remains fresh in their minds, and this could be done by combining a reminder about the policy with a real life or mocked up scenario or a news story.

Implementation is not checked by any external bodies, but if a firm is to have a fighting chance of defending an allegation of a corporate offence, then it must do the right thing even though no one is looking and implement a policy and communicate it as much is proportionately reasonable.

What are the compliance challenges?

- It is important that everyone in the firm understands the offences created by BA 2010 and the firm's policy and procedures.
- Ensuring that the firm's anti-bribery and corruption policy is well understood is key.

What resources will help?

- BA 2010 itself.
- Law Society Practice Note: Bribery Act 2010 (25 November 2019, **www.lawsociety.org.uk/en/topics/regulation/bribery-act-2010**).

Compliance tips – how to mitigate the risk of getting it wrong

- Firms should ensure that any policy when implemented is communicated across the firm, and then messaging on the policy and around the subject area of bribery risk is regularly communicated via news stories and the like.

6.6 Should we have an anti-bribery and corruption officer?

Where deemed proportionate to do so, firms should have a designated ABO who is responsible for overseeing the firm's policy on anti-bribery and corruption and ensuring that it is upheld both in word and spirit.

The ABO's responsibilities should include:

- an annual review of the policy;
- an annual review of the risk assessment of issues relating to the policy;
- overseeing training and communications relating to the topic.

Although the ABO should have responsibility to oversee bribery compliance overall, the firm may want to make it clear that ultimately all partners or equivalent senior persons in the practice remain accountable for the policy's implementation and ensuring compliance.

What are the compliance challenges?

- It is important that all aspects of compliance are proportionate.
- Firms only need to consider appointing an ABO if it is proportionate to do so based on the firm's size and bribery risk.

What resources will help?

- BA 2010 itself.
- Law Society Practice Note: Bribery Act 2010 (25 November 2019, **www.lawsociety.org.uk/en/topics/regulation/bribery-act-2010**).

Compliance tips – how to mitigate the risk of getting it wrong

- An ABO should be appointed if proportionate to do so, and that officer must understand their role in the firm's compliance with BA 2010.

6.7 What are the best methods of training?

In order to determine the most appropriate methods of training, the firm needs to consider the nature and size of its business and the nature and extent of the risks of bribery.

There is no 'one size to fit all' approach, and each firm must decide its own training programme. Below are some training ideas:

- **Online training modules** are a good way to train consistently and provide a method of recording the training undertaken. Further, they are useful if there are many people to train at any one time.
- **In-person (physical or virtual) training** is by far the most effective method of training, especially where interaction with the trainer through questions and answers is possible.
- **Attendance at team meetings** on a regular basis to discuss a latest issue or trends in compliance or to remind people of the firm's policies can also form part of the firm's training strategy.
- **Regularly written guidance pieces or short articles** on risk and compliance news stories are also a useful way to train.
- **Regular newsletters or bulletins** perhaps providing additional news and guidance and/or incorporating the items described above can also be useful.

Variety is key when training, as not everyone will learn in the same way.

What are the compliance challenges?

- Ensuring that training is engaging and meaningful – meaning the recipient is more likely to retain the information that is given.

What resources will help?

- There are many external providers who are able to provide online training modules or face-to-face training.

Compliance tips – how to mitigate the risk of getting it wrong

- Variety is key to effective training.
- Firms may determine that they want to use an online training module for consistency and recording purposes.
- This could be supplemented with attendance at team meetings and a published guidance piece with a scenario (real or fictional) once a year.

6.8 What might my firm's stance on gifts and hospitality be?

Firms need to have a policy on gifts and hospitality that is proportionate to the work undertaken and types of clients.

Gifts and hospitality are commonly used in business to build relationships and market services or products. Hospitality often takes the form of entertainment, meals and gifts. If the provider of the hospitality does not attend, then it should be regarded as a gift rather than entertainment/meals.

While this is all normal practice, it should be recognised by law firms and reflected in its policy that gifts and hospitality can be used to influence and corrupt third parties, and on occasion to manoeuvre employees into a position of obligation, or there could be a perception of any of these things.

Firms should prevent the giving or receiving of gifts, hospitality or paying of expenses if it might influence or be perceived to influence a business decision.

Firms therefore should decide what value of gifts, entertainment and hospitality either given or received must be reported to the ABO (or other person if no ABO is to be appointed) and whether this is before or after the event and recorded by either the ABO or other appropriate business services team such as business development/marketing. The value to be reported and recorded will depend on the type of client and/or work – so for example, a threshold of £500 might be appropriate for a London City law firm which has completed a piece of work that generated large fees, but might not be appropriate for a smaller firm acting for private individuals.

By reporting and recording all gifts, entertainment and hospitality, this will allow the ABO to monitor both the level and the number of instances to assess whether the nature of the relationship is appropriate.

What are the compliance challenges?

- It is important for the firm to have a policy which covers gifts and hospitality, and that instances are recorded for monitoring.

What resources will help?

- BA 2010 itself.
- Law Society Practice Note: Bribery Act 2010 (25 November 2019, **www.lawsociety.org.uk/en/topics/regulation/bribery-act-2010**).

Compliance tips – how to mitigate the risk of getting it wrong

- Firms should place any requirements and rules into its anti-bribery and corruption policy.

6.9 We are acting for a client in a jurisdiction where we have been informed 'grease payments' are common and expected. What are 'grease payments' and should we make them?

Otherwise formally known as 'facilitation payments', 'grease payments' are small payments demanded by officials to provide a service they are obligated to perform. There is no exemption for these payments under BA 2010, and *they should not be made.*

The Law Society Practice Note states that the government does recognise that there is an issue faced by organisations which operate in some parts of the world where grease payments are considered the norm and expected.

It goes on to further state that guidance for prosecutors sets out that factors that would make it more likely that a prosecution would occur include where making such payments is seen as a standard part of conducting business and payments are repeated or large. Further, an individual's failure to follow the firm's procedures on payment facilitation payments might also be a factor.

What are the compliance challenges?

- The firm must not make grease payments or they risk breaching BA 2010.

What resources will help?

- BA 2010 itself.
- Law Society Practice Note: Bribery Act 2010 (25 November 2019, **www.lawsociety.org.uk/en/topics/regulation/bribery-act-2010**).

Compliance tips – how to mitigate the risk of getting it wrong

- A firm's policy should make it clear that it will not allow grease payments, and who in the firm should be consulted if a grease payment request is made.

6.10 What due diligence should be done on third party suppliers?

The scope of BA 2010 means that firms need to identify third party business relationships which may give opportunity for a third party to use bribery while acting on the firm's behalf. Therefore, appropriate due diligence should be undertaken before a third party is engaged.

Ordinarily this would be done during the procurement phase leading to a supplier being selected, and to that end firms may wish to (a) devise a questionnaire that asks about the supplier's own anti-bribery and corruption practices (alongside other aspects of compliance and risk management, such as modern slavery compliance, money laundering prevention measures and so on); and also (b) conduct searches via open sources (such as Google) for any adverse news which might suggest bribery might be part of the supplier's practices.

Where the risk of bribery is potentially higher (perhaps because of the location of the supplier in a high-risk jurisdiction), then the firm may wish to ask the supplier to agree to follow the terms of the firm's own policy and also request they ensure that those who supply to the supplier also have appropriate measures in place to tackle bribery. Alternatively, the firm may wish to devise its own code of conduct for suppliers and ask the supplier to confirm they will follow it.

If the supplier is wholly UK-based and not in an industry linked to bribery, then the due diligence conducted can be lighter in touch.

Contracts with suppliers should also have the ability to be terminated if bribery is detected or if the firm's policy or code of conduct is not followed (if it is a term that the supplier is to follow), and should also have clear terms about what is being supplied.

What are the compliance challenges?

- Bribery in third party suppliers can constitute a weak spot in the firm's armoury against bribery. Firms can be held accountable for the bribery of others.

What resources will help?

- BA 2010 itself.
- Law Society Practice Note: Bribery Act 2010 (25 November 2019, **www.lawsociety.org.uk/en/topics/regulation/bribery-act-2010**).

Compliance tips – how to mitigate the risk of getting it wrong

- Firms should consider devising a procurement process whereby suppliers are vetted. Firms may wish to take the view that regulated suppliers such as counsel, other forms of expert or suppliers that are wholly UK based and do not have suppliers of their own that carry a high bribery risk, do not need to go through any anti-bribery process the firm devises.
- Firms may also wish to ask suppliers to adhere to its own bribery policy or code of conduct for suppliers.

6.11 What should we do if bribery is suspected? What needs to be considered?

Bribery may be suspected as occurring either internally or externally. The firm's anti-bribery and corruption policy should make it clear to whom a report of bribery concern should be made.

If a firm is faced with a report of bribery involving one of its own people, this needs to be investigated straightaway (usually by the ABO or other senior person) and a view taken as to whether the report is accurate or not.

If the firm has been informed by one of its clients that the client has accepted bribes or has itself been bribing others, then the firm needs to think about the following:

- **Privilege** – It is very likely that what has been divulged is privileged and therefore the solicitor needs to consider whether they are able to take any further steps in relation to the information and whether the crime/fraud exception applies.
- **MLROs and suspicious activity reports (SARs)** – The MLRO needs to consider whether the act of bribery has caused criminal property and a SAR needs to be made requesting a defence from the National Crime Agency (NCA).
- **SRA Principles and Codes (www.sra.org.uk/solicitors/standards-regulations/)** – The solicitor acting and the COLP need to consider whether the solicitor/firm can continue to act in the circumstances of what is known and in accordance with the SRA Principles (Principle 1 – acting in a way that upholds principle of rule of law and proper administration of justice; Principle 2 – acting in a way that upholds trust and confidence in the solicitors profession; Principle 4 – act with honesty; and Principle 5 – act with integrity) and Codes of Conduct (Code of Conduct for Solicitors, rule 1.4 prohibiting misleading others could be relevant). The COLP needs to consider also if a report needs to be made if the solicitor or firm has not met the standards required. The client may also be asking the solicitor to put forward a position which is contrary to what the client has informed them – e.g. to put forward declarations to a buyer of a business that no bribery has occurred within the business when the client has in fact confirmed that is has taken place.
- **Reputational issues** – The solicitor and firm need to consider whether they want to continue acting from a reputational standpoint. If it is known or suspected that bribery has occurred and the information is press-worthy, does the firm want to be linked to it?

What are the compliance challenges?

- If there is suspicion of bribery, then action needs to be taken swiftly.

What resources will help?

- BA 2010 itself.
- Law Society Practice Note: Bribery Act 2010 (25 November 2019, **www.lawsociety.org.uk/en/topics/regulation/bribery-act-2010**).
- Further external help may be needed by specialists in the field.

Compliance tips – how to mitigate the risk of getting it wrong

- Upon a report of suspected bribery, an investigation needs to be undertaken without delay.
- The steps above outline what needs to be considered and could be placed in the firm's anti-bribery policy or in some other internal document for future reference.

6.12 My firm currently gives Christmas gifts each year to local estate agents who refer work to us. Is this a problem?

A small token of appreciation sent to local estate agents at Christmas is unlikely to engage BA 2010. However, firms should consider carefully the intent behind gifts. They should also ensure that they have a clear policy on gifts and record both the giving and receiving of gifts.

The firm should consider:

- The purpose of the gifts – are they to strengthen good business relations, or are they intended as some form of inducement?
- Does the firm have a policy on gifts which is clear and transparent, and do these gifts comply with the policy?
- Are the recipients of the gifts given the impression that they are under some obligation to refer business to the firm as a result of accepting the gifts?
- Are the gifts extravagant in the circumstances? For example, a box of chocolates will not be of course, but an all-inclusive holiday will be.
- Is a record made of the gift?

What are the compliance challenges?

- Giving gifts must *not* be used as an inducement, or be seen to be.

What resources will help?

- BA 2010 itself.
- Law Society Practice Note: Bribery Act 2010 (25 November 2019, **www.lawsociety.org.uk/en/topics/regulation/bribery-act-2010**).

Compliance tips – how to mitigate the risk of getting it wrong

- Firms should have a clear policy on giving gifts.
- Gifts given should be proportionate to the situation at hand.

6.13 My firm is considering setting up an overseas operation in a country which has a high level of corruption. What risks should we consider?

There are particular risks that occur during the setting up of the firm, for instance:

- gaining the appropriate government licences for the firm;
- acquiring planning permission for building new offices or changing existing ones; and
- applying for visas for staff who will be working in the new offices.

These are all transactions where there is a risk of being asked to pay a bribe. Many of these issues may be dealt with by a local agent. Using a third party also creates a risk, as the firm will have less control over the third party.

What are the compliance challenges?

- Firms must not engage in bribery and must not make 'grease payments', even if that is the 'norm' in the country at hand.
- Firms must also not allow others to bribe, or be 'blind' to others bribing on their behalf.

What resources will help?

- BA 2010 itself.
- Law Society Practice Note: Bribery Act 2010 (25 November 2019, **www.lawsociety.org.uk/en/topics/regulation/bribery-act-2010**).

Compliance tips – how to mitigate the risk of getting it wrong

- Firms must have a robust policy on anti-bribery.
- Firms must also carefully vet third party suppliers who will be assisting with the set-up overseas, and if possible request that they conform to the firm's anti-bribery policy or the firm's code of conduct for suppliers.

6.14 My firm has instructed a professional firm based overseas on behalf of a client regarding a dispute in another country. There is a high level of corruption within this country. The firm is concerned that a bribe may have been paid by the professional firm in order to resolve the dispute. The firm is not clear on whose behalf the bribe has been paid. What is the position?

In most cases, the bribe is likely to have been paid on behalf of the client, as the professional firm is providing services on their behalf. However, this may vary depending on the retainer that has been put in place.

If the retainer makes it clear that the professional firm has been retained on behalf of the firm, then the firm may be liable for any bribe paid. Firms should consider carrying out appropriate due diligence on firms they refer work to. The due diligence required will depend on the risk, including:

- the country in which the firm operates;
- current knowledge – such as the firm's reputation and previous experience of dealing with the firm;
- the nature of the transaction – for example, is the work a simple research exercise or does it involve contract negotiations or dealing with government officials where the risk is likely to be higher?

What are the compliance challenges?

- Depending in the circumstances, the firm could be liable for any bribery that has taken place.

What resources will help?

- BA 2010 itself.
- Law Society Practice Note: Bribery Act 2010 (25 November 2019, **www.lawsociety.org.uk/en/topics/regulation/bribery-act-2010**).

Compliance tips – how to mitigate the risk of getting it wrong

- In circumstances such as this, it must be absolutely clear who is the client of the overseas professional firm, as this could be a critical factor if a possible act of bribery were to have taken place.
- Further, the overseas firm should be carefully vetted, given the high risk of bribery in its jurisdiction.

6.15 A client has informed the solicitor acting in the sale of his business that contracts with those the business supplies to came about after a grease payment was made. The business and contracts are in the UK. What does the firm need to do and think about?

The solicitor should report the matter to the firm's COLP and MLRO. The solicitor and COLP need to consider whether the solicitor will be drafting any warranties in the company sale documentation that warrants that bribery has not taken place, as to do so would be misleading, potentially dishonest and show a lack of integrity. If the solicitor has already done this, thought needs to be given about whether the position should be corrected. If the solicitor has not drafted such warranties, thought needs to be given as to whether the solicitor can, and what should be said to the client.

The MLRO needs to consider whether there is a suspicion of money laundering and whether criminal property is in existence. If so, the MLRO needs to consider whether a defence should be sought.

Generally, the firm and solicitor need to consider whether they want to continue acting, and if not whether it is appropriate to stop acting (it may prejudice the client's position).

What are the compliance challenges?

- Solicitors in the firm need to be alert to the possibility of bribery happening in retainers they least expect it to.
- Solicitors also need to know whom to bring their concerns to.

What resources will help?

- BA 2010 itself.
- Law Society Practice Note: Bribery Act 2010 (25 November 2019, **www.lawsociety.org.uk/en/topics/regulation/bribery-act-2010**).

Compliance tips – how to mitigate the risk of getting it wrong

- Firms must have a robust policy on anti-bribery and makes it clear what to do and whom to speak to if bribery is suspected or indeed confirmed.

CHAPTER 7

Tax evasion and the Criminal Finances Act 2017

7.1 What offences does the Criminal Finances Act 2017 create? Who is an associated person?

The Criminal Finances Act 2017 (CFA 2017) came into force on 30 September 2017 and created a criminal offence for any relevant body that fails to prevent the criminal facilitation of tax evasion by associated persons.

A 'relevant body' is an incorporated body such as companies and some partnerships. The offences under CFA 2017 cannot be committed by individuals, though individuals may commit offences under different legislation. Note that where there is a UK tax facilitation offence, it does not matter where the relevant body was incorporated or based or whether the associated person performs the facilitation of the criminal act in the UK or overseas.

At CFA 2017's core, an entity is in the frame if it fails to prevent tax evasion by its associated persons. If there is tax evasion by the associated persons, the entity's defence is that it did all it could to prevent it from happening. Therefore, entities need to do their best to ensure compliance so as to use those compliance steps as a defence.

The offence of tax evasion will be committed where an associated person:

- is knowingly concerned in, or takes steps with a view to, the fraudulent evasion of tax by another person; or
- aids, abets, counsels or procures the commission of a UK tax evasion offence by another person; or
- is involved in the commission of an offence consisting of being knowingly concerned in, or taking steps with a view to, the fraudulent evasion of tax.

There are three stages to the offence under CFA 2017:

(a) the criminal evasion of UK tax;

(b) the criminal facilitation of this offence by an associated person to the relevant body;
(c) the relevant body failing to prevent the associated person from committing that facilitation.

This is a strict liability offence, and if stages (a) and (b) have occurred then stage (c) is deemed to have taken place unless the relevant body can demonstrate they have put in place reasonable prevention measures.

Note that it is no prerequisite for bringing a prosecution under CFA 2017 for a conviction of the taxpayer to have taken place, though the prosecution would have to show that beyond all reasonable doubt the taxpayer level offence had been committed.

An 'associated person' is defined as a person who is an employee of the relevant body who is acting in the capacity of an employee (in the case of a law firm, this would include partners and consultants); an agent of the body who is acting in their capacity as an agent; or any other person who performs services for and on behalf of the body who is acting in the capacity of a person performing such services.

Those who act as an agent may be experts that the body instructs including counsel. These parties may therefore be construed as being associated persons. In the case of a law firm, most if not all such persons will be regulated persons and so will be subject to their own regulators' requirements and CFA 2017. A firm may therefore decide to consider these associated persons as being low risk.

What are the compliance challenges?

- Everyone in the firm must understand not to facilitate tax evasion, and what to do if it is suspected.

What resources will help?

- CFA 2017 itself.
- The Law Society Practice Note: Criminal Finances Act 2017 (27 January 2020, **www.lawsociety.org.uk/en/topics/tax/criminal-finances-act-2017**).

Compliance tips – how to mitigate the risk of getting it wrong

- Firms should:
  - conduct a risk assessment;
  - implement a policy; and
  - provide training for its people.
- These steps should be taken to minimise the risk of tax evasion occurring or the facilitation of it, and also to provide the firm with a defence that it did all that it could to prevent the facilitation of tax evasion.

7.2 What is an unexplained wealth order?

CFA 2017 introduced for the first time the concept of unexplained wealth orders (UWOs). This is a form of court order which compels the recipient to explain their wealth.

To obtain a UWO, the court must be satisfied that there are reasonable grounds to suspect that the known sources of the individual's income would not be enough to enable them to acquire the property that they hold (and the property value exceeds £50,000) and that the individual is either a politically exposed person (PEP) or there is a reasonable suspicion that the individual is involved in serious crime. The ability to obtain UWOs has now been made easier by the Economic Crime (Transparency and Enforcement) Act 2022.

Persons who fail to account for their wealth under one of these orders are liable to have assets seized.

The burden for proving the source of the wealth falls to the individual holding the wealth, as opposed to authorities who have suspicions about it.

What are the compliance challenges?

- A high-level explanation of an UWO should be set out the firm's policy so that the concept is understood.

What resources will help?

- CFA 2017 itself.
- The Law Society Practice Note: Criminal Finances Act 2017 (27 January 2020, **www.lawsociety.org.uk/en/topics/tax/criminal-finances-act-2017**).
- Further guidance can be found on the Transparency International UK website: 'Unexplained wealth orders: a brief guide' (30 May 2017, **www.transparency.org.uk/unexplained-wealth-orders-brief-guide**).

Compliance tips – how to mitigate the risk of getting it wrong

- A high-level explanation of an UWO should be set out in the firm's policy so that the concept is understood.

7.3 What is an account freezing order?

Also created by CFA 2017 is the ability for enforcement officers to apply to a magistrate for an account freezing order (AFO). These orders freeze funds held in bank accounts and building societies.

To obtain an AFO, the enforcement officer must have reasonable grounds to suspect that money (of which there must be more than £1,000 held in the account in question) held is 'recoverable property' (on the balance of probabilities the monies were obtained through unlawful conduct) or intended for use in unlawful conduct. No criminal conviction is required.

Once an account has been frozen, the monies contained in it can be subject to a forfeiture order if the court is satisfied that the money is recoverable or was intended to be used in unlawful conduct.

An account forfeiture notice can also be issued, and this will set out the monies to be taken and the period of time available for objection. If no objection is raised, then an order is made. The order is capable of appeal for 30 days after being made.

What are the compliance challenges?

- A high-level explanation of an AFO could be set out in the firm's policy so that the concept is understood.

What resources will help?

- CFA 2017 itself.
- The Law Society Practice Note: Criminal Finances Act 2017 (27 January 2020, **www.lawsociety.org.uk/en/topics/tax/criminal-finances-act-2017**).

Compliance tips – how to mitigate the risk of getting it wrong

- A high-level explanation of an AFO could be set out in the firm's policy so that the concept is understood.

7.4 What are the penalties for an offence under CFA 2017?

Penalties for an offence under CFA 2017 are unlimited financial penalties and ancillary orders such as confiscation orders or prevention orders. A conviction will undoubtedly bring intense interest from regulators, and bring with it reputational damage.

To mitigate penalties, early self-reporting is encouraged, and is also seen in itself to be a reasonable measure put in place to prevent further criminal acts from occurring.

It is possible to reach an agreement with prosecutors under the supervision of a judge to allow a prosecution to be suspended for a defined period (known as Deferred Prosecution Agreements) providing certain conditions are met by the relevant body. This can include the body making full reparation for the criminal behaviour without being convicted.

What are the compliance challenges?

- Firms and those within them need to understand the penalties for tax evasion and the penalties for offences under CFA 2017.

What resources will help?

- CFA 2017 itself.
- The Law Society Practice Note: Criminal Finances Act 2017 (27 January 2020, **www.lawsociety.org.uk/en/topics/tax/criminal-finances-act-2017**).

Compliance tips – how to mitigate the risk of getting it wrong

- The firm's tax-evasion policy should set out the penalties for the relevant offences.
- This should be supplemented with training.

7.5 What is the best way to assess my firm's CFA 2017/tax evasion risk?

As CFA 2017 creates a corporate 'failure to prevent' offence, it is important to assess the tax evasion risk and put in place mitigation measures.

The first step is to conduct a risk assessment to assess the extent and nature of the firm's activities, and the bribery risk they may create. This assessment should record the risk identified and the means by which the firm prevents or mitigates exposure to such risk. The assessment should be reviewed each year, and firms may wish to combine it into their firm-wide risk assessment.

The firm should then implement an anti-tax evasion policy, which sets out:

- the firm's stance on facilitating tax evasion (i.e. that it is not tolerated);
- the offences created under CFA 2017;
- what steps people should take to prevent tax evasion; and
- whom to report concerns to.

Firms should also provide regular training.

When considering risk via a risk assessment, firms may wish to consider the following questions.

Clients

- Does the firm act for clients whom the firm has reason to suspect of tax evasion in the past or present?
- Does the firm act for clients who may pose particular tax evasion risk? For example, because they are cash-based, have assets in higher risk jurisdictions or hold assets through complex or obscure ownership structures.
- Does the firm act for PEPs, and does the firm have proper procedures in place around the discovery of source of funds and wealth?

Services

- Does the firm advise clients on tax?
- Does the firm assist in creating corporate or tax structures which may be used to facilitate tax evasion?
- Does the firm act on matters connected to tax havens?
- Does the firm set up structures to minimise tax?

Employees

- Does the firm have a lack of supervision anywhere?
- Does the firm ensure that appropriate checks are carried out before employment?
- Is there a culture of compliance in the firm and can it be better?
- Do any employees display an ignorant attitude to compliance?
- Do employees receive training on tax evasion?

Firm risk

- Does the firm contract with suppliers who may pose a high tax evasion risk due to their work or geographical location?
- Does the firm have in place a procurement process to minimise the risk of being associated with a business who engages in tax evasion?

The firm may wish to incorporate some of these questions into their client and matter risk assessment (required under the Money Laundering, Terrorist Financing and Transfer of Funds (Information on the Payer) Regulations 2017, SI 2017/692 (AML Regulations)) either as standard across the firm or just for certain practice areas.

What are the compliance challenges?

- To ensure as far as possible that the facilitation of tax evasion is not occurring in the firm, firms must assess the risk of it happening and take appropriate measures. This will provide the firm with a defence also should it be accused of failing to prevent the facilitation of tax evasion.

What resources will help?

- CFA 2017 itself.
- The Law Society Practice Note: Criminal Finances Act 2017 (27 January 2020, **www.lawsociety.org.uk/en/topics/tax/criminal-finances-act-2017**).

Compliance tips – how to mitigate the risk of getting it wrong

- Firms should:
  - assess the risk;
  - implement a policy and any required procedures; and
  - train its people.

7.6 Should my firm have an anti-tax evasion policy? How could that policy be implemented and its implementation checked?

Undoubtedly yes, firms should have an anti-tax evasion policy. The reasons are twofold. Firstly, so that everyone understands what CFA 2017 says, what offences it creates, how to avoid facilitating tax evasion and what to do if it is suspected; and secondly, to partly demonstrate that the firm has done all that it can to prevent the facilitation of tax evasion in its business thereby providing it with a defence to a corporate offence allegation.

The policy (like all policies) should be communicated across the firm, and if possible positive confirmation sought from those in the firm that they have read it and understand the contents.

The policy should be periodically brought to people's attention so that it remains fresh in their minds, and this could be done by combining a reminder about the policy with a real life or mocked up scenario or a news story.

Implementation is not checked by any external bodies, but if a firm is to have a fighting chance of defending an allegation of a corporate offence of failure to prevent facilitation of tax evasion, then it should implement a policy.

What are the compliance challenges?

- Any policy must be widely communicated and understood.

What resources will help?

- CFA 2017 itself.
- The Law Society Practice Note: Criminal Finances Act 2017 (27 January 2020, **www.lawsociety.org.uk/en/topics/tax/criminal-finances-act-2017**).
- *Financial Crime: A Compliance Manual* (Rebecca Atkinson, Law Society Publishing, 2021). This includes a template policy (p.260).

Compliance tips – how to mitigate the risk of getting it wrong

- Firms should implement an anti-tax evasion policy, ensuring that this is communicated widely and understood.

7.7 What are the best methods of training?

In order to determine the most appropriate methods of training, the firm needs to consider the nature and size of its business and the nature and extent of the risks of facilitating tax evasion.

There is no 'one size fits all' approach, and each firm must decide its own training programme. Below are some training ideas:

- **Online training modules** are a good way to train consistently and provide a method of recording the training undertaken. Further, they are useful if there are many people to train at any one time.
- **In-person (physical or virtual) training** is by far the most effective method of training, especially where interaction with the trainer through questions and answers is possible.
- **Attendance at team meetings on a regular basis** to discuss a latest issue or trends in compliance or to remind people of the firm's policies can also form part of the firm's training strategy.
- **Regularly written guidance pieces or short articles** on risk and compliance news stories are also a useful way to train.
- **Regular newsletters or bulletins** perhaps providing additional news and guidance and/or incorporating the items described above can also be useful.

Variety is key when training, as not everyone will learn in the same way.

What are the compliance challenges?

- Ensuring that training is engaging and meaningful – meaning the recipient is more likely to retain the information that is given.

What resources will help?

- CFA 2017 itself.
- The Law Society Practice Note: Criminal Finances Act 2017 (27 January 2020, **www.lawsociety.org.uk/en/topics/tax/criminal-finances-act-2017**).

Compliance tips – how to mitigate the risk of getting it wrong

- Variety is key to training.
- Firms may determine that they want to use an online training module for consistency and recording purposes.
- This could be supplemented with attendance at team meetings and a published guidance piece with a scenario (real or fictional) once a year.

7.8 What are examples of the types of tax evasion that could be happening in mainstream practice areas?

Below are some practical examples of tax evasion that may arise in a law firm. These could be placed in a firm's anti-tax evasion policy.

In any practice area

- Delivering a misleading or inaccurate bill which enables a client to evade tax. For example, billing a company for work actually done for its directors or shareholders in order to assist clients to claim a tax deduction to which they are not entitled. This is likely to be value added tax (VAT) fraud.

Property

- Preparing documents which misstate the price of a property to enable a client to evade stamp duty land tax (SDLT) or capital gains tax (CGT).
- Assisting in a property being bought using nominees or other structures to enable a client to illegally avoid tax.

Corporate

- Assisting in creating corporate or trust structures designed to conceal a client's taxable income or assets.
- Referring clients to third parties in tax havens to set up accounts or structures which you know are to facilitate tax evasion, rather than tax avoidance.
- Using side letters so that aspects of a transaction with taxable effects are not apparent from reading the main agreement in order to enable a client, or anyone else, to evade tax.

Wills and probate

- Assisting in creating trusts or other structures designed to conceal a client's taxable income or assets.
- Giving clients advice on how to make lifetime transfers in ways which HM Revenue and Customs (HMRC) will find difficult to detect.
- Preparing documents which misstate the value of an estate in order to avoid inheritance tax (IHT).

Family law

- Helping a client to put forward figures which you know to be false may involve a number of offences, possibly including conspiracy to pervert the course of justice and tax evasion offences.

- Clients who have been ordered to disclose their earnings in connection with family proceedings may tell the solicitor acting that they have committed tax evasion in the past. That information will normally be privileged and is not normally reportable under money laundering regulations. However, in such cases, the solicitor should discuss the matter with the money laundering reporting officer (MLRO) or compliance officer for legal practice (COLP) to ensure that their involvement in the case will not create any liabilities or concerns.

What are the compliance challenges?

- Ensuring that people know when to spot tax evasion is key.

What resources will help?

- CFA 2017 itself.
- The Law Society Practice Note: Criminal Finances Act 2017 (27 January 2020, **www.lawsociety.org.uk/en/topics/tax/criminal-finances-act-2017**).

Compliance tips – how to mitigate the risk of getting it wrong

- To assist people in the firm, the above examples could be set out in the firm's anti-tax evasion policy.
- These could be reiterated in team meetings, and via short guidance pieces sent periodically.

7.9 What warning notices has the SRA published on this subject and what Law Society guidance will help me?

The Solicitors Regulation Authority's (SRA's) current warning notice on tax is called 'Tax avoidance your duties' (**www.sra.org.uk/solicitors/guidance/tax-avoidance-duties/**). This notice was first published on 21 September 2017 and revised on 25 November 2019 when the new SRA Standards and Regulations were implemented (**www.sra.org.uk/solicitors/standards-regulations/**). The notice is aimed at all those the SRA 'regulate involved either directly or indirectly advising clients about tax, handling client matters or transactions involving them in the design, implementation, organisation or management of tax affairs, schemes or arrangements.' All firms must read this warning notice.

Of further help is the Law Society's Practice Note on the Criminal Finances Act 2017 (27 January 2020, **www.lawsociety.org.uk/en/topics/tax/criminal-finances-act-2017**).

What are the compliance challenges?

- Firms and those within the firm must be aware at all times of SRA warning notices.

What resources will help?

- CFA 2017 itself.
- SRA warning notice: 'Tax avoidance your duties' (updated 25 November 2019, **www.sra.org.uk/solicitors/guidance/tax-avoidance-duties/**).
- The Law Society Practice Note: Criminal Finances Act 2017 (27 January 2020, **www.lawsociety.org.uk/en/topics/tax/criminal-finances-act-2017**).

Compliance tips – how to mitigate the risk of getting it wrong

- Firms should ensure that their people are made aware of SRA warning notices and the availability of additional guidance.

7.10 What should we do if tax evasion is suspected? What needs to be considered?

If a firm is faced with a report of possible tax evasion involving an associated person, this needs to be investigated straightaway and a view taken as to whether the report is accurate or not. The following should also be considered:

- **Privilege** – If a client has confirmed they have evaded tax, it is very likely that what has been divulged is privileged, and therefore the solicitor needs to consider whether he or she needs to or can take any further steps in relation to the information and whether the crime/fraud exception applies.
- **MLROs and suspicious activity reports (SARs)** – The MLRO needs to consider whether the act of tax evasion has caused criminal property and a SAR needs to be made requesting a defence from the National Crime Agency (NCA).
- **SRA Principles and Codes (www.sra.org.uk/solicitors/standards-regulations/)** – The solicitor and COLP need to consider whether the solicitor/firm can continue to act in the circumstances of what is known and in accordance with the SRA Principles (Principle 1 – act in a way that upholds principle of rule of law and proper administration of justice; Principle 2 – act in a way that upholds trust and confidence in the solicitors profession; Principle 4 – act with honesty; and Principle 5 – act with integrity). The COLP needs to consider also if a report needs to be made if the solicitor or firm has not met the standards required. The client may also be asking the solicitor to put forward a position which is contrary to what the client has informed them, e.g. to put forward declarations that tax has been paid or represent a sum to be smaller than it is in order to evade tax, and so this needs to be handled.

- **Reputational issues** – The solicitor and firm need to consider whether they want to continue acting from a reputational standpoint. If it is known or suspected that tax evasion has occurred and the information is press-worthy, does the firm want to be linked to it?

What are the compliance challenges?

- If there is suspicion of tax evasion, then action needs to be taken swiftly.

What resources will help?

- CFA 2017 itself.
- The Law Society Practice Note: Criminal Finances Act 2017 (27 January 2020, **www.lawsociety.org.uk/en/topics/tax/criminal-finances-act-2017**).
- Further external help may be needed by specialists in the field.

Compliance tips – how to mitigate the risk of getting it wrong

- Upon a report of suspected tax evasion, an investigation needs to be undertaken without delay.
- The steps above in this Q&A outline what should be considered and could be placed in the firm's anti-tax evasion policy or in some other internal document for future reference.

7.11 How often should training and messaging be repeated?

There is no set timescale by which training or messaging needs to be repeated, and this will depend on the risk profile of the firm. Firms may decide to train and message about tax evasion to higher-risk practice teams on a more frequent basis than to the firm at large. As a rule of thumb, training should occur every two years, and messaging perhaps a couple of times a year.

What are the compliance challenges?

- Firms must ensure that their people receive adequate training so as to prevent the facilitation of tax evasion, and also to provide the firm with a defence to any allegation that it has failed to prevent the offence occurring.

What resources will help?

- CFA 2017 itself.
- The Law Society Practice Note: Criminal Finances Act 2017 (27 January 2020, **www.lawsociety.org.uk/en/topics/tax/criminal-finances-act-2017**).

Compliance tips – how to mitigate the risk of getting it wrong

- Firms must roll out adequate training and messaging on a regular basis.

7.12 The client is asking that we do not include certain assets in the form E which needs to be completed for their matrimonial matter. Their reason is because 'they didn't pay tax on it'. What should we do?

Neither the firm nor the solicitor should (or be seen to) facilitate any tax evasion. The tax in theory has already been evaded, and the firm/solicitor should not perpetuate it. Further, the firm and solicitor have a duty not to mislead the court, nor the parties in the matter. It is therefore very unlikely that the firm can leave the asset out of the form E, and if the client does not consent to it being included, the firm will need to consider whether it can continue to act (in all likelihood, it cannot).

The solicitor should advise the client to seek urgent tax advice.

The solicitor should also consult the firm's MLRO to consider whether there is any suspicion of money laundering, and a SAR needs to be made. Privilege will need to be carefully considered.

What are the compliance challenges?

- Those in the firm need to be aware of how to spot a tax evasion issue, how to respond and whom to report it to.

What resources will help?

- CFA 2017 itself.
- The Law Society Practice Note: Criminal Finances Act 2017 (27 January 2020, **www.lawsociety.org.uk/en/topics/tax/criminal-finances-act-2017**).

Compliance tips – how to mitigate the risk of getting it wrong

- Firms should:
  - assess the risk;
  - implement a policy and any required procedures, and
  - train its people.

7.13 The client has asked the firm to bill their company for a will that was made. Can we amend the bill?

This is likely to result in the client's company being able to offset the VAT. This is VAT fraud, and should not be done.

What are the compliance challenges?

- Those in the firm need to be aware of how to spot a tax evasion issue, how to respond and whom to report it to.

What resources will help?

- CFA 2017 itself.
- The Law Society Practice Note: Criminal Finances Act 2017 (27 January 2020, **www.lawsociety.org.uk/en/topics/tax/criminal-finances-act-2017**).

Compliance tips – how to mitigate the risk of getting it wrong

- Firms should:
  - assess the risk;
  - implement a policy and any required procedures; and
  - train its people.

7.14 The client has asked that we readdress the bill to their parent company. Our client is the parent company's subsidiary. Can we do this?

Providing the readdressing of the bill does not allow VAT fraud, the readdressing makes commercial sense and there are no other concerns, this is ok. The firm needs to consider whether it is acting for the subsidiary company or its parent, especially if the request is on each bill rendered.

What are the compliance challenges?

- Those in the firm need to be aware of how to spot a tax evasion issue, how to respond and whom to report it to.

What resources will help?

- CFA 2017 itself.
- The Law Society Practice Note: Criminal Finances Act 2017 (27 January 2020, **www.lawsociety.org.uk/en/topics/tax/criminal-finances-act-2017**).

Compliance tips – how to mitigate the risk of getting it wrong

- Firms should:
  - assess the risk;
  - implement a policy and any required procedures; and
  - train its people.

CHAPTER 8

Sanctions

8.1 What are sanctions, why are they imposed, what types are there and who needs to comply?

Sanctions are restrictions put in place to achieve a specific foreign or national security objective.

Financial sanctions put in place by the UK and United Nations (UN) can limit the provision of certain financial services or restrict access to financial markets, funds and economic resources.

The Office of Financial Sanctions Implementation (OFSI) helps to ensure that financial sanctions are properly understood, implemented and enforced in the UK, and has issued guidance: 'UK Financial Sanctions: General guidance for financial sanctions under the Sanctions and Anti-Money Laundering Act 2018' (December 2020, available at **www.gov.uk/government/publications/financial-sanctions-faqs**).

The OFSI guidance sets out that financial sanctions are generally imposed to (para.1.1):

- **coerce** a regime, or individuals within a regime, into changing their behaviour (or aspects of it) by increasing the cost on them to such an extent that they decide to cease the offending behaviour;
- **constrain** a target by denying them access to key resources needed to continue their offending behaviour, including the financing of terrorism or nuclear proliferation;
- **signal disapproval**, stigmatising and potentially isolating a regime or individual, or as a way of sending broader political messages nationally or internationally; and/or
- **protect the value of assets** that have been misappropriated from a country until these assets can be repatriated.

The main types of financial sanctions imposed are (para.1.3):

- **Targeted asset freezes** – These apply to named individuals and entities restricting access to funds and economic resources.
- **Restrictions on a wide variety of financial markets and services** – These can apply to named individuals, entities, specified groups or sectors. These

can take the form of investment bans; restrictions on access to capital markets; directions to cease banking relationships and activities; requirements to notify or seek authorisation prior to certain payments being made or received; and restrictions on the provision of financial, insurance, brokering or advisory services and other financial services. This is not an exhaustive list.
- **Directions to cease all business** – These will specify the type of business, and can apply to a specific person, group, sector or country.

To whom the sanctions regime applies is defined under each statutory instrument. Under the Sanctions and Anti-Money Laundering Act 2018 (SAMLA 2018), those caught are as follows:

- a person who has permission under Financial Services and Markets Act 2000 (FSMA 2000), Part 4A (permission to carry on regulated activity);
- an undertaking that by way of business operates a currency exchange office, transmits money (or any representations of monetary value) by any means, or cashes cheques which are made payable to customers;
- a firm or sole practitioner that is a statutory auditor or local auditor;
- a firm or sole practitioner that provides by way of business accountancy services, legal or notarial services, advice about tax affairs or certain trust or company services;
- a firm or sole practitioner that carries out, or whose employees carry out, estate agency work;
- the holder of a casino operating licence;
- a person engaged in the business of making, supplying, selling or exchanging articles made from gold, silver, platinum, palladium or precious stones or pearls.

Those who are UK persons or entities but sit outside the UK are still subject to the sanction legislation.

Law firms are therefore clearly obligated to follow the sanctions regime in place in the UK.

What are the compliance challenges?

- It is vital that law firms do not fall foul of the sanctions regime, as the consequences can be severe.

What resources will help?

- OFSI guidance: 'UK Financial Sanctions: General guidance for financial sanctions under the Sanctions and Anti-Money Laundering Act 2018' (December 2020, available at **www.gov.uk/government/publications/financial-sanctions-faqs**).
- Law Society materials:
  - Law Society guide: 'UK sanctions regime' (29 March 2022, **www.lawsociety.org.uk/topics/anti-money-laundering/sanctions-guide**).

  - Law Society 'questions & answers' guidance: 'My client is a possible sanctions match. What should I do?' (**www.lawsociety.org.uk/en/contact-or-visit-us/helplines/practice-advice-service/q-and-as/my-client-is-a-possible-sanctions-match-what-should-i-do**).
- If in doubt, independent legal advice should be sought.

Compliance tips – how to mitigate the risk of getting it wrong

- Firms need to build into their processes appropriate sanctions checking.

8.2 Who are the sanction regime key players, and what do they do?

It is important to understand who the key government and departmental agencies involved in the sanctions regime in the UK are. These are as follows:

- Foreign, Commonwealth and Development Office (FCDO) – Responsible for the UK's international sanctions policy, including all international sanctions regimes and designations. They also negotiate all international sanctions.
- HM Treasury and OFSI – OFSI is the authority responsible for implementing the UK's financial sanctions on behalf of HM Treasury.
- Department for International Trade (Export Control Joint Unit) – Implements trade sanctions and embargoes.
- Department for Transport – Implements transport sanctions, including controlling movement of ships and aircraft in UK waters and airspace.
- Home Office – Implements travel bans.
- HM Revenue and Customs (HMRC) – Enforces breaches of trade sanctions.
- National Crime Agency (NCA) – Investigates and enforces breaches of financial sanctions.

What are the compliance challenges?

It is vital that law firms do not fall foul of the sanctions regime, as the consequences can be severe. Knowing who the key players are and what they do is important.

What resources will help?

- OFSI guidance. 'UK Financial Sanctions: General guidance for financial sanctions under the Sanctions and Anti-Money Laundering Act 2018' (December 2020, available at **www.gov.uk/government/publications/financial-sanctions-faqs**).
- Law Society guide: 'UK sanctions regime' (29 March 2022, **www.lawsociety.org.uk/topics/anti-money-laundering/sanctions-guide**).
- If in doubt, independent legal advice should be sought.

Compliance tips – how to mitigate the risk of getting it wrong

- Firms should understand the sanctions regime and its key players, and need to build into their processes appropriate sanctions checking.

8.3 What is OFAC and does it affect me and my firm?

The Office of Foreign Assets Control (OFAC) of the US Department of the Treasury, administers and enforces economic and trade sanctions based on US foreign policy and national security. Such sanctions generally attempt to freeze assets anywhere in the world in relation to individuals or entities. To act when a sanction is imposed requires a licence.

US sanctions must be complied with by all persons in the US, as well as US citizens and green card holders wherever located. These sanctions also bite on US companies and their foreign branches unless implementation is blocked by another jurisdiction – such as legislation in the UK which prevents UK entities and individuals from complying with sanctions imposed by the US on companies and individuals associated with Cuba, Iran and Libya (see the Extraterritorial US Legislation (Sanctions against Cuba, Iran and Libya) (Protection of Trading Interests) (Amendment) Order 2018, SI 2018/1357).

If a UK company has a person who is a US citizen as part of its board or senior management, this may also mean the US sanction is enforceable against the UK company.

It is possible, therefore, that a UK law firm may be caught by US sanctions – and further, if activity with a US-sanctioned person or entity involves an activity that takes place in the US (this is interpreted widely by OFAC), the UK law firm may be caught by the US sanction.

Where a UK law firm has no connection to the US and the US-sanctioned client is seeking advice that is unconnected with any US assets, the US sanctions regime will not have effect.

If, however the law firm were to be connected with the US, then the US sanctions will need to be checked and considered. Likewise, if a UK law firm is being asked to advise on US assets, a US sanction check should be considered.

What are the compliance challenges?

- Understanding the OFAC regime and whether it applies in any set of circumstances will be very fact-specific and can be challenging to ascertain.

What resources will help?

- The US government does provide some guidance found here: 'Office of Foreign Assets Control – sanctions programs and information' (**https://home.treasury.**

gov/policy-issues/office-of-foreign-assets-control-sanctions-programs-and-information).

- It may, however, be prudent to seek independent legal advice if needed.

Compliance tips – how to mitigate the risk of getting it wrong

- Firms should understand the sanctions regime, and need to build into their processes appropriate sanctions checking so that any OFAC sanction can be picked up and considered.

8.4 Where can I find sanctions lists?

OFSI maintains a consolidated list of those who are subject to financial sanctions.

In this consolidated list individuals and entities listed are known as 'designated persons'. When new UN and UK designations are made, the list is usually updated within one working day. The list can be found here: 'Financial sanctions targets: list of all asset freeze targets', updated 5 May 2022, **www.gov.uk/government/publications/financial-sanctions-consolidated-list-of-targets/consolidated-list-of-targets**.

An additional list pertaining to Russia also exists (**www.gov.uk/government/publications/financial-sanctions-ukraine-sovereignty-and-territorial-integrity**).

What are the compliance challenges?

- It is vital that law firms do not fall foul of the sanctions regime, as the consequences can be severe. Firms need to stay up-to-date with lists of those who are subject to financial sanctions.

What resources will help?

- OFSI guidance: 'UK Financial Sanctions: General guidance for financial sanctions under the Sanctions and Anti-Money Laundering Act 2018' (December 2020, available at **www.gov.uk/government/publications/financial-sanctions-faqs**).
- Law Society guide: 'UK sanctions regime' (29 March 2022, **www.lawsociety.org.uk/topics/anti-money-laundering/sanctions-guide**).
- If in doubt, independent legal advice should be sought.

Compliance tips – how to mitigate the risk of getting it wrong

- Firms should understand the sanctions regime, and need to build into their processes appropriate sanctions checking.
- The lists referenced above should be checked.

8.5 When should I check clients for sanctions? Whom, in respect of corporate clients, should I check?

Each firm needs to decide whether it will check all clients for sanctions or whether to do so on a risk-based approach. Online platforms are available at cost that enable a user to check sanctions, politically exposed person (PEP) status and adverse media at the same time. If a firm is using one of these platforms, they may decide to check all clients regardless of risk, as to do so will enable checking of PEP status and adverse media at the same time.

On a risk-based approach, firms may decide to only check the consolidated list and only check when the client is from a high-risk jurisdiction or has adverse media surrounding them.

Firms also need to decide whether to check on each new matter and/or periodically. Checking on each new matter would be advisable.

When acting for an individual client, it is the individual's name that should be checked, possibly including maiden names or known aliases. Likewise, where acting for an entity, it is the entity's name that should be checked.

Where a designated person has ownership or control over an entity, that entity will also be subject to the sanction and its assets can be frozen. It is for this reason that firms need to understand the beneficial ownership and control structure of a client so that those who are the ultimate beneficial owners or controllers can be sanction checked.

For these purposes, an entity is owned or controlled directly or indirectly by an individual in the following ways:

- the person holds (directly or indirectly) more than 25 per cent of the shares or voting rights in an entity;
- the person has the right (directly or indirectly) to appoint or remove a majority of the board of directors of the entity; or
- it is reasonable to expect that the person would be able to ensure the affairs of the entity are conducted in accordance with the person's wishes. This could, for example, include:
  - appointing, solely by exercising one's voting rights, a majority of the members of the administrative, management or supervisory bodies of an entity, who have held office during the present and previous financial year;
  - controlling alone, pursuant to an agreement with other shareholders in or members of an entity, a majority of shareholders' or members' voting rights in that entity;
  - having the right to exercise a dominant influence over an entity, pursuant to an agreement entered into with that entity, or to a provision in its memorandum or articles of association, where the law governing that entity permits its being subject to such agreement or provision;

- having the right to exercise a dominant influence referred to in the point above, without being the holder of that right (including by means of a front company);
- having the ability to direct another entity in accordance with one's wishes. This can be through any means, directly or indirectly. For example, it is possible that a designated person may have control or use of another person's bank accounts or economic resources and may be using them to circumvent financial sanctions.

Where the designated person has a minority interest in an entity, then the entity's assets may not be frozen. However, if the minority owner controls the entity because it conducts its affairs in accordance with the designated person's wishes, the entity may also find itself subject to the sanction.

When acting for an entity, taking the above into account, it is advisable to check the name of the entity, beneficial owners over 25 per cent (whom the firm would be identifying in any event to comply with the Money Laundering, Terrorist Financing and Transfer of Funds (Information on the Payer) Regulations 2017, SI 2017/692 (AML Regulations)) and the names of the directors and if possible, board members. Where possible, a risk-based approach should be taken to this task.

Sanctions lists are updated on a relatively frequent basis. It is possible, therefore, that a client may become sanctioned whilst the firm is acting for it and after checks were completed. For this reason, it is advisable for firms to sign up to alerts for when new lists are released (signing up for email alerts from HM Treasury can be done here: **https://public.govdelivery.com/accounts/UKHMTREAS/subscriber/new**) and then those lists checked against the firm's database of clients – a sort of 'reverse sanction checking'.

What are the compliance challenges?

- Firms must have processes in place that identify when a person or entity is sanctioned so that appropriate next steps can take place.
- Failure to do so could result in the firm acting in contravention of the sanction and committing a criminal offence.

What resources will help?

- OFSI guidance: 'UK Financial Sanctions: General guidance for financial sanctions under the Sanctions and Anti-Money Laundering Act 2018' (December 2020, available at **www.gov.uk/government/publications/financial-sanctions-faqs**).
- Law Society guide: 'UK sanctions regime' (29 March 2022, **www.lawsociety.org.uk/topics/anti-money-laundering/sanctions-guide**).
- If in doubt, independent legal advice should be sought.

Compliance tips – how to mitigate the risk of getting it wrong

- Firms must have processes in place that identify when a person or entity is sanctioned so that appropriate next steps can take place.
- This should include checking beneficial owners against sanctions lists, receiving alerts about newly released lists and then using newly released lists to run against the firm's database so ensuring that the firm is not acting for a newly sanctioned person or entity.

8.6 What is the obligation to report to OFSI?

All firms are required to inform OFSI as soon as reasonably practicable if it is known or reasonably suspected that a person is a designated person (that is, a person who is sanctioned) or has committed offences under the financial sanctions regulations where the information has been received in the course of carrying on the business. This requirement applies to firms and those that work in firms.

When making a report to OFSI, the firm must set out the information or other matter on which the knowledge or suspicion is based and any other information the firm holds about the person which identifies him or her. The firm must also state the nature and amount of funds or economic resources held for the client whom the firm suspects or knows is a designated person.

The OFSI guide 'UK Financial Sanctions: General guidance for financial sanctions under the Sanctions and Anti-Money Laundering Act 2018' (December 2020, available at **www.gov.uk/government/publications/financial-sanctions-faqs**) sets out the in table format examples of information to be reported (para.5.2).

The method by which a report should be made is to OFSI by email (ofsi@hm-treasury.gov.uk) including the detail outlined in the above guidance and also the designated person's unique ID from the consolidated list.

What are the compliance challenges?

- Firms who do not get this right risk committing a criminal offence.
- This will also have serious reputational consequences.

What resources will help?

- OFSI guidance: 'UK Financial Sanctions: General guidance for financial sanctions under the Sanctions and Anti-Money Laundering Act 2018' (December 2020, available at **www.gov.uk/government/publications/financial-sanctions-faqs**).

Compliance tips – how to mitigate the risk of getting it wrong

- When it is discovered that a sanction exists, the firm must take the appropriate steps to report to OFSI and seek the appropriate approval.
- Failure to do so risks committing a serious criminal offence.

8.7 How does privilege work when it comes to sanctions?

Privilege is a fundamental right and one that can only be overturned by statute. Information obtained may be privileged and therefore incapable of being disclosed without waiver by the holder of the privilege. However, the principle of iniquity/crime exception needs to be carefully considered. For further information on privilege and the exceptions, see **4.6**.

What are the compliance challenges?

- Firms need to carefully navigate privilege and any duty to report.

What resources will help?

- OFSI guidance: 'UK Financial Sanctions: General guidance for financial sanctions under the Sanctions and Anti-Money Laundering Act 2018' (December 2020, available at **www.gov.uk/government/publications/financial-sanctions-faqs**).
- Law Society guide: 'UK sanctions regime' (29 March 2022, **www.lawsociety.org.uk/topics/anti-money-laundering/sanctions-guide**).
- If in doubt, independent legal advice should be sought.

Compliance tips – how to mitigate the risk of getting it wrong

- When faced with a privilege scenario, the firm may wish to take independent legal advice.

8.8 For what do I need a licence? How do I apply for a licence?

OFSI are able to grant a licence for acts that fall within the licensing grounds set out in the legislation.

General licences issued by OFSI allow multiple parties to undertake specific acts without the need for separate licences. However, OFSI will not accept an application for a general licence, but such licences can be issued when deemed appropriate by HM Treasury.

Applications for licences need to be specific and where a relevant ground for the licence can be established. Common grounds for licences are set out in the OFSI guidance: 'UK Financial Sanctions: General guidance for financial sanctions under the Sanctions and Anti-Money Laundering Act 2018' (December 2020, available at **www.gov.uk/government/publications/financial-sanctions-faqs**). These are as follows:

- expenditure to meet basic needs;
- fees for the provision of legal services;
- routine maintenance of frozen funds and economic resources;
- extraordinary expenses (unexpected or unavoidable for example);
- pre-existing judicial decisions;
- prior obligations.

To apply for a licence, firms need to submit an 'OFSI licence application form' found here: **www.gov.uk/guidance/licences-that-allow-activity-prohibited-by-financial-sanctions** and email this to ofsi@hmtreasury.gov.uk.

The application requires the following information to be provided:

- the licensing ground(s) being relied upon in the application including supporting arguments;
- full information on the parties involved in the proposed transaction, e.g. the:
  - designated person(s);
  - any financial institution(s) involved (e.g. remitter, correspondent, beneficiary);
  - ultimate beneficiary of the transaction;
- the complete payment route including account details;
- the amount (or estimated amount) of the proposed transaction.

Licences cannot be given retrospectively, and so should a firm consider it acted without a licence, legal advice should be taken straightaway.

What are the compliance challenges?

- A licence may be needed before certain activity can take place. It is essential therefore that the appropriate licence is applied for in good time.

What resources will help?

- OFSI guidance: 'UK Financial Sanctions: General guidance for financial sanctions under the Sanctions and Anti-Money Laundering Act 2018' (December 2020, available at **www.gov.uk/government/publications/financial-sanctions-faqs**).
- Law Society guide: 'UK sanctions regime' (29 March 2022, **www.lawsociety.org.uk/topics/anti-money-laundering/sanctions-guide**).
- If in doubt, independent legal advice should be sought.

Compliance tips – how to mitigate the risk of getting it wrong

- It is a good idea to designate a specified person in the firm to handle sanctions issues, such as the money laundering reporting officer (MLRO) or money laundering compliance officer (MLCO), so that any sanctions applications can be handled by them.

8.9 My client is sanctioned and I am applying for the appropriate licence – what can I do whilst I wait for it? Can my client pay my bill?

As stated in the OFSI guidance, 'UK Financial Sanctions: General guidance for financial sanctions under the Sanctions and Money Laundering Act 2018', the legislation permits without a licence the following (para.6.1):

- a relevant firm to credit a frozen account with interest or other earnings due on the frozen account, so long as those funds are frozen immediately.
- a person to transfer funds to a relevant firm for crediting a frozen account where the transfer is in order to discharge obligations that were concluded or arose before the date the person became sanctioned.
- a relevant firm to credit a frozen account with payments from a third party, provided that the incoming funds are also frozen and that it informs OFSI of the transaction immediately without delay ...

Independent persons who wish to transfer their legal or equitable interests in frozen funds or economic resources to other persons are able to do so as long as the conditions below are met (para.6.2):

1. The independent person is not a designated person
2. The independent person holds the interest in the funds or economic resources
3. The independent person doesn't hold the interest jointly with a designated person; and
4. The independent person isn't owned or controlled, directly or indirectly by a designated person ...

Further, large banks are required to separate out their core retail banking from the rest of their business as per the Financial Services (Banking Reform) Act 2013. This is known as 'ring-fencing'.

These banks are permitted under the UK sanctions legislation to transfer funds from an account that is not ring-fenced to a ring-fenced account where both accounts are held or controlled directly or indirectly by a designated person.

It follows, therefore, that whilst law firms are not prevented from providing legal advice to a designated person, to have legal fees paid does require a licence. If a sanction prohibits specific action i.e. asset movement, then the law firm/individual advising needs to consider whether they are facilitating a breach of the sanction imposed.

Payments into court for security for costs need to be licensed specifically. Court fees are able to be paid without a licence, but only if not 'significant', which is to be determined on the facts. A scenario could arise where a client has a cause of action to which limitation is about to expire and the law firm wishes to issue a claim to preserve it. In that scenario it might not be possible to obtain a licence in time and it is likely the payment of the court fee will not require a licence. If in doubt, legal advice should be sought.

What are the compliance challenges?

- It is vital that firms do not act in contravention of the sanction imposed or they face prosecution.

What resources will help?

- OFSI guidance: 'UK Financial Sanctions: General guidance for financial sanctions under the Sanctions and Anti-Money Laundering Act 2018' (December 2020, available at **www.gov.uk/government/publications/financial-sanctions-faqs**).
- Law Society guide: 'UK sanctions regime' (29 March 2022, **www.lawsociety.org.uk/topics/anti-money-laundering/sanctions-guide**).
- If in doubt, independent legal advice should be sought.

Compliance tips – how to mitigate the risk of getting it wrong

- If the client is considered to be high risk, it might be considered worthwhile rechecking the client for sanctions before any monies are moved, whether that be to pay fees or otherwise.

8.10 My client is sanctioned by a non-UK country – can I act?

It depends on the facts. Firms need to consider the following:

- who or what country has imposed it;
- whether it has any effect on the firm;
- if it does not have any effect whether the firm wants to act anyway;
- what the activity is and whether it is caught by the sanction.

If firms are unsure, they should seek independent legal advice.

What are the compliance challenges?

- Firms must have a procedure in place to check their clients for sanctions where that is deemed appropriate.

What resources will help?

- OFSI guidance: 'UK Financial Sanctions: General guidance for financial sanctions under the Sanctions and Anti-Money Laundering Act 2018' (December

2020, available at **www.gov.uk/government/publications/financial-sanctions-faqs**).

- Law Society guide: 'UK sanctions regime' (29 March 2022, **www.lawsociety.org.uk/topics/anti-money-laundering/sanctions-guide**).
- If in doubt, independent legal advice should be sought.

Compliance tips – how to mitigate the risk of getting it wrong

- Firms must have processes in place that identify when a person or entity is sanctioned so that appropriate next steps can take place.
- This should include checking beneficial owners against sanctions lists, and also using newly released lists to run against the firm's database to ensure that the firm is not acting for a newly sanctioned person or entity.

PART III

Regulation and compliance

CHAPTER 9

Regulatory framework

9.1 What is the significance of the Legal Services Act 2007 to us?

The Legal Services Act 2007 (LSA 2007) is currently the principal piece of legislation that sets out the regulatory framework for legal services in England and Wales. It came about as a consequence of a thorough review of this topic by Sir David Clementi which resulted in the publication of a report known as the 'Review of the Regulatory Framework for Legal Services in England and Wales' (2004).

Sir David had been asked to do two things: firstly, to consider and advise on a regulatory framework which would promote competition, innovation and a new attention to public and consumer interests; and secondly, to introduce a more focused regulatory framework.

LSA 2007 enabled the following:

- the separation of representation and regulation of legal services;
- a system of approved regulators able to regulate different providers of legal services;
- regulatory objectives and professional principles to be applied by all approved regulators when discharging their obligations;
- the establishment of the Legal Services Board (LSB) to oversee the approved regulators;
- the investigation of consumer (client) complaints by an independent body – the Office for Legal Complaints – answerable to the LSB;
- the promotion of competition through the introduction of non-lawyer ownership of legal service providers (i.e. alternative business structures or ABSs).

LSA 2007 is hugely significant to all of us, as it has shaped the style of modern regulation. Whilst readers of this book, and others involved in the provision of risk and compliance support in law firms, are unlikely to discuss the Act with colleagues, knowledge of it is helpful when making decisions about how the firm will be run and what behaviours will be tolerated.

What are the compliance challenges?

- Firms must avoid misunderstanding the focus of LSA 2007 and avoid making decisions which are incompatible with the Act's objectives. This cannot be ignored by the Solicitors Regulation Authority (SRA) because of their regulatory duties as described in the same Act.

What resources will help?

- LSA 2007 itself.
- Information from the LSB website (**www.legalservicesboard.org.uk**).

Compliance tips – how to mitigate the risk of getting it wrong

- The significance of LSA 2007 relates to the regulatory framework that has been designed as a consequence.
- This knowledge supports you in your correct response to regulation and, whilst not everyone in your firm will need a working knowledge of the legislation, this will certainly help those colleagues in a risk and compliance role when giving advice to others.

9.2 What is the Legal Services Board?

The LSB is a statutory body established under LSA 2007. It is responsible – indirectly – for overseeing the regulation of all lawyers in England and Wales. Directly, it has regulatory oversight of approved regulators and certain other bodies as described in LSA 2007.

Its role and responsibilities include:

- the regulation of approved regulators (including the SRA);
- the regulation of the Solicitors Disciplinary Tribunal (SDT);
- oversight of the Office for Legal Complaints (OLC) (i.e. the Legal Ombudsman, or LeO);
- making statutory decisions about proposed new rules and regulations (including the SRA Standards and Regulations (**www.sra.org.uk/solicitors/standards-regulations/**)); practising fees; applications from approved regulators);
- assessing the regulatory performance of the approved regulators.

As already described, the LSB does not have a direct relationship with solicitors and authorised law firms and will not make any direct approaches to you or ask for information from you. Instead, all communication is with the SRA. Indirectly, this oversight of, and communication with, the SRA will have an impact on you particularly because of the LSB's ability to approve new rules, etc.

What are the compliance challenges?

- It is important to understand the role of the LSB.

What resources will help?

- Information from the LSB website (**www.legalservicesboard.org.uk**).

Compliance tips – how to mitigate the risk of getting it wrong

- Include appropriate (albeit minimal) information about the LSB in your regulatory training programmes.

9.3 What is the Solicitors Regulation Authority?

The SRA was established in 2007 and is the approved regulator (as defined in LSA 2007) of solicitors of England and Wales. It is also able to authorise law firms to provide legal services. Everyone who either owns or works in an authorised law firm is subject to SRA oversight.

As an approved regulator, the SRA has a role in ensuring that regulatory objectives and professional principles (as described in LSA 2007, s.1) are met.

In practice this means that the SRA performs a number of different functions, including the following:

- It exercises powers relating to the admission of solicitors, including a role in setting training and competency requirements which must be met.
- It issues practising certificates and has powers in connection with conditions or the removal of certification.
- It sets standards for all solicitors.
- It authorises law firms and sets standards in respect of these businesses which apply to owners and all employees.
- It exercises supervisory powers.
- For the purposes of the Money Laundering, Terrorist Financing and Transfer of Funds (Information on the Payer) Regulations 2017, SI 2017/692 (AML Regulations), it is an approved supervisor answerable to the Office for Professional Bodies Approved Supervisors (OPBAS).
- It has disciplinary powers and can take enforcement action against individuals and authorised law firms.
- It can refer individuals (including non-solicitors who own or are employed in authorised law firms) to the SDT.

Section 7 of the SRA Code of Conduct for Solicitors, RELs and RFLs (repeated in part in section 3 of the SRA Code of Conduct for Firms) contains professional duties of cooperation and accountability which show us the SRA's expectations. These include:

7.2 You are able to justify your decisions and actions in order to demonstrate compliance with your obligations under the SRA's regulatory arrangements.

7.3 You cooperate with the SRA, other regulators, ombudsmen, and those bodies with a role overseeing and supervising the delivery of, or investigating concerns in relation to, legal services.

7.4 You respond promptly to the SRA and:

(a) provide full and accurate explanations, information and documents in response to any request or requirement; and

(b) ensure that relevant information which is held by you, or by third parties carrying out functions on your behalf which are critical to the delivery of your legal services, is available for inspection by the SRA.

7.5 You do not attempt to prevent anyone from providing information to the SRA or any other body exercising regulatory, supervisory, investigatory or prosecutory functions in the public interest.

7.6 You notify the SRA promptly if:

(a) you are subject to any criminal charge, conviction or caution, subject to the Rehabilitation of Offenders Act 1974;

(b) a relevant insolvency event occurs in relation to you; or

(c) if you become aware:

(i) of any material changes to information previously provided to the SRA, by you or on your behalf, about you or your practice, including any change to information recorded in the register; and

(ii) that information provided to the SRA, by you or on your behalf, about you or your practice is or may be false, misleading, incomplete or inaccurate.

7.7 You report promptly to the SRA or another approved regulator, as appropriate, any facts or matters that you reasonably believe are capable of amounting to a serious breach of their regulatory arrangements by any person regulated by them (including you).

7.8 Notwithstanding paragraph 7.7, you inform the SRA promptly of any facts or matters that you reasonably believe should be brought to its attention in order that it may investigate whether a serious breach of its regulatory arrangements has occurred or otherwise exercise its regulatory powers.

7.9 You do not subject any person to detrimental treatment for making or proposing to make a report or providing or proposing to provide information based on a reasonably held belief under paragraph 7.7 or 7.8 above, or paragraph 3.9, 3.10, 9.1(d) or (e) or 9.2(b) or (c) of the SRA Code of Conduct for Firms, irrespective of whether the SRA or another approved regulator subsequently investigates or takes any action in relation to the facts or matters in question.

7.10 You act promptly to take any remedial action requested by the SRA. If requested to do so by the SRA you investigate whether there have been any serious breaches that should be reported to the SRA.

What are the compliance challenges?

- Misunderstanding the role of the SRA and its interest in individuals and the law firm.

- Being unable to demonstrate appropriate behaviours to the SRA.

What resources will help?

- SRA materials:
  - SRA Standards and Regulations (**www.sra.org.uk/solicitors/standards-regulations/**);
  - SRA Codes of Conduct (**www.sra.org.uk/solicitors/standards-regulations/**);
  - SRA website generally (**www.sra.org.uk**).
- *Compliance and Ethics in Law Firms*, 2nd edn (Tracey Calvert, Law Society Publishing, 2019).

Compliance tips – how to mitigate the risk of getting it wrong

- Provide training on the role of the SRA to all colleagues in the firm so that there is no confusion about its role or its regulatory reach. For example, some more experienced solicitors and other lawyers may not understand the difference between the SRA and the Law Society. Non-lawyers may have little interest in regulation.
- Ensure that your internal policies and procedures include breach reporting mechanisms.
- Promote a culture of openness and accountability so that there is prompt discussion of mistakes and high-risk decisions, and also of concerns about compliance issues.

Related questions/issues

- What is the Law Society and what is the difference between the Law Society and the SRA? (See **9.6**.)

9.4 What disciplinary action can the SRA take against us?

The SRA's role as an approved regulator is to regulate in the public interest. In doing this, it aims to ensure that clients, and the public at large, receive adequate protections when they receive legal services from solicitors and also from authorised law firms.

The SRA's regulatory reach extends to all solicitors, plus registered European lawyers (RELs), registered foreign lawyers (RFLs), authorised bodies including recognised sole practices, other types of lawyer and all non-lawyers who are either managers or employees of an authorised law firm, plus any owner of an authorised firm.

The SRA has wide investigative powers and you have a regulatory duty to be open and accountable and to cooperate in investigations. Please see the SRA Code of Conduct for Solicitors, RELs and RFLs, paras.7.3 and 7.4 (repeated in the SRA Code of Conduct for Firms, section 3):

7.3 You cooperate with the SRA, other regulators, ombudsmen, and those bodies with a role overseeing and supervising the delivery of, or investigating concerns in relation to, legal services.

7.4 You respond promptly to the SRA and:

(a) provide full and accurate explanations, information and documents in response to any request or requirement; and

(b) ensure that relevant information which is held by you, or by third parties carrying out functions on your behalf which are critical to the delivery of your legal services, is available for inspection by the SRA

The SRA's sanctions and controls (i.e. the disciplinary action it can take after an investigation has been completed) are as follows:

- issue a letter which contains advice and a warning;
- rebuke;
- conditions imposed on an individual;
- conditions imposed on a firm;
- fine;
- referral to the SDT.

As at early 2022, the SRA is consulting on its fining powers. As at that date, the SRA has powers to fine non-ABS firms (so-called traditional law firms) up to a maximum of £2,000 only. It can impose similar fines on individual solicitors regardless of how they practice. The firm/individual must be referred to the SDT if the SRA considers that a higher fine is an appropriate sanction.

This is in contrast to fining powers in respect of ABSs (described as licensed bodies in the SRA Standards and Regulations) which are derived from LSA 2007 and enables the SRA to fine a manager or an employee of an ABS up to £50 million and to fine the ABS entity up to £250 million.

The SRA's consultation is with a view to increase the threshold for their internal fining powers. If it decides to proceed, then legislation will be required and no doubt there will be much publicity about this.

What are the compliance challenges?

- SRA investigations of alleged misconduct may trigger an interest in your firm's systems and controls and in other individuals within the firm.
- The firm must avoid the SRA proving lack of openness and cooperation.
- Firms must be aware of matters that ought to be brought to the SRA's attention.

What resources will help?

- SRA materials:
  - SRA Codes of Conduct (**www.sra.org.uk/solicitors/standards-regulations/**);
  - SRA Regulatory and Disciplinary Procedure Rules (**www.sra.org.uk/solicitors/standards-regulations/regulatory-disciplinary-procedure-rules/**);

  - SRA Enforcement Strategy (7 February 2019, updated 21 January 2022, **www.sra.org.uk/sra/corporate-strategy/sra-enforcement-strategy/**);
  - SRA guidance: 'How we regulate non-authorised persons' (updated 17 November 2021, **www.sra.org.uk/solicitors/guidance/general-regulation-non-authorised-persons/**);
  - SRA guidance: 'How we gather evidence in our regulatory and disciplinary investigations' (updated 25 November 2019, **www.sra.org.uk/solicitors/guidance/investigations-gathering-evidence/**);
  - SRA guidance: 'Making decisions to investigate concerns' (updated 30 December 2021, **www.sra.org.uk/solicitors/guidance/investigations-decisions-investigate-concerns/**).
- Law Society materials:
  - Law Society Practice Note: SRA Powers of Investigation (24 November 2021, **www.lawsociety.org.uk/topics/regulation/sra-powers-of-investigation**).
  - Law Society Practice Note: Alternative Business Structures (28 July 2021, **www.lawsociety.org.uk/en/topics/business-management/alternative-business-structures**).

Compliance tips – how to mitigate the risk of getting it wrong

- Conduct induction training which emphasises the need for internal communication of concerns, breaches, etc.
- Provide awareness training on the role of the SRA.
- Engage senior management involvement in breach recording.
- Create and supply templates to support internal reporting in a consistent fashion.
- Produce a whistleblowing policy.
- Watch this space in respect of SRA fining powers – who needs to know about this within your firm?

9.5 What do we need to know about the Solicitors Disciplinary Tribunal?

The SDT is an independent statutory tribunal that has powers to make decisions about alleged misconduct on the part of solicitors, RELs or RFLs, authorised bodies, the managers of authorised bodies, and the employees of recognised sole practices and authorised bodies. It can also consider applications from former solicitors and indefinitely suspended solicitors for restoration to the roll of solicitors or the determination of that individual's suspension.

The SDT has a number of powers, including:

- reprimanding a solicitor;
- imposing restrictions on the way a solicitor may practise;
- striking off the roll of solicitors the name of the solicitor who has been found to have behaved unprofessionally;
- suspension of the solicitor from practice either indefinitely or for a fixed period of time;

- unlimited fines on solicitors, and other individuals over which the SDT has regulatory reach, payable to HM Treasury;
- exclusion of a solicitor from legal aid work, indefinitely or for a fixed period;
- making orders – a 'section 43 order' (under Solicitors Act 1974, s.43) – prohibiting the employment of a non-solicitor by a solicitor/authorised body;
- sanctions against RELs and RFLs;
- making an order to revoke the recognition of a recognised body;
- determination of an indefinite period of suspension;
- restoration to the roll of the name of a solicitor previously struck off or imposing a direction prohibiting the restoration of the individual's name;
- payment of costs or a contribution towards costs on any party to the proceedings;
- review and revocation of section 43 orders imposed on non-solicitors involved in legal practice.

Matters will usually be referred to the SDT in circumstances where the SRA concludes that this is in the public interest because the nature of the alleged misconduct is severe and it is appropriate for it to be considered by a body with greater regulatory powers than the SRA itself. The SRA Regulatory and Disciplinary Rules explain at rule 6 when the SRA (through its own internal authorised decision-makers) may consider such an application.

SRA Code of Conduct for Solicitors, RELs and RFLs sets out at section 7 the SRA's requirements about your response to communications with the SDT (repeated in the SRA Code of Conduct for Firms), so that:

> 7.3 You cooperate with the SRA, other regulators, ombudsmen, and those bodies with a role overseeing and supervising the delivery of, or investigating concerns in relation to, legal services.
>
> . . .
>
> 7.5 You do not attempt to prevent anyone from providing information to the SRA or any other body exercising regulatory, supervisory, investigatory or prosecutory functions in the public interest.

What are the compliance challenges?

- It must be understood that despite its name, the SDT's regulatory reach extends beyond solicitors to other individuals.
- The firm, or individuals within it, must not fail to comply with their duties of openness and accountability because of misunderstanding about the expected relationship with the SDT or because of fear of the consequences.

What resources will help?

- SDT materials:
  - Information on the SDT's website (**www.solicitorstribunal.org.uk**);

  - SDT *Guidance Note on Sanctions* (9th edn, December 2021, **www.solicitorstribunal.org.uk/news/publication-guidance-notes-sanctions-other-powers-and-appeals-1**);
  - SDT *Guidance Note on Other Powers of the Tribunal* (5th edn, December 2021, **www.solicitorstribunal.org.uk/news/publication-guidance-notes-sanctions-other-powers-and-appeals-1**).
- SRA materials:
  - SRA Codes of Conduct (**www.sra.org.uk/solicitors/standards-regulations/**);
  - SRA Regulatory and Disciplinary Procedure Rules (**www.sra.org.uk/solicitors/standards-regulations/regulatory-disciplinary-procedure-rules/**);
  - SRA guidance: 'Issuing Solicitors Disciplinary Tribunal proceedings' (updated 25 November 2019, **www.sra.org.uk/solicitors/guidance/disciplinary-issuing-solicitors-disciplinary-tribunal-proceedings/**);
  - SRA guidance: 'Prosecution before the Solicitors Disciplinary Tribunal' (updated 26 October 2021, **www.sra.org.uk/solicitors/enforcement/solicitors-disciplinary-tribunal/**);
  - SRA guidance: 'How we regulate non-authorised persons' (updated 17 November 2021, **www.sra.org.uk/solicitors/guidance/general-regulation-non-authorised-persons/**).

Compliance tips – how to mitigate the risk of getting it wrong

- Foster a healthy compliance culture within your firm so that internally you achieve openness and accountability with which to address issues with a prompt response.
- Create an internal reporting process.
- Create a whistleblowing process.

9.6 What is the role of the Law Society of England and Wales?

LSA 2007 contains a requirement that professional bodies separate their governance arrangements and work into regulatory and representative functions. This was to address the criticism that there was confusion about the role of these bodies.

Regulation now focuses on the promotion of appropriate standards by members of the profession and a focus on public interest so that the latter are protected when they receive legal services. In contrast, representation focuses on the promotion of the members' interests by lobbying when necessary and providing guidance and support.

In terms of the solicitors' profession in England and Wales, the Law Society gave up its regulatory role to the SRA and now exclusively concentrates on representational tasks. It provides a number of resources for its members, which are designed to promote best practice and support compliance with regulatory and professional matters.

Prior to this splitting of roles, the Law Society was both the regulator and representative body and also investigated clients' service complaints. This change of role and focus might be a surprise to some managers and employees.

What are the compliance challenges?

- It is important not to assume that all colleagues will understand the recent history of the Law Society and the fact that it is no longer our regulator. Many lawyers and others incorrectly assume that the Law Society remains the profession's regulatory body. Failing to realise this is not the case might mean that they undermine the firm's relationship with the SRA, do not appreciate the relationship which they must have with the SRA or the help that they can obtain from the Law Society, and they might mislead their clients and others.
- Ensure that the firm optimises the support and best practice advice that individuals and the firm can obtain from the Law Society.

What resources will help?

- Information from the Law Society website (**www.lawsociety.org.uk**).

Compliance tips – how to mitigate the risk of getting it wrong

- Provide education for staff to ensure that everyone understands the respective roles of the SRA and the Law Society.
- Include commentary on these roles in induction training and in your compliance and office manuals.

Related questions/issues

- What is the role of the SRA, and what is the difference between the SRA and the Law Society? (See **9.3**.)

9.7 What do we need to know about the Legal Ombudsman?

Before the changes brought about by LSA 2007, professional bodies (such as the Law Society of England and Wales in connection with the solicitor's profession in this jurisdiction) not only represented and regulated their members, but they also investigated consumer complaints (i.e. service standard complaints) about those members. This led to widespread criticism that such a service was not suitably independent and that too many conflicting roles were being performed under one roof.

LSA 2007 created a system in which the handling of consumer complaints was taken away from all the professional bodies and given to an independent complaints handling organisation known as the OLC. The OLC is led by the Legal Ombudsman (LeO) and is sometimes described as the Legal Ombudsman Service.

This organisation handles complaints in respect of services offered by all lawyers although, as may be expected, the majority of investigations relate to solicitor services because the solicitor's profession is the largest category of legal service providers in England and Wales. The OLC has wide-ranging powers to investigate consumer complaints, including complaints from individuals who have been refused legal representation by a lawyer or law firm. It provides remedies to those who have received inappropriate standards of service.

The SRA Standards and Regulations set professional standards which we must meet when dealing with the OLC. The SRA Code of Conduct for Solicitors, RELs and RFLs, para.7.3 (repeated in identical form in SRA Code of Conduct for Firms, para.3.2 and therefore relevant to everyone in your law firm) addresses cooperation and accountability expectations:

> 7.3 You cooperate with the SRA, other regulators, ombudsmen, and those bodies with a role overseeing and supervising the delivery of, or investigating concerns in relation to, legal services.

This statement means that unprofessional behaviour and, for example, lack of cooperation with the OLC, could be reviewed by the SRA as a regulatory breach.

Lack of cooperation might be evidenced through a breach of SRA Code of Conduct for Solicitors, etc. para.7.5 (Code of Conduct for Firms, para.3.11):

> 7.5 You do not attempt to prevent anyone from providing information to the SRA or any other body exercising regulatory, supervisory, investigatory or prosecutory functions in the public interest.

What are the compliance challenges?

- Ensure that the compliance officer for legal practice (COLP), compliance officer for finance and administration (COFA) and others involved in complaints handling are made aware of any issues that might give rise to a referral to, and investigation by, the OLC.
- Ensure that colleagues appreciate the role of the OLC and their investigative interest in their behaviours.

What resources will help?

- SRA Codes of Conduct (**www.sra.org.uk/solicitors/standards-regulations/**).
- Information from the LeO's website (**www.legalombudsman.org.uk**).

Compliance tips – how to mitigate the risk of getting it wrong

- Provide training on the role of the SRA to all colleagues in the firm so that there is no confusion about its role or its regulatory reach. For example, some more experienced solicitors and other lawyers may not understand the difference between the SRA and the Law Society. Non-lawyers may have little interest in regulation.
- Ensure that your internal policies and procedures include breach reporting mechanisms.

- Promote a culture of openness and accountability so that there is prompt discussion of mistakes and high-risk decisions, and also of concerns about compliance issues.

9.8 What are the different types of law firms which the SRA authorises?

The SRA has statutory powers that apply to the authorisation of law firms. These can be recognised bodies, licensed bodies and recognised sole practices.

A licensed body is a body licensed by the SRA under LSA 2007, s.71(2). Its owners and managers are not necessarily lawyers, although at least one manager (i.e. a member of a limited liability partnership (LLP), a director of a company, a partner on a partnership or, in relation to any other body, a member of its governing body) must be an authorised person (i.e. a person authorised by the SRA or another approved regulator to carry on a reserved activity). A licensed body is more commonly described as an 'alternative business structure' because not all its owners/managers are lawyers. ABSs have been eligible for licensing since the introduction of LSA 2007.

A recognised body means a body (entity) recognised by the SRA under Administration of Justice Act 1985, s.9. All the managers and interest holders are legally qualified. This is more commonly described as a traditional law firm in which all the owners/managers are lawyers.

A recognised sole practice is an entity in which a solicitor or a REL is the sole principal. Traditionally, this is described as being a sole practitioner.

What are the compliance challenges?

- It is important to understand, particularly, whether your firm is a licensed body or a recognised body and apply the SRA Standards and Regulations appropriately, e.g. obtaining the correct approvals for new owners/managers, appointing COLP or head of legal practice (HOLP), etc., understanding different breach reporting duties, etc.

What resources will help?

- SRA materials:
  - SRA Authorisation of Firms Rules (**www.sra.org.uk/solicitors/standards-regulations/authorisation-firms-rules/**);
  - SRA guidance: 'How we make our decision to authorise a firm' (updated 25 November 2019, **www.sra.org.uk/solicitors/guidance/authorisation-firms/**).
- Law Society materials:
  - Law Society Practice Note: Alternative Business Structures (28 July 2021, **www.lawsociety.org.uk/en/topics/business-management/alternative-business-structures**);

– Law Society Practice Note: Entity-based Regulation (2 January 2020, **www.lawsociety.org.uk/en/topics/business-management/entity-based-regulation**).

Compliance tips – how to mitigate the risk of getting it wrong

- Have clear information about the status of your practice printed in office manuals and compliance materials.
- Provide induction training to ensure adequate awareness of the firm's status.

9.9 What are the reserved legal activities, and why do we need to be aware of these?

'Reserved legal activities' is the phrase which describes a hotchpot of legal services activities which, for a variety of reasons, can be performed only by those who are authorised, or are otherwise exempt from authorisation.

The latest version of the statutory reservation is included in LSA 2007, s.12(1), and they are as follows:

(a) the exercise of a right of audience;
(b) the conduct of litigation;
(c) reserved instrument activities;
(d) probate activities;
(e) notarial activities;
(f) the administration of oaths.

Detailed descriptions of the extent of these reservations is found in LSA 2007, Sched.2. For example, the conduct of litigation is interpreted in the following way:

4(1) The 'conduct of litigation' means —

(a) the issuing of proceedings before any court in England and Wales,
(b) the commencement, prosecution and defence of such proceedings, and
(c) the performance of any ancillary functions in relation to such proceedings (such as entering appearances to actions).

(2) But the 'conduct of litigation' does not include any activity within paragraphs (a) to (c) of sub-paragraph (1), in relation to any particular court or in relation to any particular proceedings, if immediately before the appointed day no restriction was placed on the persons entitled to carry on that activity.

Solicitors, and other lawyers, carrying on these reserved legal activities are regulated by their approved regulators and the regulator will supervise individuals to ensure that there is no breach of this duty. Non-qualified employers working in an authorised business are able to carry on reserved activities under the supervision of an authorised person.

Bear in mind SRA Code of Conduct for Solicitors, RELs and RFLs, para.7.1 (repeated in SRA Code of Conduct for Firms, para.3.1) and the requirement that 'you keep up to date with and follow the law and regulation governing the way you work', which includes compliance with LSA 2007.

Any activity not listed in section 12 is, by default, unreserved. This list is extensive and includes legal advice generally, will writing and similar. This means that anyone – legally qualified or not legally qualified – can perform these activities.

What are the compliance challenges?

- Effective supervision is important, as a lack could lead to a breach of LSA 2007.
- Unauthorised, or non-exempt, persons must be dealt with in a way that does not facilitate a breach of the reservation.
- Ensure that there is no outsourcing of reserved legal services to unauthorised entities.

What resources will help?

- LSA 2007, s.12.
- LSB guidance: 'Reserved legal activities' (**https://legalservicesboard.org.uk/enquiries/frequently-asked-questions/reserved-legal-activities**).
- SRA materials:
  - SRA guidance: 'Does my employer need to be authorised by an approved regulator?' (updated 25 November 2019, **www.sra.org.uk/solicitors/guidance/employer-need-authorised-approved-regulator/**);
  - SRA guidance: 'Does my business need to be authorised?' (updated 25 November 2019, **www.sra.org.uk/solicitors/guidance/business-need-authorised/**).
- Law Society Practice Note: In-house Practice: Regulatory Requirements (9 September 2021, **www.lawsociety.org.uk/en/topics/in-house/in-house-practice-regulatory-requirements**).

Compliance tips – how to mitigate the risk of getting it wrong

- Provide training to ensure an appropriate understanding of this topic.
- Implement supervision policies which support compliance.

9.10 How can solicitors practise?

Solicitors can practise in a number of different ways:

- as a sole practitioner with your practice authorised as a recognised sole practice;
- as an independent (freelance) solicitor subject to compliance with SRA Authorisation of Individuals Regulations, reg.10.2 and conditions attached to the types of activities that can be performed and restrictions on particular

activities (**www.sra.org.uk/solicitors/standards-regulations/authorisation-individuals-regulations/**);

- as an employee of a recognised body or a licensed body (i.e. a private practice law firm);
- as an owner/manager of a recognised body or a licensed body;
- as an employee of an unauthorised business (i.e. an in-house solicitor);
- as an employee/manager/owner of a business authorised by another approved regulator;
- practising overseas (which for regulatory purposes is anywhere outside England and Wales).

In all these different circumstances, the individual has personal responsibilities to comply with the SRA Standards and Regulations. Some sections will be relevant irrespective of practising style – the SRA Principles and the SRA Code of Conduct for Solicitors, RELs and RFLs will apply to everyone except solicitors practising permanently overseas who will need to comply with a modified version of these as found in the SRA Overseas and Cross-border Practice Rules (**www.sra.org.uk/solicitors/standards-regulations/overseas-cross-border-practice-rules/**).

Other sections will be relevant only where the type of practice is an authorised body as described in the SRA Authorisation of Firms Rules (**www.sra.org.uk/solicitors/standards-regulations/authorisation-firms-rules/**). In these circumstances, the SRA Code of Conduct for Firms must be accommodated in compliance plans.

What are the compliance challenges?

- Ensure that you understand personal responsibilities and the application of the SRA Standards and Regulation to your style of practise.
- When dealing with other solicitors practising in a different style, ensure that you understand what they can and cannot do (e.g. whether they can hold client money or not, etc.).
- Ensure that you avoid misunderstandings leading to complaints about unprofessional behaviours.

What resources will help?

- SRA materials:
  - SRA Principles (**www.sra.org.uk/solicitors/standards-regulations/principles/**);
  - SRA Code of Conduct for Solicitors, RELs and RFLs (**www.sra.org.uk/solicitors/standards-regulations/code-conduct-solicitors/**);
  - SRA Code of Conduct for Firms (**www.sra.org.uk/solicitors/standards-regulations/code-conduct-firms/**);
  - SRA Authorisation of Individuals Regulations (**www.sra.org.uk/solicitors/standards-regulations/authorisation-individuals-regulations/**);
  - SRA Authorisation of Firms Rules (**www.sra.org.uk/solicitors/standards-regulations/authorisation-firms-rules/**);

- SRA Overseas and Cross-border Practice Rules (**www.sra.org.uk/solicitors/standards-regulations/overseas-cross-border-practice-rules/**);
- SRA guidance: 'Not for profit sector: summary' (updated 25 November 2019, **www.sra.org.uk/solicitors/guidance/not-for-profit-sector---summary/**).

- Law Society materials:
  - Law Society Practice Note: Solicitors Offering Legal Services to the Public from Unregulated Entities (13 July 2021, **www.lawsociety.org.uk/en/topics/business-management/solicitors-offering-legal-services-to-the-public-from-unregulated-entities**);
  - Law Society Practice Note: Freelance Solicitors (13 July 2021, **www.lawsociety.org.uk/en/topics/regulation/freelance-solicitors**).

Compliance tips – how to mitigate the risk of getting it wrong

- Raising awareness of the different types of practice, particularly those styles which are not private practice in nature.

Related questions/issues

- What is a freelance solicitor?
- How do we deal with a freelance solicitor/solicitor employed in an unauthorised business?
- Can a freelance solicitor/solicitor employed in an unauthorised business hold client money?

9.11 What is a freelance solicitor?

This is a fairly new concept, so do not be surprised if you find that colleagues do not understand what a freelance solicitor is or how they should treat this type of practitioner.

The concept was introduced in the SRA Standards and Regulations in 2019 as an alternative to being a recognised sole practice for solicitors who wish to practice alone.

The SRA Authorisation of Individuals Regulations are relevant and include, at reg.10.2, an exception to the default position that if you are a solicitor or a registered European lawyer (REL), you must not be a sole practitioner unless your practice is authorised as a recognised sole practice. The exception is as follows:

> 10.2 If you otherwise would be, you will not be regarded as acting as a sole practitioner and you will not therefore need to be authorised as a recognised sole practice if:
>
> (a) your practice consists entirely of carrying on activities which are not reserved legal activities; or
>
> (b) any reserved legal activities you carry on are provided through an authorised body or an authorised non-SRA firm, or in circumstances in which you:

(i) have practised as a solicitor or an REL for a minimum of three years since admission or registration;

(ii) are self-employed and practise in your own name, and not through a trading name or service company;

(iii) do not employ anyone in connection with the services that you provide;

(iv) are engaged directly by the client with your fees payable directly to you;

(v) have a practising address in the UK;

(vi) take out and maintain indemnity insurance that provides adequate and appropriate cover in respect of the services that you provide or have provided, whether or not they comprise reserved legal activities, taking into account any alternative arrangements you or your clients may make; and

(vii) do not hold client money, save that you may hold money which falls within the category of client money set out in rule 2.1(d) of the SRA Accounts Rules so long as:

(A) any money held for disbursements relates to costs or expenses incurred by you on behalf of your client and for which you are liable; and

(B) you have informed your client in advance of where and how the money will be held,

and you choose for your practice not to be authorised as a recognised sole practice.

In practical terms, this alternative means that you are able to practise as a solicitor (i.e. an authorised person) but do not need to do this through an authorised body.

If you are intending to be a freelance solicitor, you must:

- Comply with the restriction on the provision of reserved legal activities. These are the activities described in LSA 2007, s.12 (see **9.9**).
- Note the other restrictions on freelance practise which are statutory restrictions; if you provide immigration, claims management (which includes employment claims) or regulated financial services your business must be authorised by the SRA as a recognised sole practice or be regulated by another approved regulator.
- Practise in your own name and not through a limited company or similar, not using a service company, and not using a trading name.
- You must not employ anyone (although you are able to contract with others to provide administrative as opposed to legal services).
- Ensure that your clients contract directly with you and pay fees directly to you.
- Have a UK practising address which is notified to the SRA along with your notification of your intended status and whether you will deliver reserve legal services.
- Comply with the restrictions on holding client money.

- Be confident that you understand and comply with those other parts of the SRA Standards and Regulations that apply to you personally; for example, the SRA Principles, the SRA Code of Conduct for Solicitors, RELs and RFLs and the SRA Transparency Rules are all relevant to you.
- Provide your clients with relevant information about you, your type of practice, and the indemnity cover which you have (noting that you do not need to comply with the SRA Indemnity Insurance Rules because you are not an authorised practice).

What are the compliance challenges?

- Understand that despite your practice being unauthorised, you are an authorised individual in your capacity as a solicitor and that you must take care to maintain an appropriate regulatory relationship with the SRA.
- Ensure that clients and others are not misled about you and your practice. Do not forget your duties in SRA Code for Solicitors, para.8.8: 'you ensure that any publicity in relation to your practice is accurate and not misleading . . .'.
- Do not forget your professional obligations more generally – you: will be bound to comply with SRA requirements in respect of undertakings; will have duties of confidentiality; must consider conflicts; and must be satisfied that you have identified your clients.
- You also must comply with the law relevant to your practice – e.g. is data protection covered by your risk management techniques? Do you understand advertising legislation? Do you apply the Equality Act 2010 appropriately?, etc.

What resources will help?

- SRA materials:
  - SRA Principles (**www.sra.org.uk/solicitors/standards-regulations/principles/**);
  - SRA Code of Conduct for Solicitors, RELs and RFLs (**www.sra.org.uk/solicitors/standards-regulations/code-conduct-solicitors/**);
  - SRA Accounts Rules (**www.sra.org.uk/solicitors/standards-regulations/accounts-rules/**);
  - SRA Transparency Rules (**www.sra.org.uk/solicitors/standards-regulations/transparency-rules/**);
  - SRA Authorisation of Individuals Regulations (**www.sra.org.uk/solicitors/standards-regulations/authorisation-individuals-regulations/**);
  - SRA guidance: 'Preparing to become a sole practitioner or an SRA-regulated freelance solicitor' (updated 25 November 2019, **www.sra.org.uk/solicitors/guidance/preparing-sole-practitioner-regulated-independent-solicitor/**);
  - SRA guidance: 'Transparency in price and service' (updated 3 August 2021, **www.sra.org.uk/solicitors/guidance/transparency-in-price-and-service/**).
- Law Society Practice Note: Freelance Solicitors (13 July 2021, **www.lawsociety.org.uk/en/topics/regulation/freelance-solicitors**).

Compliance tips – how to mitigate the risk of getting it wrong

- Conduct thorough research before starting your business.
- Work with the SRA to ensure that it is satisfied with your decisions and that you are registered appropriately.
- Use a template for client information.
- Develop risk resources and the means by which to record risk decision-making.

Related questions/issues

- Can a freelance solicitor hold client money?

9.12 Do we need to register new partners, directors or members with the SRA?

The answer to this question requires the need to understand what the SRA means by the use of two words: manager and, separately but additionally, owner.

The SRA uses the term 'manager' to describe any of the following:

- the sole principal of a recognised sole practice;
- a member of a limited liability partnership;
- a director of a company;
- a partner in a partnership;
- in relation to any other body, a member of its governing body.

Similarly, the correct meaning of 'owner' for these purposes is:

- any person who holds a material interest (as defined in LSA 2007, Sched.13) in an authorised body and, in the case of a partnership, any partner regardless of whether they hold a material interest in the partnership.

If you are considering the position of a new manager and/or owner (whether this is someone appointed as a lateral hire or refers to a promotion of an existing employee), your next decision is whether the SRA simply needs to be notified of a new appointment or whether you need to obtain the SRA's approval before the appointment is made.

Approval is not needed when an individual has been deemed to be a fit and proper person in accordance with SRA Authorisation of Firms Rules, rule 13.2:

> 13.2 The SRA will deem a person to be fit and proper to be a manager or owner of an authorised body if the person is:
>
> (a) a solicitor, an REL, RFL or an authorised body; or
> (b) a person who has previously been approved by the SRA under rule 13.1 and is:
>
> (i) authorised and regulated by another approved regulator; or

(ii) authorised and regulated by a regulatory body which operates a regulatory regime recognised by the SRA as reasonably equivalent to that of an approved regulator,

and who is not subject to a regulatory or disciplinary investigation, or adverse finding or decision of the SRA, the Tribunal or another regulatory body.

In these circumstances, your obligation is to notify the SRA promptly of the new designation. Additionally, you will of course want to update your publicity and notify any clients for whom this information might be relevant.

Where an individual is not in a position to comply with rule 13.2, it is necessary to notify the SRA of your intention to appoint them as a manager and owner, and for the SRA to grant approval before the individual (described in these circumstances as the candidate) is entitled to take up their appointment. The application is made via the 'mySRA' portal. The SRA's service level agreement aims at a 30-day consideration time, although the process can take up to 90 days if additional information is required.

Your firm will be in breach of the SRA Authorisation of Firms Rules if it fails to comply with these obligations and doesn't notify and/or seek approval of new role-holders.

What are the compliance challenges?

- Do not delegate this task (perhaps to office managers or your HR team) and ensure that notification/approval duties are understood.
- Do not publish new appointments too early and thereby place yourself in breach of SRA's regulatory arrangements.

What resources will help?

- SRA materials:
  - SRA Authorisation of Firms Rules (**www.sra.org.uk/solicitors/standards-regulations/authorisation-firms-rules/**);
  - SRA guidance: 'Apply to add a manager/owner' (updated 21 February 2022, **www.sra.org.uk/solicitors/firm-based-authorisation/existing-firms-applications/approval-manager-owner**);
  - SRA guidance: 'Approval of role holders' (updated 12 March 2021, **www.sra.org.uk/solicitors/guidance/authorisation-approval-role-holders/**);
  - SRA guidance: 'Does your interest in a licensed body require approval?' (8 March 2021, **www.sra.org.uk/solicitors/guidance/interest-licensed-body-require-approval**).
- Law Society Practice Note: Information on Letterheads, Emails and Websites (26 January 2021, **www.lawsociety.org.uk/en/topics/client-care/information-on-letterheads-emails-and-websites**).

Compliance tips – how to mitigate the risk of getting it wrong

- Provide training to relevant staff involved in the application process.
- Create a procedure for the appointment of new managers/owners.

9.13 What compliance training should we deliver to support staff/lateral hires/temporary staff/qualified lawyers, and why?

There is very little in the way of prescribed training. The only obvious exception arises in respect of the training specified in AML Regulations 2017, reg.24 for colleagues undertaking relevant business for these purposes, and there is an implied need to consider training to comply with SRA Financial Services (Conduct of Business) Rules, rule 21 for colleagues undertaking insurance distribution activities.

However, it is surely best practice to roll out regular training on a wider range of regulatory subjects and this will support the managers and owners demonstrate compliance with not only SRA Code of Conduct for Firms, section 2 (compliance and business systems), but also the following:

> 4.3 You ensure that your managers and employees are competent to carry out their role, and keep their professional knowledge and skills, as well as understanding of their legal, ethical and regulatory obligations, up to date.

Plus, more specifically, there are duties contained in the SRA Code of Conduct for Solicitors, RELs and RFLs which must be demonstrated by these types of lawyers:

> 3.3 You maintain your competence to carry out your role and keep your professional knowledge and skills up to date.
>
> ...
>
> 3.5 Where you supervise or manage others providing legal services:
>
> (a) you remain accountable for the work carried out through them; and
> (b) you effectively supervise work being done for clients'
>
> 3.6 You ensure that the individuals you manage are competent to carry out their role, and keep their professional knowledge and skills, as well as understanding of their legal, ethical and regulatory obligations, up to date.

Solicitors must maintain continuing competency with reference to the SRA Statement of Solicitor Competence.

Misunderstandings about these duties are not only potentially damaging commercially and for reputational reasons, but there are also regulatory implications for firms if the actions of their employees are deemed improper.

Training topics (in addition to anti-money laundering and insurance distribution activities where relevant) will be a matter to be decided by each firm. The decision will be based on the needs of your staff; the type of services provided and how they are provided; the intelligence about weaknesses gathered from compliance exercises such as review of supervisory findings, complaints and negligence data and records of breaches. The following are suggestions of some useful subjects which ought to be considered to ensure an appropriate knowledge of regulatory and compliance topics (and noting that there will be associated legal topics to add, such as training on data protection and the Equality Act):

- **Support staff:** the significance of working in an SRA-authorised law firm, the SRA Principles, conduct outside of practice, the SRA Code of Conduct for Firms, the SRA Accounts Rules, the firm's internal compliance response (including, where relevant, the link to your accreditation scheme memberships), the COLP and COFA and compliance support, internal procedures, the importance of openness and cooperation.
- **IT staff:** particular emphasis on SRA's requirements in respect of confidentiality.
- **Marketing staff:** particular emphasis on confidentiality and publicity requirements (including the SRA's concern about social media).
- **HR staff:** particular emphasis on equality, diversity and inclusion duties, duties to treat each other fairly, SRA concerns about harassment in the workplace, misuse of non-disclosure agreements.
- **Qualified lawyers and fee earners/casehandlers:** all of the above but with more focus on the client-facing duties, supervision, risk management, etc.
- **Temporary staff:** all of the above.
- **Lateral hires:** all of the above.
- **Accounts staff:** all of the above, plus more detailed training on the Accounts Rules and COFA risk topics.

What are the compliance challenges?

- Getting managers/owners buy-in to the costs of providing training (the cost of dealing with issues that arise but could be remedied by training is greater).
- Ensuring that training is appropriate to the target audience.

What resources will help?

- SRA materials:
  - SRA Standards and Regulations (**www.sra.org.uk/solicitors/standards-regulations/**); in particular:
    - SRA Principles (**www.sra.org.uk/solicitors/standards-regulations/principles/**);
    - SRA Code of Conduct for Solicitors, RELs and RFLs (**www.sra.org.uk/solicitors/standards-regulations/code-conduct-solicitors/**);
    - SRA Code of Conduct for Firms (**www.sra.org.uk/solicitors/standards-regulations/code-conduct-firms/**); and
    - SRA Accounts Rules (**www.sra.org.uk/solicitors/standards-regulations/accounts-rules/**).

- Statement of Solicitor Competence (**www.sra.org.uk/solicitors/resources/continuing-competence/cpd/competence-statement/**);
- SRA guidance: 'How we regulate non-authorised persons' (updated 17 November 2021, **www.sra.org.uk/solicitors/guidance/general-regulation-non-authorised-persons/**);
- SRA guidance: 'The SRA's approach to equality, diversity and inclusion' (updated 25 November 2019, **www.sra.org.uk/solicitors/guidance/sra-approach-equality-diversity-inclusion/**);
- SRA warning notice: 'Offensive communications' (updated 25 November 2019, **www.sra.org.uk/solicitors/guidance/offensive-communications/**);
- SRA case study – 'Sexual harassment' (23 July 2019, **www.sra.org.uk/solicitors/guidance/sexual-harassment/**);
- SRA warning notice: 'Use of non disclosure agreements (NDAs)' (updated 12 November 2020, **www.sra.org.uk/solicitors/guidance/non-disclosure-agreements-ndas/**).

- Use disciplinary decisions from the Law Society *Gazette* to demonstrate the effects of non-compliance.
- *Compliance and Ethics in Law Firms*, 2nd edn (Tracey Calvert, Law Society Publishing, 2019).

Compliance tips – how to mitigate the risk of getting it wrong

- Conduct induction training on SRA regulation and professional ethics and the firm's internal policies, controls and procedures (PCPs).
- Provide regular update training on these issues.
- Share disciplinary decisions that are relevant to staff so that the importance of complying with SRA requirements is reinforced.
- Ensure the visibility of the COLP, COFA and risk and compliance team – the main messages to deliver are about the need to be open and accountable, mistakes will happen, discussing concerns, reporting issues, etc.
- Conduct supervisory oversight of individual compliance with the acknowledgement that information about breaches, lack of an appropriate response, training needs, etc. must be shared with the compliance team.
- Implement a reporting and notification procedure.

9.14 Do we need to help non-solicitors understand the importance of the SRA and professional ethics?

It is not mandatory to ensure that your non-solicitors understand regulatory and ethical expectations, but there are a number of best practice reasons why law firms should educate non-solicitor employees about the SRA and professional ethics:

- The SRA Code of Conduct for Firms applies to all owners and employees of your firm, regardless of legal qualification or what these individuals might be employed to do.

- It is unreasonable to assume that non-solicitors will have knowledge of regulation and sensible to deliver training to ensure gaps in knowledge are filled; this benefits not only the individual but also the firm and the firm's regulatory relationship with the SRA.
- The SRA Principles are also relevant and trigger the need for all owners and employees to consider their behaviours both in the office and in their personal lives.
- You may employ individuals who are regulated by other professional bodies (e.g. qualified lawyers from other jurisdictions; barristers regulated by the Bar Standards Board; legal executives regulated by the Institute of Legal Executives; accountants regulated by the ICAEW and other bodies; etc.). It is essential that they appreciate that they now have to consider that there is oversight by the SRA as well as their own regulatory body, and that a breach of regulatory duties in which the SRA has primary oversight might have consequences for them with their primary regulator.
- The SRA has the power to prevent an authorised law firm from employing such an individual, so unprofessional behaviour has an effect on the employability of the individual concerned.

Ensuring that non-solicitors understand the importance of the SRA and professional ethics will support the owners of the business demonstrate compliance with SRA Code of Conduct for Firms, para.4.3: 'You ensure that your managers and employees are competent to carry out their role, and keep their professional knowledge and skills, as well as understanding of their legal, ethical and regulatory obligations, up to date'.

What are the compliance challenges?

- Ensure that non-solicitors appreciate the impact of their own behaviour on their employment.
- Ensure that non-solicitors appreciate the impact of their own behaviour on their employer's authorised status; failings on the part of any employee might lead to scrutiny of supervision and internal governance and disciplinary repercussions for the firm itself.

What resources will help?

- SRA materials:
  - SRA Principles (**www.sra.org.uk/solicitors/standards-regulations/principles/**);
  - SRA Code of Conduct for Solicitors, RELs and RFLs (**www.sra.org.uk/solicitors/standards-regulations/code-conduct-solicitors/**);
  - SRA Code of Conduct for Firms (**www.sra.org.uk/solicitors/standards-regulations/code-conduct-firms/**);
  - SRA Accounts Rules (**www.sra.org.uk/solicitors/standards-regulations/accounts-rules/**);

- SRA Guidance: 'How we regulate non-authorised persons' (updated 17 November 2021, **www.sra.org.uk/solicitors/guidance/general-regulation-non-authorised-persons/**);
- SRA guidance: 'The SRA's approach to equality, diversity and inclusion' (updated 25 November 2019, **www.sra.org.uk/solicitors/guidance/sra-approach-equality-diversity-inclusion/**);
- SRA warning notice: 'Offensive communications' (updated 25 November 2019, **www.sra.org.uk/solicitors/guidance/offensive-communications/**);
- SRA case study – 'Sexual harassment' (23 July 2019, **www.sra.org.uk/solicitors/guidance/sexual-harassment/**).

- Disciplinary decisions reported in the Law Society *Gazette* used to illustrate consequences of non-compliance.
- *Compliance and Ethics in Law Firms*, 2nd edn (Tracey Calvert, Law Society Publishing, 2019).

Compliance tips – how to mitigate the risk of getting it wrong

- Conduct pre-employment screening of all staff – this is of course mandatory for those staff who are subject to the AML Regulations, and it is prudent to apply the same type of screening to all employees for broader purposes.
- Provide induction training on SRA regulation and professional ethics and the firm's internal PCPs.
- Provide regular update training on these issues.
- Share disciplinary decisions that are relevant to staff so that the importance of complying with SRA requirements is reinforced.
- Ensure the visibility of the COLP, COFA and risk and compliance team – the main messages to deliver are about the need to be open and accountable, mistakes will happen, discussing concerns, reporting issues, etc.
- Conduct supervisory oversight of individual compliance with the acknowledgement that information about breaches, lack of an appropriate response, training needs, etc. must be shared with the compliance team.
- Implement reporting and notification procedures.

9.15 Do we need to maintain training records and why?

If your firm is subject to the AML Regulations (as amended), then for the purposes of fulfilling your legal duties you must maintain training records to demonstrate compliance with regs.24 and 25.

In addition, it is sensible to maintain more general training records for the following reasons:

- Your trainee solicitors have individual responsibilities to keep a record of their training, and it is prudent for the firm to also maintain a log should there ever be scrutiny over the experience gained or similar.
- Your solicitors must demonstrate that they maintain continuing competency. For example, the SRA Code of Conduct for Solicitors, RELs and RFLs includes the following requirement at para.3.3: 'You maintain your

competence to carry out your role and keep your professional knowledge and skills up to date'.

- This continuing competency question is addressed annually as part of the practising certificate renewal exercise and the SRA is entitled to ask for such information at any time as part of its supervisory work. For this reason, it is best practice to encourage the keeping of training records that provide evidence of continuing competency measures.
- In addition, SRA Code of Conduct for Firms, para.4.3 applies to the owners of the business and all manager and employees of the firm: 'You ensure that your managers and employees are competent to carry out their role, and keep their professional knowledge and skills, as well as understanding of their legal, ethical and regulatory obligations, up to date'. In order to demonstrate compliance with this, it is prudent to maintain further records to demonstrate training delivered to all staff. This might also serve to show the development of the correct response to compliance throughout the business.
- More specifically, take note of SRA Financial Services (Conduct of Business) Rules, rule 20 (professional and organisational requirements), which contains an obligation in connection with the provision of insurance distribution activities that you ensure 'the firm and each relevant employee possesses appropriate knowledge and ability in order to complete their tasks and perform duties adequately'.

What are the compliance challenges?

- Having insufficient budget to meet training needs. Training need not be expensive or supplied by external consultants; it can take the form of personal reading, research, sharing of experiences, etc.
- Colleagues not attending training; in terms of anti-money laundering training, their non-attendance is likely to place them in breach of the AML Regulations. In respect of other topics, lack of training might result in other legal breaches, or regulatory breaches, or actions that might give rise to client complaints and/or acts or omissions which give rise to a negligence claim.

What resources will help?

- SRA Standards and Regulations (**www.sra.org.uk/solicitors/standards-regulations/**).
- AML Regulations.
- *Compliance and Ethics in Law Firms*, 2nd edn (Tracey Calvert, Law Society Publishing, 2019).

Compliance tips – how to mitigate the risk of getting it wrong

- Have a training policy which explains to colleagues your expectations about how training attendance will be recorded.
- Create a centralised system for recording all training so that non-attendance, etc. can be identified and remedied.

- Allocate ownership of the maintenance of training records to a team or individual, perhaps with the COLP or compliance team or maybe with HR, learning and development, or your practice manager.
- Supervisory oversight of training needs feeding into training programmes, with this information being shared with anyone involved in risk and compliance, the COLP/COFA/MLRO, and senior managers and the owners of the firm.

Related questions/issues

- What training should we deliver to our colleagues?

CHAPTER 10

Practising certificates, certificate renewals and continuing competency regime

10.1 Do solicitors always need a practising certificate to work in the law firm?

Any individual who is admitted to the roll and employed in connection with the provision of any legal services in an authorised law firm must have a current practising certificate. This is a legal obligation which is contained in Solicitors Act 1974, s.1A.

The interpretation of this requirement is wide. In private practice, this means that an individual admitted to the roll must have a practising certificate even if:

- they do not use the solicitor title;
- they are employed in a backroom or non-client facing role;
- they fulfil compliance and risk-management duties only;
- they are employed only as the firm's compliance officer for legal practice (COLP) or compliance officer for finance and administration (COFA) or both;
- they do the same work as a non-solicitor;
- they are a locum or otherwise recruited for a fixed term.

It is a criminal offence to practise in such circumstances without a current practising certificate.

It is a sensible compliance function to ensure that this legal requirement – and the breadth of application as described above – is understood not only by solicitors but also by others with responsibilities in respect of the firm's recruitment process and all human resources functions associated with this.

A connected compliance consideration is whether an individual on the roll is subject to any regulatory restraints on their employment. An individual's current regulatory status can be checked by using the Solicitors Register and by making enquiries of the Solicitors Regulation Authority (SRA). In addition to confirming that an individual holds a current practising certificate, you should also check whether there are regulatory findings which restrict or prohibit their employment in any way.

What are the compliance challenges?

- Ensure that you understand the Solicitors Act 1974.
- Do not rely on misinformation provided by an individual, instead make your own checks with the SRA.
- Ensure that your recruitment processes include checking the certification status of individuals.

What resources will help us?

- Solicitors Act 1974.
- SRA materials:
  - SRA Authorisation of Individuals Regulations (**www.sra.org.uk/solicitors/standards-regulations/authorisation-individuals-regulations/**);
  - SRA guidance: 'When do I need a practising certificate?' (updated 25 November 2019, **www.sra.org.uk/solicitors/guidance/practising-certificate/**);
  - SRA guidance: 'Admission as a solicitor' (updated 25 November 2019, **www.sra.org.uk/solicitors/guidance/admission-solicitor/**).

Compliance tips – how to mitigate the risk of getting it wrong

- Implement recruitment processes which include appropriate regulatory checks.
- Have proper regard to the annual practising certificate renewal exercise.

Related questions/issues

- Does a locum solicitor need a practising certificate?

10.2 Can we ask retired solicitors to provide locum or similar support?

Yes, subject to making the correct decision about their eligibility (i.e. practising certificate status) and their competency.

A retired solicitor who remains on the roll of solicitors must hold a current practising certificate in order to comply with Solicitors Act 1974, s.1A and provide any legal services in an authorised law firm. This is a personal duty, but there will be regulatory concerns if any firm hires an individual – albeit even on a temporary basis – without being satisfied that they are correctly certificated.

Conversely, a retired solicitor who has removed their name from the roll can be hired, and does not need to reapply to be admitted to the roll and will not need a practising certificate before accepting a temporary role. However, both they and the firm must not do anything, or use any title or description, that would hold the individual out as a practising solicitor. The individual cannot undertake reserved legal activities unless this is under the supervision of a qualified person.

By way of reminder, reserved legal services are those activities which by statute (Legal Services Act (LSA) 2007, s.12) can only be provided by authorised persons (such as solicitors):

(a) the exercise of a right of audience;
(b) the conduct of litigation;
(c) reserved instrument activities;
(d) probate activities;
(e) notarial activities;
(f) the administration of oaths.

In addition to practising certificate requirements, you will also need to consider whether you are satisfied about the retired solicitor's competency to provide a proper standard of service and satisfy the relevant regulatory and professional requirements as described in the SRA Standards and Regulations. For example, SRA Code of Conduct for Solicitors, RELs and RFLs (repeated at para.4.2 in the SRA Code of Conduct for Firms and therefore relevant to everyone in the firm) contains the duty that: 'You ensure that the service you provide to clients is competent and delivered in a timely manner' (para.3.2) and takes 'account of your client's attributes, needs and circumstances' (para.3.4).

Given that lack of compliance will not only cause regulatory difficulties for the individual, but may also trigger regulatory interest in the firm (e.g. does it have effective compliance and business systems as required by SRA Code of Conduct for Firms, section 2) and also of course might create negative or adverse publicity amongst your client base, it is sensible to be satisfied that the individual is aware of your compliance expectations. Your supervisory procedures should extend to temporary employees and be appropriate to manage risks of non-compliance.

What are the compliance challenges?

- Ensure there is no lack of compliance coverage of temporary staff.
- Ensure there are no misunderstandings or lack of current knowledge about the SRA Standards and Regulations.
- Ensure that there is no uncertificated practising.
- Never use misleading job titles.

What resources will help?

- SRA Authorisation of Individuals Regulations (**www.sra.org.uk/solicitors/standards-regulations/authorisation-individuals-regulations/**);
- SRA Codes of Conduct (**www.sra.org.uk/solicitors/standards-regulations/**): SRA Code of Conduct for Solicitors, RELs and RFLs (**www.sra.org.uk/solicitors/standards-regulations/code-conduct-solicitors/**) and SRA Code of Conduct for Firms (**www.sra.org.uk/solicitors/standards-regulations/code-conduct-firms/**);

- SRA guidance: 'When do I need a practising certificate?' (updated 25 November 2019, **www.sra.org.uk/solicitors/guidance/practising-certificate/**).

Compliance tips – how to mitigate the risk of getting it wrong

- Implement an internal procedure for recruiting temporary staff which includes checking certification status with the SRA.

Related questions/issues

- Do solicitors need practising certificates?

10.3 What are the requirements on firms to reauthorise each year with the SRA and renew solicitors' practising certificates?

Each year a firm needs to reauthorise with the SRA and renew all their solicitors' practising certificates via the SRA's bulk renewal process. The application is completed online via 'mySRA' and generally opens for completion on 1 October each year and is open for one month. The SRA contacts firms to confirm the renewal dates as these may change.

The categories of information that the firm needs to have available when completing the application are as follows (note this list may change):

- largest, smallest and average client account balance for last accounting period;
- the firm's turnover and whether more than 20 per cent comes from any single client, group of clients or referral source;
- areas of work that make your turnover, i.e. conveyancing, family, personal injury;
- professional indemnity insurance details;
- information about associations (such as introduction arrangements);
- details about any arrangements, relationships or connections that might influence the running of the firm;
- details about separate businesses clients are signposted to and the like;
- how many legally qualified and non-legally qualified fee earners the firm has;
- how many claims have been made in the last indemnity period and how many claims have been paid out in the last indemnity period regardless of when the claim was made;
- details about complaints that have gone through the firm's internal complaints process, what those complaints were about (i.e. delay, failure to advise, costs information) and which complaints went to the Legal Ombudsman;
- details of solicitors for which a practising certificate is being sought.

Once the form is completed, the firm must pay the reauthorisation and practising certificate fee. Details of the fees can be found here **www.sra.org.uk/mysra/fees/current-fees/**.

What are the compliance challenges?

- Gathering the information needed can be time-consuming.

What resources will help?

- SRA FAQs (**www.sra.org.uk/mysra/services/faqs/**).

Compliance tips – how to mitigate the risk of getting it wrong

- A person should be designated to the task of reauthorising the firm with the SRA and the renewal of solicitors' practising certificates (PCs). This will ensure that it is done on time. The firm's COLP will ordinarily be set up in mySRA as the 'authorised signatory' and will need to submit the application when it is completed.

10.4 What should we expect from our solicitors in relation of continuing competency?

The continuing professional development (CPD) 16-hour-a-year requirement was replaced in November 2016 with the continuing competence regime. This regime requires solicitors to reflect on the quality of their practice and identify any learning and development needs. With no minimum hour requirement, this was a sea change for practitioners, and some firms decided to keep minimum hours of training.

Each firm should provide its people (solicitors and others) with the mechanism by which they can record their learning and development needs and journey. This could be by way of a learning platform or a simple Word form.

When the firm renews their solicitor's PC, the firm needs to tick a box to confirm that the solicitor has provided the following declaration: 'Have you reflected on your practice and addressed any identified learning and development needs?' Whoever is completing the firm's reauthorisation and PC renewal process needs to be made aware that solicitors in the firm have indeed reflected and addressed any learning and development needs. Presumably if the answer to the question is 'no', then no PC will be granted.

What are the compliance challenges?

- It can be a challenge for some people to reflect on the quality of their practice and identify any learning and development needs. Solicitors will need guidance.

What resources will help?

- SRA guidance: 'Continuing competence' (**www.sra.org.uk/solicitors/resources/continuing-competence/cpd/continuing-competence/**).

Compliance tips – how to mitigate the risk of getting it wrong

- The consequences to solicitors not staying up-to-date with the law or ensuring their skills remain competent could be very serious. Guidance will need to be given to solicitors and periodic checks for compliance made.

10.5 How do we manage the SRA annual renewal exercise effectively?

The bulk renewal process is a phrase used to describe the position when the authorised law firm completes one form to pay their periodic fees and renew PCs and other registrations for all managers and employees.

The majority of law firms apply for PCs for their solicitors using the bulk renewal process rather than asking colleagues to complete this process individually. This makes sense, and will help avoid any repercussions of non-completion or late completion of individual returns.

The bulk renewal process is completed through the 'mySRA' portal and can be undertaken by your nominated Authorised Signatory or the Organisation Contact. This is an administrative task which can be daunting. The process is made more straightforward through effective pre-planning initiatives, such as:

- When solicitors join the firm or trainees qualify, make sure they amend their SRA record to show they are a solicitor at the firm and opt in to the firm's bulk renewal.
- Check the SRA website, and SRA communications such as the monthly SRA Update, for advance warning of the commencement of the renewal season. The paperwork can usually be accessed early, and early scrutiny will help in deciding what information is needed.
- Ensure you have early communication with those individuals whose details will be submitted to the SRA to ensure that their details are correct, to confirm that their personal reporting and notifications have been met, and to check their training records are complete and will justify their competency statements.
- Conduct communication which is supported by senior oversight of completion; e.g. the manager partner and/or the COLP reminding colleagues of the need to assist and the consequences of non-compliance for individuals and for the business.
- Prepare a checklist of the firm-wide information that is requested in any particular year – usually these relate to indemnity; client money; introductions and fee sharing arrangements; complaints; areas of work and turnover, etc. Sometimes one-off questions are asked. Once the information required is

known, the checklist approach can help with the delegation of responsibilities for information gathering and timing of collection of information.

What are the compliance challenges?

- Take steps to avoid tardiness and/or lack of interest on the part of those you are relying on to provide you with information.
- Be alive to potential lack of support for the process from senior managers.

What resources will help?

- SRA guidance: 'Apply for bulk renewal and pay your periodic fees' (**www.sra.org.uk/mysra/manage-account/organisation-account/step-by-step-guide/apply-for-bulk-renewal-pay-your-periodic-fees/**).
- SRA guidance: 'Annual fees' (**www.sra.org.uk/mysra/fees/**).
- SRA FAQs (**www.sra.org.uk/mysra/services/faqs/**).

Compliance tips – how to mitigate the risk of getting it wrong

- Ensure that there is owner/manager support for completion of this project (which, by implication, needs input from a number of colleagues in your firm).
- Implement an effective communication strategy.
- Allow sufficient resources with which to complete the task.
- Conduct training on the keeping of competency records.

CHAPTER 11

SRA Accounts Rules

11.1 Who needs to know about the SRA Accounts Rules and why?

The Solicitors Regulation Authority (SRA) Accounts Rules apply to everyone employed in your law firm.

These rules are designed to ensure that client money is safe, and that the SRA, clients and the public at large have confidence in firms when holding client money. Because of this duty of trust, the Accounts Rules contain obligations which support everyone in their personal duty to 'safeguard money and assets entrusted to you by clients and others' (as described in SRA Code of Conduct for Solicitors, para.4.2; and SRA Code of Conduct for Firms, para.5.2).

Consider the following circumstances when it is important that individuals in different teams understand this duty and apply the Accounts Rules correctly:

- **Reception and front-of-house staff** – When receiving payments from clients in respect of the firm's fees and disbursements, these members of staff will need to know about your banking processes.
- **Support staff** – When providing information about the client account to clients and others, these members of staff must understand the risks associated with providing this information and banking issues.
- **Caseworkers and fee earning staff** – When acting on client monies and handling client monies, these members of staff will want to ensure that they comply with requirements relating to clarity about payments, providing correct information, being wary about payments for third parties and/or requests that might be indicative of banking activities, and their duties in respect of payments out of client account.
- **Accounts and finance staff** – When providing accounting services, these members of staff must understand the need for proper accounting records and systems, and be mindful of risk activities such as unexplained payments from third parties and banking activities.
- **Owners of the firm** – These individuals have overall responsibility for the firm's accounting systems and will want to understand the requirements of

the Accounts Rules and be satisfied that the accounting records and systems are sufficient to demonstrate compliance in practice.

What are the compliance challenges?

- Lack of evidence of senior management collective responsibility for compliance.
- Mismanagement of accounts staff so that book-keeping and accounting records fail.
- Lack of understanding of all staff about the seriousness of holding other people's money.

What resources will help?

- SRA materials:
  - SRA Codes of Conduct (**www.sra.org.uk/solicitors/standards-regulations/**), SRA Code of Conduct for Solicitors, RELs and RFLs (**www.sra.org.uk/solicitors/standards-regulations/code-conduct-solicitors/**) and SRA Code of Conduct for Firms (**www.sra.org.uk/solicitors/standards-regulations/code-conduct-firms/**);
  - SRA Accounts Rules (**www.sra.org.uk/solicitors/standards-regulations/accounts-rules/**);
  - SRA guidance: 'Helping you keep accurate client accounting records' (updated 25 November 2019, **www.sra.org.uk/solicitors/guidance/accurate-client-accounting-records/**).
- *Compliance and Ethics in Law Firms*, 2nd edn (Tracey Calvert, Law Society Publishing, 2019).

Compliance tips – how to mitigate the risk of getting it wrong

- Conduct induction training for all staff on the SRA Accounts Rules. Essential topics include the following:
  - the meaning of client money;
  - disbursements;
  - the firm's policy on monies on account of costs and disbursements and/or fixed fees;
  - the proper use of the client account including expectations about prompt payments into the account;
  - the banking prohibition;
  - proper payments out of client account;
  - when funds can be retained after the end of a matter; and
  - housekeeping matters more generally when closing a file.
- Create procedures to ensure that client monies are paid into client account promptly, withdrawn in accordance with a consistent process, etc.
- Ensure visibility of the compliance officer for finance and administration (COFA) and a 'no blame' culture so that concerns and queries can be remedied.

11.2 Should we send client monies to an in-house solicitor?

When dealing with in-house solicitors (perhaps solicitors employed by developers or by a local authority), it might be necessary to send client monies to them for completion of a transaction or similar.

Solicitors who are not employed in SRA-authorised law firms are usually not permitted to hold client monies in an account in their personal name. This restriction is contained in the SRA Code of Conduct for Solicitors, RELs and RFLs at para.4.3:

> 4.3 You do not personally hold client money save as permitted under regulation 10.2(b)(vii) of the Authorisation of Individuals Regulations, unless you work in an authorised body, or in an organisation of a kind prescribed under this rule on any terms that may be prescribed accordingly.

These circumstances mean that monies sent to an unauthorised entity will be held in a bank account in the business's name, although an in-house solicitor can be a signatory to this account. This business account will not be subject to the SRA Accounts Rules, although the in-house solicitor will be required to display personal professional behaviours in keeping with the requirements of the SRA Principles (such as Principle 2 on duties of trust and confidence; Principle 4 on the duty of honesty; and Principle 5 on the duty of integrity) and the SRA Code of Conduct for Solicitors, RELs and RFLs. With the latter, they are subject to para.4.2 of this Code which is the requirement to 'safeguard money and assets entrusted to you by clients and others'.

When considering whether to send monies to an in-house solicitor, you will want to consider your client's best interests and make enquiries of the in-house solicitor as to their internal arrangements. It may be useful to remember that an in-house solicitor will be bound by any undertakings that they give in respect of the protection of client monies in the same way as any counterpart employed in an authorised firm.

What are the compliance challenges?

- Ensure there is no lack of understanding on your part, or on the part of the in-house solicitor, about the restrictions on the holding of client money by the latter.
- Take steps to avoid making decisions that put client money at risk.
- Do not act in an unprofessional or discourteous manner towards another member of the profession because of lack of understanding about their status as an in-house solicitor.

What resources will help?

- SRA materials:
  - SRA Code of Conduct for Solicitors, RELs and RFLs (**www.sra.org.uk/solicitors/standards-regulations/code-conduct-solicitors/**);

- SRA guidance: 'Unregulated organisations for employers of SRA regulated lawyers' (updated 25 November 2019, **www.sra.org.uk/solicitors/guidance/unregulated-organisations-employers-sra-regulated-lawyers/**);
- SRA guidance: 'Helping you keep accurate client accounting records' (updated 25 November 2019, **www.sra.org.uk/solicitors/guidance/accurate-client-accounting-records/**).

- Law Society materials:
  - Law Society Practice Note: In-house Practice: Regulatory Requirements (9 September 2021, **www.lawsociety.org.uk/en/topics/in-house/in-house-practice-regulatory-requirements**);
  - Law Society Practice Note: Solicitors Offering Legal Services to the Public from Unregulated Entities (13 July 2021, **www.lawsociety.org.uk/en/topics/business-management/solicitors-offering-legal-services-to-the-public-from-unregulated-entities**).

Compliance tips – how to mitigate the risk of getting it wrong

- Provide training to relevant staff (e.g. those who regularly deal with developers, on new plot sales, purchases from local authorities and similar).
- Conduct supervisory oversight.

Related questions/issues

- How can solicitors practise?
- What is the position of a solicitor employed within an unauthorised business?

11.3 Can we round up disbursements in bills to clients?

No. This is a breach not only of the SRA Accounts Rules but is also likely to breach basic ethical principles such as the duty to act with trust and confidence (SRA Principle 2), with integrity (Principle 5) and the duty to act in each client's best interests (Principle 7).

This is because a disbursement is defined in the following way: 'any costs or expenses paid or to be paid to a third party on behalf of the client or trust (including any VAT element) save for office expenses such as postage and courier fees' (SRA Glossary). The amount recovered from the client (or paying third party) must be the exact amount you are charged.

What are the compliance challenges?

- It is an incorrect assumption that a service charge element can be added to a request for a disbursement.

What resources will help?

- SRA Accounts Rules (**www.sra.org.uk/solicitors/standards-regulations/accounts-rules/**);
- SRA Transparency Rules (**www.sra.org.uk/solicitors/standards-regulations/transparency-rules/**);
- SRA guidance: 'Helping you keep accurate client accounting records' (updated 25 November 2019, **www.sra.org.uk/solicitors/guidance/accurate-client-accounting-records/**).

Compliance tips – how to mitigate the risk of getting it wrong

- Conduct training of everyone who discusses disbursements with clients, drafts bills, advertises process on the firm's website, etc.
- Check content of bills.

11.4 If we hold client money in respect of our costs, does this have to be placed in a client account?

Yes, unless you are able to take advantage of a specific provision in the SRA Accounts Rules.

SRA Accounts Rules rule 2.1 defines 'client money'. The definition includes – at rule 2.1(d) – money held or received by you 'in respect of your fees and any unpaid disbursements if held or received prior to delivery of a bill for the same'.

The default position to consider is that all client money including funds received in respect of fees, etc. must be held in a client account.

However, there is an exception to this general rule which can be used in respect of money that is held in respect of fees but only if you can justify changing your position (and significantly, that of your clients) through the correct application of SRA Accounts Rules, rule 2.2 which contains the following wording:

> 2.2 In circumstances where the only client money you hold or receive falls within rule 2.1(d) above, and:
>
> (a) any money held for disbursements relates to costs or expenses incurred by you on behalf of your client and for which you are liable; and
> (b) you do not for any other reason maintain a client account;
>
> you are not required to hold this money in a client account if you have informed your client in advance of where and how the money will be held. Rules 2.3, 2.4, 4.1, 7, 8.1(b) and (c) and 12 do not apply to client money held outside of a client account in accordance with this rule.

In other words, if you are satisfied that this is the only category of client money which you hold, and there is no other reason for you to maintain a client account, you can place this into your business (i.e. office) account prior to the delivery of a bill, whilst noting the following:

- Any money held for disbursements (in other words, costs, etc. to be paid to a third party on behalf of the client such as search fees, Land Registry fees, payments to counsel, etc. you instruct in your client's matter) relates to payments incurred by you on behalf of this client and in respect of which you are liable to the third party.
- You must notify the client in advance about where and how the money will be held.
- You note that the carve-out means that the following rules are disapplied:
  - rule 2.3 – the general obligation to pay client money promptly into a client account;
  - rule 2.4 – the general obligation to ensure that client money is available on demand;
  - rule 4.1 – the requirement that client money is kept separate from money belonging to the firm;
  - rule 7 – duties that apply to the payment of interest;
  - rule 8.1(b) – you maintain a list of all the balances shown by the client ledger accounts of the liabilities to clients and third parties with a running total of the balances;
  - rule 12 – the duty to obtain an accountant's report does not apply to the client money held outside of a client account.

What are the compliance challenges?

- Ensure that you do not adopt rule 2.2 without satisfying the conditions attached to it, for example not providing clients with appropriate information.
- Ensure that you do not misinterpret rule 2.2 by applying it to some client matters but not others.
- Do not place client money in your own account without managing the risks appropriately.
- Be able to demonstrate that this decision has been made having considered what is reasonable.

What resources will help?

- SRA Accounts Rules (**www.sra.org.uk/solicitors/standards-regulations/accounts-rules/**);
- SRA guidance: 'Taking money for your firm's costs' (14 September 2020, **www.sra.org.uk/solicitors/guidance/taking-money-for-your-firms-costs/**);
- SRA guidance: 'Accountant's report and the exemption to obtain one' (updated 25 November 2019, **www.sra.org.uk/solicitors/guidance/accountant-report-exemption-obtain-one/**);
- SRA guidance: 'Do I need to operate a client account?' (updated 25 November 2019, **www.sra.org.uk/solicitors/guidance/operate-client-account/**).

Compliance tips – how to mitigate the risk of getting it wrong

- Ensure that the owners/managers understand rule 2.2 and have made a decision about whether they wish to take advantage of this having correctly identified that the firm can meet all the conditions and does not need to operate a client account for any other purpose.
- Train staff about this decision.
- Include a statement about the firm's decision in client literature.
- Conduct supervisory oversight.

11.5 Can we retain completion funds in our client account if our client intends to use the money to buy another property?

This situation might arise in circumstances where the firm has acted for a client in a sale transaction and the client requests that the firm retains funds pending a future instruction.

In these circumstances, care must be taken to avoid breaching the banking prohibition in SRA Accounts Rules, rule 3.3: 'You must not use a client account to provide banking facilities to clients or third parties. Payments into, and transfers or withdrawals from a client account must be in respect of the delivery by you of regulated services.'

Where future instructions are imminent, it seems unlikely that the firm would be in breach of rule 3.3. if funds are retained for a very short time. However, if any future transaction is only speculative or not imminent, then it is likely that the firm will be in breach of rule 3.3 if funds are retained in client account.

In practice, this is a high-risk activity and great care must be taken to monitor the retention of any monies after completion of a regulated service. Your COFA, and those involved in risk and compliance management, will want to be aware of all such matters.

What are the compliance challenges?

- Do not misunderstand rule 3.3; it is essential to understand the meaning of the 'regulated services' phrase.
- Ensure that you challenge inappropriate client instructions when to carry out a client's wish places the individual in breach of rule 3.3.
- Do not allow fee earners to override firm policies designed to prevent a breach of rule 3.3.
- Prevent the holding of such monies for a period longer than that which is justifiable or holding the money in circumstances in which it is not justifiable.

What resources will help?

- SRA materials:
  - SRA Accounts Rules (**www.sra.org.uk/solicitors/standards-regulations/accounts-rules/**);

  - SRA warning notice: 'Improper use of client account as a banking facility' (updated 25 November 2019, **www.sra.org.uk/solicitors/guidance/improper-client-account-banking-facility/**).
- SDT disciplinary decisions and case reports on the consequences of breaching this prohibition. It is good practice to monitor the Law Society *Gazette* and other legal journals where such cases are reported, so that relevant cases can be shared with colleagues.

Compliance tips – how to mitigate the risk of getting it wrong

- Implement a client money policy in which approval for retention of monies at the end of a retainer can be given only by a senior manager/the COFA.
- Create client account record-keeping to monitor such monies.

11.6 Can we donate small client balances to charity?

It is possible to seek the express consent of the individual client/third party to donate small balances to charity. However, it is essential to show that it was reasonable to ask the client/third party and that the client/third party gave informed consent.

However, seeking blanket consent for this practice (for example, by adding a clause to the firm's terms of business), or simply having a 'house rule' that small amounts will not be repaid to the client, is likely to place the firm in breach of the SRA Accounts Rules.

This is because rule 2.5 says: 'You ensure that client money is returned promptly to the client, or the third party for whom the money is held, as soon as there is no longer any proper reason to hold those funds.'

This rule applies to all sums of money regardless of the amount. This is because the money does not belong to the firm and the firm must account to the client/third party.

What are the compliance challenges?

- Do not apply a blanket policy regarding all client monies – this is unlikely to be regarded by the SRA as compatible either with SRA Accounts Rules rule 2.5 or with SRA Principle 7 (you must act in the best interests of each client).
- Do not get in the position of donating money to charity with the client's consent but not having evidence that the consent was obtained and/or not being able to show that the client gave informed consent (i.e. the client gave consent knowing that a) this was their money; b) the exact amount owing; and c) the firm's duty is to return it to them) and with the firm being unable to demonstrate that it was reasonable to ask the client for permission to vary their duty to comply with rule 2.5.
- Avoid confusing this situation with the position described in SRA Accounts Rules rule 5.1(c) and/or misusing this rule. Rule 5.1(c) states that: 'You only

withdraw client money from a client account: ... (c) on the SRA's prior written authorisation or in prescribed circumstances.' This rule permits law firms to withdraw residual client account balances of £500 or less on any client money provided the balance is paid to a charity. This rule can only be used if you have not returned monies at the end of a retainer and it is now difficult for the firm to do this as they cannot identify or trace the client.

What resources will help?

- SRA materials:
  - SRA Accounts Rules (**www.sra.org.uk/solicitors/standards-regulations/accounts-rules/**);
  - SRA guidance: 'The prescribed circumstances in which you can withdraw client money from client account to pay to a charity of your choice' (**www.sra.org.uk/solicitors/standards-regulations/withdraw-client-money/**).
- Law Society Practice Note: Residual Client Balances (9 September 2021, **www.lawsociety.org.uk/en/topics/client-care/residual-client-balances**).

Compliance tips – how to mitigate the risk of getting it wrong

- Implement a file closure procedure which includes a requirement to deal with client balances promptly.
- Conduct training of fee earners on file closure.
- Engage in supervision to include consideration of client money issues.
- Create a client money policy with a statement about firm's policy on small balances.
- Where permission is requested, create a template letter to show that this is with informed consent.

Related questions/issues

- What steps should we take to trace former clients for whom we are holding money?
- When do we need to speak to the SRA about residual balances?

11.7 What is a third party managed account, and what should we take into account when considering whether it is appropriate to use this type of account?

Third party managed accounts (TPMAs) were introduced in the SRA Accounts Rules in 2019 as an alternative – subject to conditions – to the holding of client money in a client account.

Understanding of TPMAs is helped by the fact this is it a defined term in the SRA Glossary which is part of the SRA Standards and Regulations:

> **third party managed account** means an account held at a bank or building society in the name of a third party which is an authorised payment institution or small payment institution that has chosen to implement safeguarding arrangement in accordance with

> the Payment Services Regulations (as each defined in the Payment Services Regulations 2017) regulated by the FCA, in which monies are owned beneficially by the third party, and which is operated upon terms agreed between the third party, you and your client as an escrow payment service.

The conditions of use are in SRA Accounts Rules, rule 11.1 which states that a TPMA can be used:

> ... for the purpose of receiving payments from or on behalf of, or making payments to or on behalf of, the client ... only if:
>
> (a) use of the account does not result in you receiving or holding the client's money; and
>
> (b) you take reasonable steps to ensure, before accepting instructions, that the client is informed of and understands:
>
> (i) the terms of the contractual arrangements relating to the use of the third party managed account, and in particular how any fees for use of the third party managed account will be paid and who will bear them; and
>
> (ii) the client's right to terminate the agreement and dispute payment requests made by you.

Rule 11.2 contains the requirement that you must obtain regular statements and you must ensure the accuracy of these.

Using a TPMA and not otherwise holding client money in other circumstances, means that the majority of the SRA Accounts Rules will not apply to you. In circumstances where your need to hold client money is minimal, this alternative might be an attractive proposition. However, it is still necessary to undertake certain key compliance steps and be able to justify that your use of a TPMA has been considered carefully and that this is in the best interests of your client as well as a business decision that has been made for your own benefit.

Steps to consider:

- You should do appropriate due diligence checks on the TPMA provider so that you:
  - are satisfied that they are correctly regulated by the Financial Conduct Authority;
  - know that the account held is in a bank as defined in the Solicitors Act 1974 or a building society as defined in the Building Societies Act 1986;
  - have checked that the account is operated as an escrow payment service so that the third party receives and deals with money on behalf of you and your client;
  - are satisfied that the monies in the account are owned beneficially by the third party and that the use of the account does not mean that you are receiving or holding client money.
- You must take all reasonable steps to make sure that your client understands about the use of the TPMA and their rights and obligations and the relevance

of its use to their matter. In particular, your client must understand how their money will be held, how the transaction works, their right to terminate the agreement, their right to dispute payment requests, regulatory matters and complaints procedures, and how regulatory protections in respect of the TPMA are different to regulatory protections available in respect of monies held in client account .The client is additionally advised about whether they are required to authorise payments, and any charges or other fees they are liable to pay.

- You must notify the SRA that you are using a TPMA and, if more than one, provide details of all TPMAs. This notification can be done through the completion of the SRA's prescribed form.

In addition, use of a TPMA should be aligned with your compliance with client information and publicity duties described in SRA Code of Conduct for Solicitors, RELs and RFLs, section 8 (referred to in the SRA Code of Conduct for Firms, para.7.1(c)), so that:

> 8.6 You give clients information in a way they can understand. You ensure they are in a position to make informed decisions about the services they need, how their matter will be handled and the options available to them.
>
> 8.7 You ensure that clients receive the best possible information about how their matter will be priced and, both at the time of engagement and when appropriate as their matter progresses, about the likely overall cost of the matter and any costs incurred.
>
> 8.8 You ensure that any publicity in relation to your practice is accurate and not misleading, including that relating to your charges and the circumstances in which interest is payable by or to clients.

What are the compliance challenges?

- Ensure that you only use TPMAs in inappropriate circumstances.
- Avoid using TPMAs without appropriate vetting of the provider and finding that the account is not in fact a TPMA or that any of the conditions described in rule 11 are not met.
- Ensure that you give the client sufficient information about the TPMA.
- TPMAs being used without the permission and/or knowledge of relevant managers/employees such as the COFA, risk and compliance team, or the accounts/finance team.
- Do not assume that the use of a TPMA removes the need for risk and compliance oversight and management.

What resources will help?

- SRA Codes of Conduct: SRA Code of Conduct for Solicitors, RELs and RFLs (**www.sra.org.uk/solicitors/standards-regulations/code-conduct-solicitors/**); SRA Code of Conduct for Firms (**www.sra.org.uk/solicitors/standards-regulations/code-conduct-firms/**).
- SRA Accounts Rules (**www.sra.org.uk/solicitors/standards-regulations/accounts-rules/**).

- SRA guidance: 'Third party managed accounts' (updated 25 November 2019, **www.sra.org.uk/solicitors/guidance/third-party-managed-accounts/**).

Compliance tips – how to mitigate the risk of getting it wrong

- Ensure that the owners/managers understand TPMAs and have made a decision about whether they wish to take advantage of such accounts and, if so, in what circumstances.
- Document the firm's position on the use of TPMAs.
- Have an internal procedure to ensure timely notification of TPMA use to the SRA.
- Create template documentation to ensure that clients receive appropriate information about your suggestion that a TPMA is used.
- Require notes to be added to client files to record the reasons to justify the use of a TPMA.
- Conduct supervisory oversight.

Related questions/issues

- Do we need to put money on account of our costs in a client account?

CHAPTER 12

Data protection

12.1 What should be included in an effective firm-wide data protection response?

Every firm, of whatever size or type, must manage the risks which arise in connection with data processing. This is because you must comply with the Data Protection Act (DPA) 2018 and the UK General Data Protection Regulation (GDPR).

Not only might the wrong response place you in breach of this legislation, this can also trigger regulatory concerns. There are individual and firm-wide duties to comply with the law, and have effective systems and controls to support such compliance, in the Solicitors Regulation Authority (SRA) Standards and Regulations, so for example, note needs to be taken of:

- SRA Principle 1 – you act 'in a way that upholds the constitutional principle of the rule of law, and the proper administration of justice';
- SRA Code of Conduct for Solicitors, RELs and RFLs, para.7.1 (repeated in the SRA Code of Conduct for Firms, para.3.1) – 'You keep up to date with and follow the law and regulation governing the way you work';
- SRA Code of Conduct for Firms, para.2.5 – 'You identify, monitor and manage all material risks to your business, including those which may arise from your connected practices.'

Dealing with the legal and regulatory risks effectively triggers the need to be confident that you have dealt with the following considerations:

- Data processors (such as your law firm) must be registered with the Information Commissioner's Office (ICO) and pay an annual registration fee. In some (but not all) cases, you must also appoint a data protection officer (DPO).
- You must have identified and made records of the data you are processing; not only will this be client data, but it also extends to personal data in connection with third parties, with suppliers and others with whom you communicate, and of course managers, employees and former colleagues.

- You must know where this data is held and must have made records of these locations; not only will this require an understanding of how client-related data is held and where it is held (e.g. on paper and/or electronic case management systems, in office-based locations and systems, or otherwise outside of the office framework), plus the identification of other systems such as those maintained by your accounts and human resources colleagues.
- You need to have made an assessment about data security and recorded these findings – How is data protected in all its different formats? Are your IT strategies providing sufficient security from cyber attack and similar risk events?
- You need to have considered and documented the lawful basis you are relying on to process personal data; the law provides six legal bases for processing – i.e. consent; performance of a contract; legitimate interest; vital interest; legal requirement; and a public interest – and it will be necessary for you to justify data processing against these.
- Considering the benefits of training of all managers and employees is advisable; this is training on the law, the relevance in SRA-authorised law firms, and the firm's internal policies and procedures.
- You need to have drafted a suite of policies and procedures that will demonstrate the right response to this topic and make it easier for all managers and employees to act in a consistent and risk-averse manner. Policies might include:
  - a data protection policy;
  - an information security policy (including password protection requirements, etc.);
  - email usage policy;
  - acceptable use policy;
  - privacy notices (for public-facing use and separately for use with data held in respect of managers and employees);
  - subject access request procedure;
  - data erasure request policy;
  - data breach notification procedure;
  - data retention and destruction policy.
- You need to have considered how you will deal with data subject access and data erasure requests. Data subjects have a variety of legal rights, and these are the most frequently used. It is sensible to have a procedure to ensure an appropriate response.
- Data breaches might place you in breach of legal and regulatory duties, so it is advisable to have a procedure for dealing with this which includes timely internal notification, testing of business continuity plans and similar.
- More generally, data protection relies on having effective IT security. It is important to be confident that your IT is secure, well-maintained and upgraded as necessary.

What are the compliance challenges?

- Avoid being unable to demonstrate an effective response, either because you have no response at all, or because you have used a template-based solution which is not appropriate for your needs, or because there is lack of individual adherence to your solutions.
- Avoid individuals misunderstanding this topic or your policies.

What resources will help?

- SRA Codes of Conduct: SRA Code of Conduct for Solicitors, RELs and RFLs (**www.sra.org.uk/solicitors/standards-regulations/code-conduct-solicitors/**); and SRA Code of Conduct for Firms (**www.sra.org.uk/solicitors/standards-regulations/code-conduct-firms/**).
- Resources available from the ICO website (**www.ico.org.uk**).
- *Data Protection Toolkit*, 2nd edn (Alison Matthews, Law Society Publishing, 2019).

Compliance tips – how to mitigate the risk of getting it wrong

- Involve managers in the decision-making process and in developing an agreed strategy to the data protection topic.
- Delegate responsibility for this topic, and the need to show compliance in practice is happening, to an individual or a team; e.g. maybe the compliance officer for legal practice (COLP), another senior manager, the data protection officer if appointed, or the risk and compliance team.
- Diarise an annual review schedule.
- Conduct a training programme for all managers and employees on the law, SRA regulatory requirements, and the firm's internal response.
- Conduct supervisory oversight.

12.2 Do we need to appoint a data protection officer?

Not necessarily, but you will need to consider your legal obligations and make your decision based on these requirements. For example, you must appoint a DPO if your core activities require large-scale, regular and systematic monitoring of individuals (unlikely but this will be your judgment call) or your core activities consist of large-scale processing of special categories of data or data relating to criminal convictions and offences (again, probably unlikely, but there are no definitions to assist with this analysis and this is another judgment call).

Where appointed, the DPO has tasks that are set in the UK GDPR:

- to inform and advise the firm about its obligations to comply with data protection legislation;
- to monitor compliance with data protection legislation, and with the firm's data protection policies;
- to advise on, and to monitor, data protection impact assessments;
- to cooperate with the ICO;

- to be the first point of contact for supervisory authorities and for data subjects.

In assessing whether or not you require a DPO, it would be advisable to keep records of why a decision is made (particularly if the decision is that you are not bound to comply with a legal duty to appoint a DPO) and to review this decision regularly. Even if you are confident that you do not need a DPO to comply with the law, you are still able to take a decision to appoint one on a voluntary basis. In these circumstances, and to avoid any confusion as to status, it might be prudent to use another title (perhaps 'data compliance officer').

Where a DPO is not appointed, it will nevertheless be prudent to ensure that the firm is demonstrating an appropriate response to this topic. Bear in mind SRA Code of Conduct for Firms, para.2.5 – 'You identify, monitor and manage all material risks to your business, including those which may arise from your connected practices' – and consider whether it might be sensible to add data protection duties to the COLP's job description, or delegate oversight responsibilities to another senior colleague and/or the risk and compliance team.

What are the compliance challenges?

- Ensure that you are interpreting the law correctly so that the correct decision is made about a DPO appointment.
- Ensure that you have sufficient evidence to justify any decision not to appoint a DPO, particularly if that decision is subsequently challenged.
- Do not appoint someone who has lack of knowledge.
- Do not appoint someone who is unable to fulfil his or her duties because of lack of seniority, influence over decision-making, etc.
- Do not make a voluntary appointment or appoint someone to have non-DPO responsibilities without clarity about his or her status, etc.

What resources will help?

- UK General Data Protection Regulation and DPA 2018.
- Information from ICO website (**www.ico.org.uk**).
- SRA Codes of Conduct: SRA Code of Conduct for Solicitors, RELs and RFLs (**www.sra.org.uk/solicitors/standards-regulations/code-conduct-solicitors/**); SRA Code of Conduct for Firms (**www.sra.org.uk/solicitors/standards-regulations/code-conduct-firms/**).
- *Data Protection Toolkit*, 2nd edn (Alison Matthews, Law Society Publishing, 2019).

Compliance tips – how to mitigate the risk of getting it wrong

- Take legal advice if uncertain whether you are processing data on a large scale.
- Involve managers in the decision-making process and develop an agreed strategy to the data protection topic.
- Provide tailored training of the DPO, any voluntary appointee or anyone involved in the firm's data compliance response.
- Ensure visibility of key personnel so that effective communication is enabled.

- Provide training of all managers/employees on data protection legislation and this role.

12.3 How should we respond to a data subject access request?

All data subjects have a legal right to make a data subject access request (DSAR).

Your response is governed by the DPA 2018 which has a default requirement within it that you must ordinarily respond within one calendar month with the data requested (subject to exceptions such as where the data is excessive or the request complex, etc.).

Because we are dealing with time-critical requests, it makes sense to have an internal procedure to ensure that this limited time is used wisely. A suggested procedure/checklist is as follows:

- It is important that everyone within the firm knows the internal point of contact in order that they can transfer the DSAR to the individual with responsibilities to manage the process which will follow.
- The DSAR must be reviewed – is the person making the request a data subject, and what information are they requesting? Whilst it is possible for third parties to make requests on behalf of others, it would be necessary in these circumstances for you to be satisfied that the underlying data subject is aware of the request and confirms that they have given their authority for the request.
- The DSAR should be in writing.
- The DSAR should be acknowledged.
- The DSAR should be carefully considered as it might be necessary to ask for more information; for example, you can ask for further information to satisfy yourself on the identity of the individual who is making the request.
- If you consider that the DSAR is extensive or complex, your timescales can be extended, but you will want to explain this to the person making the request. Bear in mind that this decision may need to be justified to the ICO, so you will want to protect your position by making notes of your reasoning.
- If you consider that the request is unfounded, then this should also be explained. As the data subject is exercising a legal right, you may feel it is prudent to take legal advice if you decide to refuse to reply as again this decision may be scrutinised by the ICO.
- You will need to be able to search all sources of data, so bear in mind the need to sift through files, emails and other electronic and other storage means.
- You will need to distinguish personal data that relates to the data subject and others, and respond accordingly. This might trigger the need to seek consent from the other parties, to redact their information, or to consider whether it is

nonetheless reasonable to make a disclosure. This decision might be better made with legal advice to support your decision-making

- You will want to consider the exemptions to providing data. These include circumstances where either litigation or legal privilege applies; requests for confidential references; information which is publicly available; personal data that is processed for management reasons; negotiations with the individual making the DSAR; etc.

What are the compliance challenges?

- There are tight timescales which are legally binding, so there are challenges associated with missing deadlines (perhaps because of late or missed internal transfers of the DSAR).
- Ensure that colleagues understand when they are in receipt of such a request and therefore deal with the request with recourse to the right people and resources.

What resources will help?

- SRA Codes of Conduct: SRA Code of Conduct for Solicitors, RELs and RFLs (**www.sra.org.uk/solicitors/standards-regulations/code-conduct-solicitors/**); SRA Code of Conduct for Firms (**www.sra.org.uk/solicitors/standards-regulations/code-conduct-firms/**).
- DPA 2018.
- Information from the ICO website (**www.ico.org.uk**).

Compliance tips – how to mitigate the risk of getting it wrong

- Take legal advice if uncertain of your position with regard to a DSAR, particularly high-risk decisions such as right to extend timescale, imposing a fee because of complexity, or your refusal.
- Involve managers in the decision-making process and develop an agreed procedure to deal with DSARs.
- Provide tailored training of the DPO, any voluntary appointee or anyone involved in the firm's DSAR response.
- Provide training on the law and the firm's internal procedure.
- Ensure visibility of key personnel so that effective communication is enabled.
- Conduct supervisory oversight.

Related questions/issues

- How should we deal with data erasure requests?

12.4 What steps must we take if we have a data breach incident?

Data breaches trigger a need for you to consider regulatory expectations and professional behaviours, together with the need to comply with data protection legislation.

Regulatory expectations are largely focused on your relationship with your client, but with this topic there are also public interest issues that must be taken into account. Your compliance with the SRA Principles will be considered in the event of a serious data breach – have you, for example, acted in a way that upholds trust and confidence in the solicitors' profession (Principle 2)? In relation to your professional conduct in practice, individuals will be expected to comply with the two SRA Codes of Conduct (i.e. the SRA Code of Conduct for Solicitors, RELs and RFLs and the SRA Code of Conduct for Firms). A data breach incident might also suggest an issue with your confidentiality duties (para.6.3 in each of the two Codes). Authorised law firms are required to have compliance and business systems as described in SRA Code of Conduct for Firms, section 2 which include having effective governance structures, etc. (para.2.1), compliance record-keeping (para.2.2) and the need to identify, monitor and manage all material risks (para.2.5).

In addition, a data breach is indicative of a breach of the UK GDPR. This legislation imposes a statutory duty on you to report serious personal data breaches to the ICO within 72 hours of becoming aware of the breach, plus the duty to keep a record of all personal data breaches regardless of whether these are reportable.

This means that you will need to be in a position to take the following steps:

- Record all data breach events in a compliance log (preferably maintained centrally by the compliance team or COLP so that patterns of behaviour and effectiveness of compliance systems can be kept under review).
- Consider which individuals have been affected by the breach (e.g. clients and other data subjects) and whether and how you should contact them.
- Consider the confidentiality issues – is this a serious and therefore reportable breach so that we should be making contact with the SRA?
- Consider also whether this is a serious breach of our legal duties so that we must notify the ICO within 72 hours of becoming aware of the incident.
- Keep an audit trail of your actions after becoming aware of the breach so that you have evidence to justify your response if this is challenged by either the SRA or the ICO.

What are the compliance challenges?

- Ensure that data breaches are reported as required.
- Ensure that data breaches are reported in a timely fashion.
- Notify the affected individuals, or the SRA and ICO.

What resources will help?

- SRA Codes of Conduct: SRA Code of Conduct for Solicitors, RELs and RFLs (**www.sra.org.uk/solicitors/standards-regulations/code-conduct-solicitors/**);

SRA Code of Conduct for Firms (**www.sra.org.uk/solicitors/standards-regulations/code-conduct-firms/**).
- Information from the ICO website (**www.ico.org.uk**).
- *Data Protection Toolkit*, 2nd edn (Alison Matthews, Law Society Publishing, 2019).

Compliance tips – how to mitigate the risk of getting it wrong

- Provide training on data protection legislation for all staff.
- Implement a data policy which includes a procedure to deal with data incidents.
- Include references to data issues within your confidentiality policy.
- Create an internal reporting system for data incidents.
- Conduct IT oversight.
- Conduct supervisory oversight.
- Keep compliance records to demonstrate risk management and mitigation, plus records of all data breach incidents.

Related questions/issues

- What are the issues if we have sent an email to the wrong recipient?
- Breaching duties of confidentiality owed to current and former clients in order to comply with para.6.3 in each of the SRA Codes of Conduct.

CHAPTER 13

Financial services

13.1 Do we need to include financial services in our compliance response?

Yes, you need to be confident that you understand whether anyone in the firm is delivering such services to their clients.

This is because anyone providing financial services must comply with the Financial Services and Markets Act 2000 (FSMA 2000) and consider the regulatory framework within which financial services are provided. This means that at the very least your compliance planning must include an assessment of whether your firm provides any services which trigger the need to consider FSMA 2000.

If you are confident that it doesn't, then it would be best practice to record this assessment in your compliance materials and make it clear to all colleagues that this is not an area in which they should be involved. Colleagues might also need to understand in specific terms what they are prohibited from doing for their clients and why this is so.

In other circumstances, and without being directly and separately authorised by the Financial Conduct Authority (FCA), solicitors employed in Solicitors Regulation Authority (SRA) authorised law firms are only able to provide exempt regulated activities. When undertaking such activities, you must comply with the SRA Financial Services (Scope) Rules ('the Scope Rules') and the SRA Financial Services (Conduct of Business) Rules ('the COB Rules'). Because of the risks involved in breaching these regulatory requirements, and the possible breach of FSMA 2000 that may be a consequence, you will want to be confident that your compliance management is robust with full understanding of the limits of what activities you can perform and the conditions attached to performance.

Key points to note:

- You must not perform prohibited activities as described in Scope Rules, rule 3, or corporate finance activities as described in rule 4.
- When providing other services, this must only be in circumstances where the activities arise out of, or are complementary to, the professional services you are providing to a particular client. In other words, you are prohibited from

doing standalone financial services and these must directly arise in connection with the specific and current legal services you are providing to a particular client.

- You may only carry on certain insurance distribution activities and subject to the law firm being on the FCA's Financial Services Register, and with the appointment of an insurance distribution officer and with certain conditions contained in the COB Rules being met as to training, status information and similar –Scope Rules, rule 5 and COB Rules, Part 3.
- You may only carry on certain credit-regulated financial services activities as described in Scope Rules, rule 6 and subject to the conditions in COB Rules, Part 4.

What are the compliance challenges?

- Lack of competency when providing exempt regulated activities is likely to create difficulties with duties of client care contained in SRA Code of Conduct for Solicitors, RELs and RFLs, section 3 and SRA Code of Conduct for Firms, section 4. Are you satisfied that you are delivering a competent service?
- Misunderstandings about the limit of the financial services that may be provided without being directly authorised by the FCA will be problematic. If performance of regulated activities is in breach of FSMA 2000, the individual might be committing a criminal offence and any contract is unlikely to be enforceable. A breach of FSMA 2000 will also have regulatory consequences for the individual and the firm as it would be a matter that would be reportable to the SRA.
- Misunderstanding the conditions attached to the performance of exempt regulated activities will be problematic. For example, providing standalone financial services which are unconnected to a current legal service is a breach of FSMA 2000 and the Scope Rules, and it is important that exempt regulated activities can be shown to arise out of, and be complementary to, a current legal service. This might include for example arranging indemnity cover for a defective title when acting for a client on the sale of their property. This would be acceptable, whereas arranging indemnity cover unconnected with a particular transaction would not be acceptable.

What resources will help?

- SRA Financial Services (Scope) Rules (**www.sra.org.uk/solicitors/standards-regulations/financial-services-scope-rules/**).
- SRA Financial Services (Conduct of Business) Rules (**www.sra.org.uk/solicitors/standards-regulations/financial-services-conduct-business-rules/**).
- SRA guidance: 'Law firms carrying on insurance distribution activities' (updated 25 November 2019, **www.sra.org.uk/solicitors/guidance/law-firms-carrying-insurance-distribution-activities/**).
- SRA guidance: 'Regulated financial services activities' (updated 4 January 2021, **www.sra.org.uk/solicitors/resources/financial-services-rules/regulated-financial-services-activites/**).
- SRA website resources page: 'Financial services' (**www.sra.org.uk/solicitors/resources/financial-services/**).

Compliance tips – how to mitigate the risk of getting it wrong

- This subject is sometimes overlooked in terms of risk management and compliance strategies – consider a compliance project to ascertain which teams might be providing financial services, competency standards and training needs, record-keeping, etc.
- Implement a financial services policy.
- Provide appropriate training.
- Create template documentation for information that must be provided to clients when delivering financial services.
- Conduct supervisory oversight and reporting of training needs.
- Monitor the Law Society *Gazette* for cases which highlight misunderstandings about this topic – these cases can be usefully shared to ensure that staff vigilance remains high.

Related questions/issues

- The need to demonstrate effective compliance and risk management with appropriate resources.

13.2 What is the appropriate compliance response when considering how to provide financial services correctly?

It is foolish to provide financial services without having the correct compliance oversight. This is because the majority of law firms are not authorised by the FCA to provide financial services, and will be committing offences under FSMA 2000 if they do not restrict what they do to the exempt regulated activities which professional firms are permitted to do but only on condition that they comply with the rules of their own regulatory body. These rules are found in the SRA Standards and Regulations and are the SRA Scope Rules and the SRA COB Rules.

The Scope Rules set out the financial services which law firms which are not authorised by the FCA are able to perform (known as exempt regulated activities) and the conditions which must be met if they are to be provided. The COB Rules explains the compliance requirements which attach to the performance of these exempt regulated activities.

It is essential that the firm's compliance plans extend to appropriate oversight of the provision of exempt regulated activities. The following steps are recommended:

- Identify the exempt regulated activities that are performed and by whom.
- Benchmark the performance of these activities against the SRA Scope Rules and the SRA COB Rules.
- For example: are you confident that the services are being provided in compliance with the basic conditions in Scope Rules, rule 2 and are you satisfied

that you are correctly fulfilling the status disclosure requirements in COB Rules, rule 2?

- The COB Rules require that you maintain a number of records and on specific terms – are you keeping accurate records of transactions as per rule 4; records of commissions (if any) as per rule 5; and are you dealing with any execution-only transactions which will trigger the need to comply with rule 7?
- In terms of insurance distribution activities, is the firm registered with the FCA and has an individual been appointed as the insurance distribution officer (Scope Rules, rule 5)? Have the conditions in COB Rules, Part 3 been considered so that, for example, correct status disclosure information is provided, complete information is provided to the client about any personal recommendation and demands and needs, training is provided, etc.?
- Deliver appropriate training to all staff performing exempt regulated activities, plus supervisors and the insurance distribution officer (IDO) and the firm's compliance officer for legal practice (COLP).
- Perform ongoing monitoring of both individual actions, and the firm's compliance position.

What are the compliance challenges?

- This is a discrete area of knowledge. In order to manage risks appropriately, it is necessary to understand financial services regulation and the specific SRA rules.
- It is also necessary to ensure that the areas of the firm which perform exempt regulated activities have been identified and appropriate policies, controls and procedures (PCPs) are adopted to ensure that compliance in practice can be demonstrated. It may be necessary to upskill colleagues and the compliance team to ensure appropriate competencies.

What resources will help?

- SRA Financial Services (Scope) Rules (**www.sra.org.uk/solicitors/standards-regulations/financial-services-scope-rules/**).
- SRA Financial Services (Conduct of Business) Rules (**www.sra.org.uk/solicitors/standards-regulations/financial-services-conduct-business-rules/**).
- SRA guidance: 'Law firms carrying on insurance distribution activities' (updated 25 November 2019, **www.sra.org.uk/solicitors/guidance/law-firms-carrying-insurance-distribution-activities/**).
- SRA guidance: 'Regulated financial services activities' (updated 4 January 2021, **www.sra.org.uk/solicitors/resources/financial-services-rules/regulated-financial-services-activites/**).
- SRA website resources page: 'Financial services' (**www.sra.org.uk/solicitors/resources/financial-services/**).

Compliance tips – how to mitigate the risk of getting it wrong

- Conduct a benchmarking exercise to identify gaps in knowledge and record-keeping.
- Implement a training programme.

Related questions/issues

- Developing an appropriate training programme to support risk and compliance initiatives.

13.3 Must we appoint an insurance distribution officer, and what does this role involve?

This is a mandatory appointment, but only if your firm performs insurance distribution activities.

SRA Scope Rules, rule 5.1 allows firms which are authorised by the SRA, but not also authorised by the FCA, to carry on insurance distribution activities as an ancillary insurance intermediary subject to compliance with the Scope Rules and, where relevant, other parts of the SRA Standards and Regulations, including the SRA Principles, SRA Codes of Conduct, the SRA Accounts Rules and the SRA COB Rules.

SRA Scope Rules, rule 5.2 states:

> 5.2 You must not carry on any insurance distribution activities unless you:
>
> (a) are registered in the Financial Services Register; and
> (b) have appointed an insurance distribution officer who will be responsible for your insurance distribution activities.

In other words, if your firm is carrying on insurance distribution activities, it must appoint an IDO whose details must be registered with the FCA. Notification is effected by way of notification to the SRA on form FA8.

This decision requires an understanding of defined terms as follows.

'Insurance distribution activities' are financial service activities which are carried out in respect of contracts of insurance (e.g. contracts relating to after the event insurance, defective title insurance and similar and in respect of rights and interests in a life policy (both described generically as investments in the rules)), specifically the following activities:

- dealing in the investment as agent;
- arranging (bringing about) deals in investments;
- making arrangements with a view to transactions in investments;
- assisting in the administration and performance of a contract of insurance;
- advising on investments (except peer to peer agreements);
- agreeing to carry on a regulated activity as described in the preceding bullet points.

Common examples of insurance distribution activities include advising on insurance policies designed to deal with defects in title and other property issues; arranging policies for clients; and advising on and arranging after the event insurance.

The meaning of 'ancillary insurance intermediary' for the purposes of rule 5.1 uses the definition of 'IDD ancillary insurance intermediary' contained in the FCA Handbook, and ought not cause a problem to law firms:

> any natural or legal person, other than a credit institution or an investment firm who, for remuneration, takes up or pursues the activity of insurance distribution on an ancillary basis, provided that all the following conditions are met:
>
> (a) the principal professional activity of that natural or legal person is other than insurance distribution;
> (b) the natural or legal person only distributes certain insurance products that are complementary to a good or service; and
> (c) the insurance products concerned do not cover life assurance or liability risks, unless that cover complements the good or service which the intermediary provides as its principal professional activity.

SRA Scope Rules, rule 5.2(b) clarifies that the IDO is responsible for the insurance distribution activities. This responsibility requires a good understanding of the SRA COB Rules which regulate the way in which exempt professional firms (such as your law firm if it is not directly regulated by the FCA) carry on exempt regulated activities so that they are not in breach of FSMA 2000.

Key knowledge includes the following points in the SRA COB Rules:

- rule 2.2 – a prescribed status disclosure statement must be given to clients before you provide an insurance distribution activity
- rule 9.1 – communications must be clear, fair and not misleading;
- rule 10 – general information about your reasons for making a recommendation must be provided to the client;
- rule 11 – you must explain to the client why you are recommending a particular investment;
- rule 12 – you must provide the client with a statement of demands and needs to explain why a particular investment is suitable for them and their specific circumstances;
- rule 13 – any intermediaries which you use must have the correct permissions from the FCA and you are required to check the Financial Services Register for this confirmation;
- rule 14 – you must treat complaints about the provision of exempt regulated activities fairly;
- rule 15 – your remuneration arrangement must not create any obstacles with the duty to act in the client's best interests (in other words, you are discouraged from having any arrangements with the providers of insurance providers that might encourage you to choose them if that is not the most suitable product for your specific client);
- rule 16 – you must provide the client with any information about remuneration (which, for the most part, will be your disclosure about the cost of your legal services);

- rule 17 – any fees that a client might have to pay for the investment product must be disclosed;
- rule 18 – information must be provided on paper or some other durable format (in order to assist with your audit trail needs);
- rule 19 – applies if you are undertaking what is described as cross-selling and offer a non-insurance ancillary product with an insurance product, and includes conditions attached to the whole package;
- rule 20 – you must ensure that the firm and relevant employees have appropriate knowledge to complete tasks 'adequately' and that they are individuals of 'good repute' (e.g. they have a clean criminal record and have not been previously declared bankrupt);
- rule 21 – you must ensure that your client is given objective and relevant information so that they can make informed decisions.

What are the compliance challenges?

- Not identifying that you are undertaking an insurance distribution activity would be problematic. This concerns either a contract of insurance (a long-term insurance contract under which rights are treated as contractually based investments or a general insurance contract such as an after the event insurance policy or a defective title product) or a life policy. In practice, many of these types of investments are provided to clients as a matter of course during a retainer (such as after the event insurance for dispute resolution clients) and the point might be missed.
- Ensure that there are no misunderstandings about the limit of the financial services that be provided without being directly authorised by the FCA. If performance of regulated activities is in breach of FSMA 2000, the individual might be committing a criminal offence and any contract is unlikely to be enforceable. A breach of FSMA 2000 will also have regulatory consequences for the individual and the firm. For example, arranging a standalone insurance product for an individual which is unconnected to any current legal service is a breach of FSMA 2000 and the SRA Scope Rules.
- Misunderstanding the conditions attached to the performance of exempt regulated activities would be problematic; for example, not providing a statement of demands and needs as required by the SRA COB.
- Ensure that you document records and communications appropriately and are able to justify your actions.
- Ensure to note that employee screening (with which you will be familiar for the purposes of compliance with the Money Laundering, Terrorist Financing and Transfer of Funds (Information on the Payer) Regulations 2017, SI 2017/692 (AML Regulations)) is also necessary to satisfy SRA COB Rules, rule 20.

What resources will help?

- SRA materials:
  - SRA Financial Services (Scope) Rules (**www.sra.org.uk/solicitors/standards-regulations/financial-services-scope-rules/**);

- SRA Financial Services (Conduct of Business) Rules (**www.sra.org.uk/solicitors/standards-regulations/financial-services-conduct-business-rules/**);
- SRA guidance: 'Law firms carrying on insurance distribution activities' (updated 25 November 2019, **www.sra.org.uk/solicitors/guidance/law-firms-carrying-insurance-distribution-activities/**);
- SRA guidance: 'Regulated financial services activities' (updated 4 January 2021, **www.sra.org.uk/solicitors/resources/financial-services-rules/regulated-financial-services-activites/**);
- SRA website resources page: 'Financial services' (**www.sra.org.uk/solicitors/resources/financial-services/**).

- Information obtained from the FCA's website (**www.fca.org.uk**).

Compliance tips – how to mitigate the risk of getting it wrong

- This subject is sometimes overlooked in terms of risk management and compliance strategies; consider a compliance project to ascertain which teams might be providing financial services, competency standards and training needs, record-keeping, etc.
- Implement a financial services policy.
- Write an IDO job description and include the role and role-holder in your compliance materials.
- Provide training – tailored to the needs of relevant staff, plus the compliance team and the COLP, and your IDO.
- Create template documentation for information that must be provided to clients when delivering financial services.
- Conduct supervisory oversight and report training needs.
- Monitor the Law Society *Gazette* for cases which highlight misunderstandings about this topic – these cases can be usefully shared to ensure that staff vigilance remains high.

13.4 What financial services training should we provide to colleagues?

There are three points to consider when considering training on this topic:

1. SRA COB Rules, rule 20.1 applies to the performance of insurance distribution exempt regulated activities, and you must ensure that the firm and each relevant employee 'possesses appropriate knowledge and ability'. If you are subject to this rule, this would suggest that it is prudent to assess competence and deliver training.
2. SRA Code of Conduct for Firms, para.4.3 applies the following responsibilities: 'You ensure that your managers and employees are competent to carry out their role, and keep their professional knowledge and skills, as well as understanding of their legal, ethical and regulatory obligations, up to date'. This triggers the need to consider whether training is necessary to ensure individual skills meet the appropriate standards to meet client needs and demonstrate professionalism.

3. SRA Code of Conduct for Solicitors, RELs and RFLs, para.3.2 (repeated at SRA Code of Conduct for Firms, para.4.2, and therefore relevant to everyone in the firm) says that you must 'ensure that the service you provide to clients is competent'.

Training can support competency and professional development. It also supports firms in their firm-wide compliance strategy in that it facilitates learning about key legal and regulatory subjects and also the firm's own requirements.

Decisions about training on specific topics are made on the basis of a combination of factors: your benchmarking exercises and gap analysis work; feedback from individuals perhaps through the appraisal system; supervisory feedback; file reviews; complaints and breach diagnosis; and as a response to changes in law or regulation or service provision.

Having said that, the following are suggestions of possible training topics relevant to all staff with an interest in this area:

- the financial services regulatory regime;
- the relevance of FSMA 2000 to solicitors and law firms;
- what solicitors and law firms can do if they are not directly regulated by the FCA;
- the SRA's role in supervising our exempt regulated activities – the SRA Scope Rules and the SRA COB Rules;
- SRA Scope Rules – basic conditions, prohibited and restricted activities, conditions attached to insurance distribution and credit-regulated activities;
- SRA COB Rules – conditions about how we deal with these activities, with particular emphasis on insurance distribution and credit-related activities;
- the role of the IDO (if relevant);
- the overlap with other parts of the SRA Standards and Regulations;
- your firm's own compliance response.

In addition, it might be appropriate to consider training of the managers, the COLP and the IDO to ensure that their own competencies are appropriate to oversee and implement appropriate risk management strategies.

What are the compliance challenges?

- Ensure that you have proper buy-in to developing skills in this area and have sufficient resources to ensure competency.
- Ensure supervisory oversight of this topic.
- Take steps to counteract a general potential lack of interest in this topic.

What resources will help?

- SRA materials:
  - SRA Financial Services (Scope) Rules (**www.sra.org.uk/solicitors/standards-regulations/financial-services-scope-rules/**);

- SRA Financial Services (Conduct of Business) Rules (**www.sra.org.uk/solicitors/standards-regulations/financial-services-conduct-business-rules/**);
- SRA guidance: 'Law firms carrying on insurance distribution activities' (updated 25 November 2019, **www.sra.org.uk/solicitors/guidance/law-firms-carrying-insurance-distribution-activities/**);
- SRA guidance: 'Regulated financial services activities' (updated 4 January 2021, **www.sra.org.uk/solicitors/resources/financial-services-rules/regulated-financial-services-activites/**);
- SRA website resources page: 'Financial services' (**www.sra.org.uk/solicitors/resources/financial-services/**).

- Information obtained from the FCA's website (**www.fca.org.uk**).

Compliance tips – how to mitigate the risk of getting it wrong

- This subject is sometimes overlooked in terms of risk management and compliance strategies, and as a consequence might be missed when considering training needs – consider adding it to your training programme.
- Implement a financial services policy which includes training commitments.
- Implement a training policy which includes this topic.
- Record and analyse feedback from file reviews, complaint and breach handling that identifies weaknesses that can be improved through training.
- Conduct other supervisory oversight and reporting of training needs.

CHAPTER 14

Modern slavery

14.1 What is the aim and purpose of the Modern Slavery Act 2015?

The Modern Slavery Act 2015 (MSA 2015) seeks to tackle modern slavery by creating criminal offences of:

- slavery, servitude and forced or compulsory labour;
- human trafficking: arranging or facilitating the travel of another person with a view to that person being exploited;
- exploitation: slavery, servitude and forced or compulsory labour, certain sexual offences, removal of organs or tissue, and obtaining services or benefits by threats, force or deception.

These apply whether or not the offences take place in England and Wales.

MSA 2015 seeks to address the role of businesses in preventing modern slavery from occurring in their supply chains and organisations.

MSA 2015 requires businesses in the UK with a total annual turnover of £36 million or more to report annually (by way of statement) on steps taken by the business to ensure that slavery and human trafficking is not taking place in either its business or its supply chains.

What are the compliance challenges?

- All firms that meet the criteria of MSA 2015 need to ensure that they produce a modern slavery statement annually.

What resources will help?

- The Law Society has produced guidance: 'Victims of modern slavery – guidance for solicitors' (30 April 2020, **www.lawsociety.org.uk/en/topics/immigration/victims-of-modern-slavery-guidance-for-solicitors**).

Compliance tips – how to mitigate the risk of getting it wrong

- Firms must understand MSA 2015 and publish an annual statement if the firm meets the turnover criteria.

14.2 Which firms must comply with the annual statement requirement?

The reporting obligation (by way of annual statement) applies to companies, limited liability partnerships (LLPs) and partnerships which:

- carry on a business or part of a business in the UK;
- supply goods or services; and
- have an annual turnover of £36 million or more.

An organisation's turnover for these purposes includes the turnover of that organisation and all of its subsidiaries, whether those are located in or outside the UK.

Each organisation within a group that conducts business in whole or in part in the UK and exceeds the turnover threshold is required to publish a slavery and human trafficking statement. There is the option, however, to take a group approach to this requirement, say where a parent company and its subsidiary are both required to produce a statement, one statement can be published as long as it covers the supply chains of both.

If turnover drops below £36 million, the governmental recommendation is that the organisation should continue to report and publish a statement.

What are the compliance challenges?

- All firms that meet the criteria of MSA 2015 need to ensure they produce a modern slavery statement annually.

What resources will help?

- The Law Society has produced guidance: 'Victims of modern slavery – guidance for solicitors' (30 April 2020, **www.lawsociety.org.uk/en/topics/immigration/victims-of-modern-slavery-guidance-for-solicitors**).

Compliance tips – how to mitigate the risk of getting it wrong

- Firms must understand MSA 2015 and publish an annual statement if the firm meets the turnover criteria.

14.3 Should we have a modern slavery/anti-slavery policy?

Although it is not a requirement of MSA 2015 to have a modern slavery/anti-slavery policy, it is a good way of bringing awareness of the issue internally and also a good way of setting out the firm's stance on slavery practices and a firm's tolerances to such practices. The policy can also be a method of training people on what modern slavery is.

What are the compliance challenges?

- Getting the message across in a law firm can be tricky especially when fee earners are busy and may not consider the subject of slavery to be relevant to their day-to-day work.

What resources will help?

- The Law Society has produced guidance: 'Victims of modern slavery – guidance for solicitors' (30 April 2020, **www.lawsociety.org.uk/en/topics/immigration/victims-of-modern-slavery-guidance-for-solicitors**).

Compliance tips – how to mitigate the risk of getting it wrong

- Implementing a firm-wide anti-slavery policy can be a good way of getting across the message about modern slavery and the firm's stance on it.

14.4 What should be placed in our Modern Slavery Act statement? Who should endorse it/sign it? Where should it be published?

MSA 2015 requires as a minimum for the statement to set out the steps taken by the business in the relevant financial year to ensure that slavery and human trafficking is not taking place in either its business or its supply chains or, if no such steps have been taken in that financial year, to specify that no steps have been taken.

For corporate entities, the statement must be approved by the board and signed by a director. An LLP's statement must be approved by its members and signed by a designated member. A partnership's statement must be signed by a partner.

The statement may also include information about:

- the organisation's structure, business and supply chains;
- relevant policies, including supplier due diligence, auditing and procurement processes;
- training provided to those in supply chain management;
- key risks related to slavery and human trafficking including how those are evaluated and managed;

- relevant key performance indicators to enable readers to assess the effectiveness of the business' anti-slavery activities.

The organisation is not required to guarantee that there is no slavery or human trafficking in the business or its supply chains and businesses are encouraged to take a risk-based approach to their management of the risk of slavery and human trafficking.

The statement must be published following each financial year of the business. Government guidance states that:

- organisations should publish their statements as soon as possible after the end of the financial year and at most, within six months of the organisation's financial year end;
- organisations may wish to publish the statement alongside their annual or non-financial reports;
- it is recommended that historic statements from previous financial years should remain available online even when new statements are published to permit the public to compare statements from different years (alternatively your current statement could set out that prior statements are available on request and to whom such a request can be made).

If the firm has a website, it must publish the statement on that website and include a link to the statement in a prominent place on the homepage. The link should be clearly labelled so that the contents are apparent and so no hiding it behind another area of the firm's website – it needs to be at the front.

If the firm does not have a website, then it must provide a copy of the statement to anyone who requests it in writing, within 30 days of receiving the request.

What are the compliance challenges?

- The Home Office conduct checks to make sure those who should publish a statement have done so. It is essential that firms who are required to, publish a statement each year.

What resources will help?

- The government has published useful guidance: 'Publish an annual modern slavery statement' (Home Office, updated 28 July 2021, **www.gov.uk/guidance/publish-an-annual-modern-slavery-statement**).

Compliance tips – how to mitigate the risk of getting it wrong

- A designated person should be responsible each year for drafting the modern slavery statement and making sure it is appropriately approved internally and published. This person could be the firm's compliance officer for legal practice (COLP) or someone delegated by that person.

14.5 What are the sanctions for non-compliance?

The secretary of state has the power to bring civil proceedings in the High Court for an injunction requiring an organisation to publish a statement. A subsequent failure to comply with any court order would risk being in contempt of court, punishable by an unlimited fine.

Of course, the biggest sanction is reputational damage. Negative attention because a firm does not have a published statement would be severely damaging especially if it matters to the firm's client base due to the type of clients a firm has and work the firm does.

What are the compliance challenges?

- The Home Office conduct checks to make sure those who should publish a statement have done so. It is essential that firms who are required to, publish a statement each year.

What resources will help?

- The government has published useful guidance: 'Publish an annual modern slavery statement' (Home Office, updated 28 July 2021, **www.gov.uk/guidance/publish-an-annual-modern-slavery-statement**).

Compliance tips – how to mitigate the risk of getting it wrong

- A designated person should be responsible each year for drafting the modern slavery statement and making sure it is appropriately approved internally and published. This person could be the firm's COLP or someone delegated by that person.

14.6 How should compliance with MSA 2015 be approached?

Below is a suggested plan of action if tackling MSA 2015 for the first time or refreshing compliance:

1. Analyse supply chains:
   - Ask your finance/accounts team to provide you with a report showing those you have been supplied to by reference to turnover and country.
   - Analyse those results and decide on the basis of turnover and/or country (as per the Global Slavery Index) whether to send the supplier a questionnaire. Suggested questions below.
2. Compose an MSA questionnaire and send this to current suppliers as identified above. See below for possible questions.

3. Analyse the results of the questionnaires. Consider responses to the questions and whether they give rise to a concern of slavery or human trafficking in the supply chain. If they do, consider next steps.
4. Review your policy, or create one.
5. Decide what training will be provided to those who are involved in procurement or other areas of the business where modern slavery is deemed to be a risk.
6. Create an MSA statement (see above).
7. Publish the statement.

Possible questionnaire questions for suppliers:

1. In which industry do you operate?
2. In which countries do you operate?
3. Can you trace every stage of the production process for your goods/services?
4. What is the composition of your work force? e.g. women, migrants, etc.
5. What do you know about how the workers in your supply chain are paid?
6. What do you know about how the workers in your supply chain are recruited?
7. Do you have an anti-slavery and human trafficking policy, and if so what does it say?
8. Who in your organisation is responsible for compliance with MSA 2015?
9. What key performance indicators (KPIs) has your organisation set to track your progress with ensuring there is no slavery or human trafficking in your supply chains?

These questions could also form part of a procurement questionnaire going forward.

What are the compliance challenges?

- Firms need to take steps to ensure that no modern slavery is occurring in their firm or supply chains.

What resources will help?

- MSA 2015 itself is a resource that should be utilised.
- Further, the government has issued guidance: 'Collection: modern slavery' (**www.gov.uk/government/collections/modern-slavery**).
- The Law Society has also produced guidance: 'Victims of modern slavery – guidance for solicitors' (30 April 2020, **www.lawsociety.org.uk/en/topics/immigration/victims-of-modern-slavery-guidance-for-solicitors**).

Compliance tips – how to mitigate the risk of getting it wrong

- Firms should consider conducting the steps above.

- Firms should also consider implementing a procurement process which assesses any modern slavery risk.
- Further, a designated person should be responsible each year for drafting the modern slavery statement and making sure it is appropriately approved internally and published. This person could be the firm's COLP or someone delegated by that person.

CHAPTER 15

Price transparency

15.1 What are the regulatory requirements in respect of price transparency?

The Solicitors Regulation Authority (SRA) Transparency Rules were made by the SRA Board on 30 May 2018.

As set out in the rules, firms need to place in a prominent position on their website price information about the following types of service undertaken:

- For members of the public:
  - residential conveyancing (freehold sale or purchase, leasehold sale or purchase, mortgages and re-mortgages);
  - probate (uncontested cases with all assets in the UK);
  - employment tribunals (claims for unfair or wrongful dismissal);
  - immigration (excluding asylum applications).
- For small businesses:
  - debt recovery (up to £100,000);
  - employment tribunals (defending claims for unfair or wrongful dismissal).

The information you produce and place on your website must include:

- what services are included within the displayed price;
- any services not included in the price that might reasonably be expected to be included;
- typical timescales and key stages for the given legal service (you are not required to provide cost information for each individual stage, just a total cost);
- the experience and qualifications of all individuals who carry out work within the areas specified under the Transparency Rules (think about whether the information already on our website is enough, also consider whether it is appropriate to set out a fee earner's post qualified experience (PQE) as this could lead to discrimination);

- the experience and qualifications of those who supervise the individuals who will be carrying out the work, although you do not need to necessarily specify who supervises whom.

All firms who undertake the work set out above must comply. The SRA check compliance and will take regulatory action for non-compliance.

What are the compliance challenges?

- The SRA Transparency Rules placed a regulatory requirement on firms for the first time to publish price information on their website. Making price information meaningful and yet not a guarantee of the cost of the work undertaken is the key challenge.

What resources will help?

- SRA Transparency Rules (**www.sra.org.uk/solicitors/standards-regulations/transparency-rules/**).
- SRA Codes of Conduct: SRA Code of Conduct for Solicitors, RELs and RFLs (**www.sra.org.uk/solicitors/standards-regulations/code-conduct-solicitors/**); SRA Code of Conduct for Firms (**www.sra.org.uk/solicitors/standards-regulations/code-conduct-firms/**).
- SRA guidance: 'Transparency in price and service' (updated 3 August 2021, **www.sra.org.uk/solicitors/guidance/transparency-in-price-and-service/**).

Compliance tips – how to mitigate the risk of getting it wrong

- The drafting of the information for the website should be undertaken by those who practise in those areas in the firm. The information published should be revisited each year and updated.
- Provide appropriate training.
- Conduct supervisory oversight of price information.

15.2 What complaints information must be on our website?

The SRA Transparency Rules require each firm to publish on its website details of its complaints handling procedure, including details of how and when a complaint can be made to the Legal Ombudsman and the SRA.

What are the compliance challenges?

- Firms may not wish to have this information on the website or at the front – but this is where it needs to be.
- Information might fall off the website.

What resources will help?

- SRA materials:
  - SRA Transparency Rules (**www.sra.org.uk/solicitors/standards-regulations/transparency-rules/**);
  - SRA guidance: 'Transparency in price and service' (updated 3 August 2021, **www.sra.org.uk/solicitors/guidance/transparency-in-price-and-service/**).
- Law Society Practice Note: Price and Service Transparency (11 May 2021, **www.lawsociety.org.uk/topics/price-and-service-transparency/price-and-service-transparency**).

Compliance tips – how to mitigate the risk of getting it wrong

- A designated person in the firm should be responsible for gathering the information required and seeing that it is published alongside the firm's complaints process.
- Ensure regular monitoring of website.

15.3 What else are we required to publish?

The SRA Transparency Rules also require firms to place on their website the firm's SRA number and the SRA's digital badge (also called a clickable logo). Details about how to obtain this digital badge can be found here: 'Clickable logo', **www.sra.org.uk/solicitors/resources/transparency/clickable-logo/**.

The aim of the badge is to show visitors to the firm's website that the firm is verified as being regulated by the SRA and when clicked on it will provide details of the protections that this affords.

What are the compliance challenges?

- These items need to be added to every firm's website. The SRA periodically checks compliance.
- The logo may fall off the website, meaning that the firm is in breach of regulatory requirements.

What resources will help?

- SRA Transparency Rules (**www.sra.org.uk/solicitors/standards-regulations/transparency-rules/**).
- SRA guidance: 'Transparency in price and service' (updated 3 August 2021, **www.sra.org.uk/solicitors/guidance/transparency-in-price-and-service/**).
- SRA resources: 'Clickable logo' (**www.sra.org.uk/solicitors/resources/transparency/clickable-logo/**).

Compliance tips – how to mitigate the risk of getting it wrong

- Navigate to the SRA website outlined above.

- Conduct regular monitoring of the website.
- Ensure that marketing and website staff, and any external consultants who build or maintain the website, are aware of this requirement.

15.4 We have acted on a conveyancing transaction and charged more than the price published on our website – is this a problem?

It depends.

The SRA Transparency Rules apply to residential conveyancing services (freehold sale and purchase, leasehold sale and purchase, mortgages and remortgages) offered to members of the public.

The rules are designed to help consumers make choices about legal representation. The price information you publish will help individuals make informed choices.

If the final fee for the conveyancing transaction is different to that shown on the website, this will need to be justified. It might be the case that the scope of the retainer changed. In these circumstances you are not bound to provide the changed legal services at the originally quoted price, but you will want to show that you complied with SRA Code of Conduct for Solicitors, RELs and RFLs, para.8.7 (referred to in the SRA Code of Conduct for Firms, para.7.1(c)) which is that:

> 8.7 You ensure that clients receive the best possible information about how their matter will be priced and, both at the time of engagement and when appropriate as their matter progresses, about the likely overall cost of the matter and any costs incurred.

So, in other words, it would be wrong to charge more than the price quoted on the website in ordinary circumstances but it is possible to charge differently if the services provided are different to those originally agreed with the client. Evidence of communication of the changes, and the impact on pricing, is essential in such circumstances.

What are the compliance challenges?

- Put in place measures to prevent retainer creepage.
- Avoid ineffective communication with the client about the scope of services.
- Ensure there are no client misunderstandings giving rise to complaints

What resources will help?

- SRA Codes of Conduct: SRA Code of Conduct for Solicitors, RELs and RFLs (**www.sra.org.uk/solicitors/standards-regulations/code-conduct-solicitors/**); SRA Code of Conduct for Firms (**www.sra.org.uk/solicitors/standards-regulations/code-conduct-firms/**).

- SRA Transparency Rules (**www.sra.org.uk/solicitors/standards-regulations/transparency-rules/**).
- SRA guidance: 'Transparency in price and service' (updated 3 August 2021, **www.sra.org.uk/solicitors/guidance/transparency-in-price-and-service/**).

Compliance tips – how to mitigate the risk of getting it wrong

- Provide training of relevant staff on all regulatory requirements.
- Ensure that retainers are scoped properly.
- Put in place onboarding checks to satisfy that there is consistency with published prices.
- Conduct ongoing monitoring of accuracy of pricing information.
- Conduct supervisory oversight.

CHAPTER 16

Conflicts of interest

16.1 How does the SRA define a significant risk for the purposes of the conflict of interest duties?

It doesn't, and this means that you must exercise your judgment when considering whether there is a significant risk of a conflict of interest.

Our duties in respect of conflicts of interest are described in paras.6.1 and 6.2 of each of the Solicitors Regulation Authority (SRA) Codes of Conduct. In para.6.1, you have the prohibition of acting for a client 'if there is an own interest conflict or a significant risk of such a conflict'. In para.6.2, you have the prohibition of acting in a client conflict (subject to exceptions) 'if you have a conflict of interest or a significant risk of such a conflict'.

This wording means that not only do you need to ascertain whether an actual conflict exists, but also whether there is a significant risk that a conflict might arise at some point during instructions.

Previously you have been asked to consider how likely it is that conflict will arise if instructions are accepted. This means that you must consider whether this likelihood is more than fanciful.

What are the compliance challenges?

- Avoid misunderstandings about the depth of analysis which is required.
- Ensure that a lack of experience does not lead to an individual reaching the wrong conclusion about the likelihood of a conflict arising.
- Ensure that there is proper conflict monitoring throughout the retainer; this is not a one-off decision, and all decisions must be kept under review.
- Being unable to justify a decision to act, particularly if the SRA challenges on the grounds that it believes that a significant risk was present.

What resources will help?

- SRA materials:
  - SRA Codes of Conduct: SRA Code of Conduct for Solicitors, RELs and RFLs (**www.sra.org.uk/solicitors/standards-regulations/code-**

conduct-solicitors/); SRA Code of Conduct for Firms (**www.sra.org.uk/solicitors/standards-regulations/code-conduct-firms/**);
- SRA guidance: 'Conflicts of interest' (updated 2 March 2020, **www.sra.org.uk/solicitors/guidance/conflicts-interest/**).

- Law Society Practice Note: Conflict of Interests (18 October 2021, **www.lawsociety.org.uk/en/topics/client-care/conflict-of-interests**).

Compliance tips – how to mitigate the risk of getting it wrong

- Provide appropriate training to all staff on this duty.
- Have a conflicts policy which gives examples of when it is likely that a significant risk might be present.
- Involve the compliance officer for legal practice (COLP) and the risk and compliance team in decision-making.
- Conduct supervisory oversight of conflict analysis and ongoing monitoring.

16.2 How does the SRA define a related matter for the purposes of the conflict of interest duties?

The SRA does not define the phrase 'related matter', but you are asked to consider whether a conflict of interest arises not only in respect of current instructions but also with 'related matters'.

Conflict of interest duties are described in paras.6.1 and 6.2 of the two SRA Codes of Conduct. In para.6.1, you have a duty not to act where there is an 'own interest conflict', of which the defined meaning (in the SRA Glossary) is 'any situation where your duty to act in the best interests of any client in relation to a matter conflicts, or there is a significant risk that it may conflict, with your own interests in relation to that or a related matter'.

In para.6.2, and conflicts of interest (i.e. client conflict), you are asked to use the following definition of 'conflicts of interest' (in the SRA Glossary): 'a situation where your separate duties to act in the best interests of two or more clients in relation to the same or a related matters conflicts'.

It will be obvious as to the application of the definition to the actual instructions but the consideration of related matters will be a more sophisticated judgment call, particularly as the SRA's current wording provides no further help. In these circumstances, it might be sensible to remember help given in previous resources such as guidance to the Solicitors' Code of Conduct 2007, which provided the following suggestions:

- two matters concerning the same asset or liability are related;
- there needs to be a reasonable degree of relationship for a conflict to arise.

What are the compliance challenges?

- Ensure that staff do not misunderstand their professional duty to consider conflicts of interest in this wider context.
- Ensure that conflict searches are sufficient to enable this decision to be made.

What resources will help?

- SRA materials:
  - SRA Codes of Conduct: SRA Code of Conduct for Solicitors, RELs and RFLs (**www.sra.org.uk/solicitors/standards-regulations/code-conduct-solicitors/**); SRA Code of Conduct for Firms (**www.sra.org.uk/solicitors/standards-regulations/code-conduct-firms/**);
  - SRA guidance: 'Conflicts of interest' (updated 2 March 2020, **www.sra.org.uk/solicitors/guidance/conflicts-interest/**).
- Law Society Practice Note: Conflict of Interests (18 October 2021, **www.lawsociety.org.uk/en/topics/client-care/conflict-of-interests**).
- *Compliance and Ethics in Law Firms*, 2nd edn (Tracey Calvert, Law Society Publishing, 2019).

Compliance tips – how to mitigate the risk of getting it wrong

- Provide training to all staff on this duty.
- Have a conflicts policy which explains the firm's view on the interpretation of this wording.
- Implement a conflicts search procedure that will provide this information.
- Involve the COLP and the risk and compliance team in decision-making.
- Conduct supervisory oversight of conflict analysis and ongoing monitoring.

16.3 Can we act for buyer and seller of a property if they instruct different offices of our firm?

Because of the nature of these instructions, it is highly unlikely that a firm can act on both sides of a conveyancing transaction. The fact that both parties have instructed different offices of the firm is not relevant when considering this ethical position. This fact does not alter the analysis. Furthermore, if this suggestion was presented to the clients by the firm as a way in which it would be possible for each side to be represented by the firm, it is unlikely to be considered positively by the SRA.

This scenario requires a consideration of your role to provide legal services in two separate retainers; firstly, instructions to act for a client wishing to sell a property and, secondly and separately, instructions to act for a client wishing to buy the same property.

The decision to act on both sides will depend on the specific circumstances of the two matters, and any firm that routinely acts for the buyer and seller of a property in any circumstances will find it difficult to justify this decision. This is because you must not act for two or more clients (here, the buyer and seller) if there is a conflict of interest or a significant risk of a conflict arising.

This decision is based on an analysis of SRA Code of Conduct for Solicitors, RELs and RFLs, para.6.2 (which is repeated with identical wording in the SRA Code of Conduct for Firms, and therefore applies to everyone in an authorised law firm).

The relevant section of para.6.2 is:

> 6.2 You do not act in relation to a matter or a particular aspect of it if you have a conflict of interest or a significant risk of such a conflict in relation to that matter or aspect of it ...

A conflict of interest means any situation where your separate duties to act in the best interests of two or more clients in relation to the same or a related matters conflict.

If a client conflict, or a significant risk of such a conflict (i.e. the possibility is more than a fanciful concept), exists, then members of the firm must not act for all of the clients unless the matter falls within one of two limited exceptions. These are also described in para.6.2 and known as 'the substantially common interest exception' and the 'competing for the same objective exception'. Neither of these exceptions apply; the buyer and seller of a property have different interests in the transaction and they are not competing against each other.

This means that the decision whether to act for both parties should take the following considerations into account:

- Are the clients' interests different?
- Will the ability to give independent advice to both clients be restricted because we are acting for both of them?
- Is there a need to negotiate, or a significant possibility that we will need to negotiate on behalf of either party?

What are the compliance challenges?

- There are a number of misunderstandings about para.6.2, in particular in connection with property transactions and acting for buyer and seller. These include:
  - misunderstanding the conflict of interest duty and believing that this is altered in circumstances where both sides are established clients – it is not altered;
  - identifying a conflict of interests (such as acting on both sides of a property transaction) and believing that client consent will override compliance with para.6.2 – it will not;
  - misunderstanding a conflict of interests by assuming that it is overridden if lawyers in two branch offices of the same firm act for each party – this does not cure a conflict of interests;
  - believing that an information barrier will resolve the conflict of interests – it will not;

- believing that a conflict of interests will not arise if two different offices of the same firm are instructed.

What resources will help?

- SRA materials:
  - SRA Codes of Conduct: SRA Code of Conduct for Solicitors, RELs and RFLs (**www.sra.org.uk/solicitors/standards-regulations/code-conduct-solicitors/**); SRA Code of Conduct for Firms (**www.sra.org.uk/solicitors/standards-regulations/code-conduct-firms/**);
  - SRA guidance: 'Conflicts of interest' (updated 2 March 2020, **www.sra.org.uk/solicitors/guidance/conflicts-interest/**).
- Law Society Practice Note: Conflict of Interests (18 October 2021, **www.lawsociety.org.uk/en/topics/client-care/conflict-of-interests**).
- *Compliance and Ethics in Law Firms*, 2nd edn (Tracey Calvert, Law Society Publishing, 2019).

Compliance tips – how to mitigate the risk of getting it wrong

- Deal with the firm's expectations in an internal conflicts of interest policy which includes a statement about the firm's expectations when a conflict of interest is identified, whether there is a policy of never acting for buyer and seller, decision-makers whose authority must be sought before the firm acts for buyer and for seller, the means of documenting decisions, etc.
- Insist on rigorous conflict searches as part of the client onboarding process.
- Provide training of fee earners on conflict of interest. For example, the misunderstandings about acting for established clients often originate from knowledge of a set of practice rules which have now been superseded but in respect of which there were specific duties attached to established clients in conveyancing matters. These practice rules no longer apply and all conflict issues must be considered by reference to para.6.2.
- Where a conflict of interest, or a significant risk of such a conflict, is identified, it is possible to represent both parties if a restricted retainer is agreed and so that the firm only acts on those aspects of the transaction where there is no conflict. This is a higher-risk strategy to adopt and you must consider whether it is reasonable, and in each client's best interests, to suggest this, both parties understand the implications of the limitation, and that the considerations and their agreement are adequately documented.

Related questions/issues

- All scenarios where the firm is acting for two or more clients in the same or a related matter must be reviewed against para.6.2 and the duty to act in each client's best interests.

16.4 Can we act for seller and buyer of a property using the 'substantially common interest exception'?

No, this is not a correct application of the substantially common interest exception.

In these circumstances, the firm will be considering instructions to act in two separate matters; firstly, for a client wishing to sell a property and secondly, and separately, for a client wishing to buy a property. The circumstances of this situation do not match the wording of the definition of 'substantially common interest', which is as follows: 'means a situation where there is a clear common purpose between the clients and a strong consensus on how it is to be achieved' (SRA Glossary).

Here, the two clients do not have a common purpose because they are instructing the firm with different objectives in mind; one client wishes to dispose of a property whilst the other client wishes to acquire the property. For this reason, it would be an incorrect to use the exception and act for both clients in reliance of the same.

This means that a decision to act for both clients can only be based on your consideration of the definition of 'conflict of interest' (i.e. 'a situation where your separate duties to act in the best interests of two or more clients in relation to the same or a related matters conflicts' (SRA Glossary)) and your judgment that such a conflict does not exists in the specific circumstances.

What are the compliance challenges?

- Ensure that the substantially common interest exception is not misunderstood and hence applied incorrectly.
- Lack of supervisory or other management oversight of files leading to misuse of the exception being undetected.
- Lack of appropriate conflict searches so that two members of the firm accept instructions.

What resources will help?

- SRA materials:
  - SRA Codes of Conduct: SRA Code of Conduct for Solicitors, RELs and RFLs (**www.sra.org.uk/solicitors/standards-regulations/code-conduct-solicitors/**); SRA Code of Conduct for Firms (**www.sra.org.uk/solicitors/standards-regulations/code-conduct-firms/**);
  - SRA guidance: 'Conflicts of interest' (updated 2 March 2020, **www.sra.org.uk/solicitors/guidance/conflicts-interest/**).
- Law Society Practice Note: Conflict of Interests (18 October 2021, **www.lawsociety.org.uk/en/topics/client-care/conflict-of-interests**).

Compliance tips – how to mitigate the risk of getting it wrong

- Provide training on the conflict duties described in the SRA Codes and the firm's policy on conflicts.
- Implement an internal conflict management policy which explains the procedure for decision-making when a conflict of interest is identified and preferably involves the COLP and/or your risk and compliance team.
- Conduct supervisory oversight.

16.5 Can we act in a contract race using the 'competing for the same objective exception'?

No, this is not a correct application of the competing for the same objective exception.

Acting for two buyers competing in a contract race for a residential property is not the type of objective anticipated. Bear in mind the relevant section of the definition of 'competing for the same objective' that is used with this exception: ' "objective" means an asset, contract or business opportunity which two or more clients are seeking to acquire or recover through a liquidation (or some other form of insolvency process) or by means of an auction or tender process or a bid or offer, but not a public takeover' (SRA Glossary).

Because use of this exception is ruled out, an individual or firm with instructions to act for two prospective buyers of the same property, is faced with the need to consider the definition of 'conflict of interest' (as defined in the SRA Glossary for the purposes of para.6.2 of each of the SRA Codes of Conduct which is a 'situation where your separate duties to act in the best interests of two or more clients in relation to the same or a related matters conflicts') and whether there is such a conflict in these related instructions.

Given that it will not be possible to act in the best interests of both clients in a contract race (because only one of your clients, if either, will be successful in their wish to purchase the property), it seems inevitable that a conflict of interest does arise in these circumstances. This means that it would be hard, if not impossible, to justify acting for more than one client.

What are the compliance challenges?

- Ensure there is no misunderstanding of the use of the competing for the same objective exception.
- Lack of supervisory or management oversight of file meaning that the use of this exception passes unnoticed.
- Lack of appropriate conflict searches so that two members of the firm accept instructions

What resources will help?

- SRA materials:
  - SRA Codes of Conduct, para.6.2: SRA Code of Conduct for Solicitors, RELs and RFLs (**www.sra.org.uk/solicitors/standards-regulations/code-conduct-solicitors/**); SRA Code of Conduct for Firms (**www.sra.org.uk/solicitors/standards-regulations/code-conduct-firms/**);
  - SRA guidance: 'Conflicts of interest' (updated 2 March 2020, **www.sra.org.uk/solicitors/guidance/conflicts-interest/**).
- Law Society Practice Note: Conflict of Interests (18 October 2021, **www.lawsociety.org.uk/en/topics/client-care/conflict-of-interests**).

Compliance tips – how to mitigate the risk of getting it wrong

- Provide training on the conflict duties described in the SRA Codes and the firm's policy on conflicts.
- Implement an internal conflict management policy which explains the procedure for decision-making when a conflict of interest is identified and, preferably, involves your COLP or the firm's risk and compliance team.
- Conduct supervisory oversight.

16.6 Is it a conflict to continue acting for a client after we have discovered that we have made a mistake?

Once a mistake has been identified, your regulatory next step is compliance with SRA Code of Conduct for Solicitors, RELs and RFLs, para.7.11 (repeated in identical terms at SRA Code of Conduct for Firms, para.3.5) which states: 'You are honest and open with clients if things go wrong, and if a client suffers loss or harm as a result you put matters right (if possible) and explain fully and promptly what has happened and the likely impact'.

Compliance with this duty will require an analysis of para.6.1 of each of the SRA Codes of Conflict, which states as follows: 'You do not act if there is an own interest conflict or a significant risk of such a conflict.' In other words, you must evaluate whether the mistake gives rise to a conflict.

What remedial steps are available to the client? If an option is for the client to make a claim for professional negligence, then clearly this gives rise to an own interest conflict, or a significant risk of one, and the client should be advised to take independent legal advice. If other remedial steps are available, then you must consider whether these have an impact on your duty to act in the client's best interests offering impartial advice unfettered by your own position and the mistake that has arisen.

This analysis means that the next steps after a mistake has occurred will reflect your consideration of your professional duties to the client. An incorrect decision, particularly if it results in a breach of the prohibition of acting when an own interest conflict, or a serious risk of the same, has been identified, is likely to create regulatory difficulties for the individual and your firm.

What are the compliance challenges?

- Ensure that your next steps after a mistake demonstrate compliance with the SRA's expectations.
- Mistakes must be brought to the attention of the COLP and compliance officer for finance and administration (COFA) and anyone with responsibilities in connection with the handling of negligence claims.

What resources will help?

- SRA materials:
  - SRA Codes of Conduct: SRA Code of Conduct for Solicitors, RELs and RFLs (**www.sra.org.uk/solicitors/standards-regulations/code-conduct-solicitors/**); SRA Code of Conduct for Firms (**www.sra.org.uk/solicitors/standards-regulations/code-conduct-firms/**);
  - SRA guidance: 'Putting matters right when things go wrong, and own interest conflicts' (25 November 2019, **www.sra.org.uk/solicitors/guidance/putting-matters-right-own-interest-conflicts/**);
  - SRA guidance: 'Conflicts of interest' (updated 2 March 2020, **www.sra.org.uk/solicitors/guidance/conflicts-interest/**).
- Law Society Practice Note: Conflict of Interests (18 October 2021, **www.lawsociety.org.uk/en/topics/client-care/conflict-of-interests**).
- Advice from your professional indemnity insurers.

Compliance tips – how to mitigate the risk of getting it wrong

- Provide training on the SRA expectations as contained in the SRA Codes of Conduct.
- Implement an internal reporting procedure for mistakes and similar.
- Ensure that all colleagues understand your procedural requirements when a mistake is made.
- Create an internal checklist to ensure that client and all other relevant parties are notified of mistake in a timely manner.
- Comply with requirements to record decision-making in writing.
- Conduct supervisory oversight.

16.7 Is it a conflict to act against the interests of a former client?

Not automatically, but this question needs unpicking by answering the following questions:

Does an own interest conflict exist?

Paragraph 6.1 of each of the SRA Codes of Conduct contains a prohibition on acting if an own interest conflict, or a significant risk of one, exists: 'You do not act if there is an own interest conflict or a significant risk of such a conflict'. Does anything about your relationship with the former client, or the services which you provided to them, prevent you from acting in the best interests of your current client?

Do you have a conflict of duties?

Paragraph 6.3 of each of the Codes applies to current and former clients and is your duty of confidentiality: 'You keep the affairs of current and former clients confidential unless disclosure is required or permitted by law or the client consents.' Paragraph 6.4 of each of the Codes applies to current clients and is your duty of disclosure: 'Where you are acting for a client on a matter, you make the client aware of all information material to the matter of which you have knowledge ... '. In acting for your current client, do you have any information gained whilst acting for your former client (and in respect of which your duty of confidentiality applies) which is material to the current client?

Do the current and former clients have adverse interests?

Whilst this does not prevent you from acting, it does create the need to manage the protection of confidential information with an appropriate information barrier and by agreeing with the current client a limited retainer so that you are not required to disclose material information. This is because of the inclusion of para.6.5 in each of the Codes. This paragraph contains the following duties:

> 6.5 You do not act for a client in a matter where that client has an interest adverse to the interest of another current or former client of you or your business or employer, for whom you or your business or employer holds confidential information which is material to that matter, unless:
>
> (a) effective measures have been taken which result in there being no real risk of disclosure of the confidential information; or
>
> (b) the current or former client whose information you or your business or employer holds has given informed consent, given or evidenced in writing, to you acting, including to any measures taken to protect their information.

As part of your analysis, you do not need to consider whether there is a conflict of interest (i.e. a client conflict). This is because para.6.2 of each of the SRA Codes of Conduct deals with conflicts of interest and the definition, and therefore your duties, are applied to current clients only. They do not extend to considering the interests of former clients. For this reason, this duty is not relevant and it is not unprofessional to act against the interests of a former client provided that you are satisfied on the own interest point and you have reconciled the potentially conflicting duties of confidentiality and disclosure, and where appropriate, managed the protection of confidential information appropriately.

Of course, in addition to this ethical starting point, as a firm you will want to consider other issues when deciding whether it is appropriate to act against the interests of a former client, for example:

- the firm might be asked to justify its decision and demonstrate that any confidential information is being protected effectively;
- the firm might in fact have given the former client assurances – by way of a commercial agreement – that it will not accept instructions of this type;
- reputational issues;

- the former client might be disinclined to instruct you in the future thus ending a good solicitor-client relationship.

What are the compliance challenges?

- Take steps to avoid misunderstanding the nature of the residual professional duties owed to former clients.
- Do not make a high-risk decision to act whilst needing to protect confidential information without having proper safeguards in place.
- Do not ask clients for consent to act without understanding the conduct requirements and/or not having appropriate informed consents.
- Do not erect information barriers where this is not appropriate because of your circumstances.

What resources will help?

- SRA materials:
  - SRA Codes of Conduct: SRA Codes of Conduct: SRA Code of Conduct for Solicitors, RELs and RFLs (**www.sra.org.uk/solicitors/standards-regulations/code-conduct-solicitors/**); SRA Code of Conduct for Firms (**www.sra.org.uk/solicitors/standards-regulations/code-conduct-firms/**);
  - SRA guidance: 'Conflicts of interest' (updated 2 March 2020, **www.sra.org.uk/solicitors/guidance/conflicts-interest/**).
- Law Society Practice Note: Conflict of Interests (18 October 2021, **www.lawsociety.org.uk/en/topics/client-care/conflict-of-interests**).
- *Compliance and Ethics in Law Firms*, 2nd edn (Tracey Calvert, Law Society Publishing, 2019).

Compliance tips – how to mitigate the risk of getting it wrong

- Provide training on the conflict of interest and conflict of duties issues.
- Implement an internal conflict management policy which explains the procedure for decision-making when a conflict of interest is identified.
- Have an agreed internal position on acting against the interests of former clients.
- Ensure that your conflict searches will capture these circumstances.
- Create an internal procedure for the use of information barriers.
- Conduct supervisory oversight.

CHAPTER 17

Confidentiality, disclosure and conflict of duties

17.1 What is the proper use of an information barrier, and how do we manage the associated risks?

An information barrier is used to protect confidential information from inadvertent disclosure.

It is commonly used when you, or someone in the firm, have agreed to act in a situation where you have reached agreement with a client not to disclose all material information to the client because that information has been gained whilst acting for another client to whom the duty of confidentiality is owed.

The Solicitors Regulation Authority (SRA) will expect each firm to design appropriate means to ensure that confidential information is not disclosed. The requirement is to comply with the duty at para.6.3 of each of the SRA Codes of Conduct which is that: 'You keep the affairs of current and former clients confidential unless disclosure is required or permitted by law or the client consents'.

An information barrier can also be used to deal with the risks associated with acting in a situation where clients have adverse interests. This is regarded as a higher risk scenario and because of the issues associated with disclosure in these circumstances (which are likely to extend to adverse publicity for the firm and the profession as a whole), the SRA has added a more prescriptive duty at para.6.5 of each of the SRA Codes of Conduct (which means that this duty applies to everyone in the firm):

> 6.5 You do not act for a client in a matter where that client has an interest adverse to the interest of another current or former client of you or your business or employer, for whom you or your business or employer holds confidential information which is material to that matter, unless:
>
> (a) effective measures have been taken which result in there being no real risk of disclosure of the confidential information; or
>
> (b) the current or former client whose information you or your business or employer holds has given informed consent, given or evidenced in writ-

ing, to you acting, including to any measures taken to protect their information.

Unfortunately the phrase 'adverse interests' is not defined, but common sense suggests that this will be arise with matters involving dispute resolution and similar.

The test is high – you will need to show that the information barrier is effective and adequate to protect the client to whom confidentiality is owed, especially if you are relying on para.6.5(a) rather than that client's informed consent as described in para.6.5(b).

If an information barrier is used, the responsibility will rest with you to demonstrate that this is reasonable and that confidential information is effectively protected. Ongoing monitoring of the decision will be expected because this is a high-risk decision which might bring (negative) attention to the firm.

The risks attached to the use of the information barrier cannot be overestimated. Bear in mind the following points:

- a decision to act might be unpopular and attract regulatory scrutiny;
- the former client might seek a legal remedy to prevent you from acting;
- adverse publicity;
- commercial consequences;
- the client for whom you decide to act might decide that you did not in fact act in their best interests and complain;
- you may not be able to show that informed consent was obtained and it was reasonable to act.

What are the compliance challenges?

- The test is high – you will need to show that the information barrier is effective and adequate to protect the client to whom confidentiality is owed, especially if you are relying on para.6.5(a) rather than that client's informed consent as described in para.6.5(b).
- Colleagues might misunderstand the circumstances in which an information barrier is relevant. For example, it is not a device to enable them to act in a conflict of interest scenario. Provide information to prevent such misunderstandings.
- Ensure that the right people are involved in the decision; because this decision alters the firm's risk position, best practice is that it should be made only by senior individuals who are in a position to evaluate not only the regulatory consequences but also such considerations as whether a controversial decision might result in legal action and/or adverse publicity and/or the loss of a client, etc.

What resources will help?

- SRA Codes of Conduct: SRA Codes of Conduct: SRA Code of Conduct for Solicitors, RELs and RFLs (**www.sra.org.uk/solicitors/standards-regulations/code-conduct-solicitors/**); SRA Code of Conduct for Firms (**www.sra.org.uk/solicitors/standards-regulations/code-conduct-firms/**).

- SRA guidance: 'Confidentiality of client information' (updated 5 April 2022, **www.sra.org.uk/solicitors/guidance/confidentiality-client-information/**).

Compliance tips – how to mitigate the risk of getting it wrong

- State the firm's policy on the use of information policies.
- Involve the COLP and/or compliance colleagues in decisions to use information barriers.
- Provide staff training on risks – generally and in respect of specific scenarios.
- Evidence the conditions attached to use of specific information barriers.
- Conduct ongoing monitoring of the appropriateness of the initial decision to use information barriers and whether the compliance solutions are effective in managing risks of inadvertent disclosure of confidential information.
- Seek undertakings from all affected staff that they will comply with the terms of the information barrier.
- Conduct supervisory oversight.
- Conduct IT oversight of security of your information technology solutions.

17.2 When does the duty of confidentiality end?

The duty of confidentiality is described in para.6.3 of each of the SRA Codes of Conduct and applies to everyone: 'You keep the affairs of current and former clients confidential unless disclosure is required or permitted by law or the client consents.'

This duty supports compliance with some of the core values described in the SRA Principles, such as trust and confidence in the profession (Principle 2), integrity (Principle 5) and the duty to act in each client's best interests (Principle 7).

The clue to the duration of the duty is in the wording of para.6.3 and the reference to 'former clients'. This duty continues despite the end of any current instructions and it is misconduct to breach confidentiality duties in respect of the affairs of former clients. Such a breach might also be a data protection issue. The duty extends to the protection of clients' written records as well as non-disclosure by other means. Breaches can occur in a number of ways: through disclosures to other clients, overheard conversations, cyber attacks and the improper storage and then uncontrolled destruction of clients' files.

This means that the duty of confidentiality ends only if the current or former client (or, with regard to a deceased client or deceased former client, if their personal representatives) gives informed consent to disclosure of their affairs or if you are legally obliged or permitted to disclose such information to a third party.

What are the compliance challenges?

- Provide staff with the information to prevent them from misunderstanding their professional duty so that they appreciate that confidentiality continues despite the end of the instructions, the death of the client concerned, or their employment with you.
- Ensure that you have the resources to ensure that client files – both paper and electronically based files – are stored securely and destroyed appropriately.
- Defend against cyber attacks and the stealing of client information.
- Staff lapses which go unreported.

What resources will help?

- SRA Principles (**www.sra.org.uk/solicitors/standards-regulations/principles/**).
- SRA Codes of Conduct: SRA Codes of Conduct: SRA Code of Conduct for Solicitors, RELs and RFLs (**www.sra.org.uk/solicitors/standards-regulations/code-conduct-solicitors/**); SRA Code of Conduct for Firms (**www.sra.org.uk/solicitors/standards-regulations/code-conduct-firms/**).
- SRA guidance: 'Confidentiality of client information' (updated 5 April 2022, **www.sra.org.uk/solicitors/guidance/confidentiality-client-information/**).

Compliance tips – how to mitigate the risk of getting it wrong

- Provide training to all staff on this duty. For example, we have already discussed the merits of training non-qualified staff on SRA regulation and professional ethics; the confidentiality topic is a sensible starting-point.
- Implement a confidentiality policy and similar which explain the importance of this duty and include a reminder about the need to report breaches.
- Include a statement in human resources and similar employment-related policies about the firm's expectations.
- IT – including mobile phones and laptops – should include security applications to safeguard confidential information.
- Implement a storage and retention policy.
- Monitor any third party which assists with storage and destruction services.

17.3 What are the issues if we have sent an email to the wrong recipient?

Aside from the obvious reputational consequences that are connected with such a mistake, the information contained in the email might create regulatory issues if it relates to another client, and also legal issues if there has been a breach of data protection legislation.

This is because of your duty to preserve confidentiality as described in para.6.3 of each of the SRA Codes of Conduct which is as follows: 'You keep the affairs of current and former clients confidential unless disclosure is required or permitted by law or the client consents.' Even the disclosure of a client's name is a breach of this duty.

Your legal duty in connection with data protection is even wider – confidentiality duties apply to your current and former clients. Data protection duties apply to data subjects which extends responsibilities beyond clients and former clients to any living individual whose data is being processed.

For these reasons, it is important that the firm keeps records of compliance (as required in SRA Code of Conduct for Firms, para.2.2). With regard to the misdirection of emails, these records should include entries relating to all the occasions when emails have been sent to the wrong recipient. This should extend to emails which might have been sent to the right recipient but with extra recipients incorrectly added or with incorrect extra information included in the email chain.

Each incorrectly sent or received email should be reviewed to ascertain the seriousness of the mistake. It is necessary to consider what next steps should be taken to mitigate the damage done – this might include making contact with the wrong recipient and asking them to delete the correspondence; contacting the client/data subject whose information has been shared with the wrong recipient; making a report of a serious breach to the SRA; making a report of a data breach to the Information Commissioner's Office (ICO).

What are the compliance challenges?

- Inaccurate records of breaches are problematic; inaccuracy puts the compliance officer for legal practice (COLP) in a position where they do not have accurate information about this type of concern because of under-reporting of this type of mistake.
- Ensure that other managers or employees do not deal with their mistake without notifying the COLP and the risk and compliance team.

What resources will help?

- SRA materials:
  - SRA Principles (**www.sra.org.uk/solicitors/standards-regulations/principles/**);
  - SRA Codes of Conduct: SRA Codes of Conduct: SRA Code of Conduct for Solicitors, RELs and RFLs (**www.sra.org.uk/solicitors/standards-regulations/code-conduct-solicitors/**); SRA Code of Conduct for Firms (**www.sra.org.uk/solicitors/standards-regulations/code-conduct-firms/**);
  - SRA guidance: 'Confidentiality of client information' (updated 5 April 2022, **www.sra.org.uk/solicitors/guidance/confidentiality-client-information/**).
- UK General Data Protection Regulation (GDPR) and other data legislation (**www.ico.org.uk**).

Compliance tips – how to mitigate the risk of getting it wrong

- Provide appropriate training on this subject.
- Have a confidentiality policy, information security policy and data protection resources which describe the firm's expectations about the procedure which will be followed in the event of a breach of this nature.

- Develop a template notification form to capture information about the breach – for example, when did it happen, form of communication; parties involved; information shared, etc.
- Involve the COLP and risk and compliance team in next steps and risk management and mitigation response.
- Deliver messages endorsing openness and accountability values.
- Conduct supervisory oversight.

17.4 What do we need to consider when seeking a client's informed consent to disclosure of their confidential information?

The duty of confidentiality is described in para.6.3 of each of the SRA Codes of Conduct and applies to everyone: 'You keep the affairs of current and former clients confidential unless disclosure is required or permitted by law or the client consents.'

This duty supports compliance with some of the core values described in the SRA Principles, such as trust and confidence in the profession (Principle 2), integrity (Principle 5) and the duty to act in each client's best interests (Principle 7).

Bearing in mind these principles, in particular the duty to act in each client's best interests, there are a number of risks associated with asking your client for consent to disclosure of their confidential information and thereby releasing you from your professional obligation.

The implication is that if the client agrees then they will be giving their informed consent. This sets you a number of challenges and the way in which to obtain informed consent is to be satisfied that you have considered the following points:

- Is it reasonable to ask a current or former client to give permission to the alteration of your duty to them?
- Why are they being asked?
- Do they realise the significance of agreeing, because the decision cannot be reversed after information has been shared with others?
- Are you and the client very clear about exactly what information is being requested and why this is so?

What are the compliance challenges?

- Provide staff with information to prevent them from misunderstanding their professional duty so that they appreciate that confidentiality continues despite the end of the instructions, the death of the client concerned, or their employment with you.

- Ensure that if you obtain client consent verbally, that you also have other evidence to confirm this.
- Ensure that if you obtain consent, that you also have evidence to justify that it was a reasonable request or that the client was not vulnerable, etc.

What resources will help?

- SRA Principles (**www.sra.org.uk/solicitors/standards-regulations/principles/**).
- SRA Codes of Conduct: SRA Codes of Conduct: SRA Code of Conduct for Solicitors, RELs and RFLs (**www.sra.org.uk/solicitors/standards-regulations/code-conduct-solicitors/**); SRA Code of Conduct for Firms (**www.sra.org.uk/solicitors/standards-regulations/code-conduct-firms/**).
- SRA guidance: 'Confidentiality of client information' (updated 5 April 2022, **www.sra.org.uk/solicitors/guidance/confidentiality-client-information/**).

Compliance tips – how to mitigate the risk of getting it wrong

- Provide training to all staff on this duty.
- Implement a confidentiality policy and similar which explain procedural steps which the firm requires if client consent to disclosure is requested.
- Create template documentation to ensure that consent of the client is documented.
- Perhaps enter into a confidentiality agreement with the third party with whom this information will be shared.
- Conduct supervisory oversight.

17.5 What do we need to consider when seeking a client's informed consent to non-disclosure of information material to their retainer?

The duty of disclosure which is owed to each current client of the firm is described in para.6.4 of each of the SRA Codes of Conduct and applies to everyone:

> 6.4 Where you are acting for a client on a matter, you make the client aware of all information material to the matter of which you have knowledge, except when:
>
> (a) the disclosure of the information is prohibited by legal restrictions imposed in the interests of national security or the prevention of crime;
> (b) your client gives informed consent, given or evidenced in writing, to the information not being disclosed to them;
> (c) you have reason to believe that serious physical or mental injury will be caused to your client or another if the information is disclosed; or
> (d) the information is contained in a privileged document that you have knowledge of only because it has been mistakenly disclosed.

This duty supports compliance with some of the core values described in the SRA Principles, such as trust and confidence in the profession (Principle 2), integrity (Principle 5) and the duty to act in each client's best interests (Principle 7).

Bearing in mind these principles, in particular the duty to act in each client's best interests, there are a number of risks associated with asking your client for consent to non-disclosure of material confidential information and thereby releasing you from your professional obligation. This is a particularly risky decision, as you are relying on demonstrating that it was appropriate to apply para.6.4(b) and you will need to show your client's informed consent.

This sets you a number of challenges. In practice, a variation of your duty at para.6.4, and continuing to act, means that you have changed the standard professional position and created a more restricted or limited retainer. This is risky and if you do continue to represent the client, having varied your default position, you will want to be satisfied that this is a justifiable position and that you have considered the following points:

- Is it reasonable to ask the client to give permission to the alteration of your duty to them without being able to disclose what information will be withheld?
- Why are they being asked?
- Do they realise the significance of agreeing, because the decision cannot be reversed after information has been shared with others?
- Are you and they very clear about exactly what information is being withheld and why this is so?
- Have you considered the increased risks of client criticism and complaint and regulatory scrutiny?

What are the compliance challenges?

- Provide information to prevent staff misunderstanding their professional duty so that they appreciate that the client must give express permission to continuing to act.
- If you obtain client consent verbally, make sure you have other evidence to confirm that this is required by para.6.4(d).
- If you obtain consent, make sure you have evidence to justify that it was a reasonable request or that the client was not vulnerable, etc.
- Ensure that you have evidence that the scope of the retainer has been evidenced.
- Ensuring that this non-disclosure scenario does not arise in circumstances where respective clients have adverse interests as described in para.6.5.

What resources will help?

- SRA Principles (**www.sra.org.uk/solicitors/standards-regulations/principles/**)
- SRA Codes of Conduct. SRA Code of Conduct for Solicitors, RELs and RFLs (**www.sra.org.uk/solicitors/standards-regulations/code-conduct-solicitors/**); SRA Code of Conduct for Firms (**www.sra.org.uk/solicitors/standards-regulations/code-conduct-firms/**).

Compliance tips – how to mitigate the risk of getting it wrong

- Provide training to all staff on this duty.
- Implement a confidentiality policy or similar which explains procedural steps which the firm requires if client consent to non-disclosure is requested.
- Create template documentation to ensure consent of the client is documented.

17.6 We are acting on a joint retainer. What is our duty of confidentiality in respect of the clients' affairs?

Your starting point for considering your ethical duties is described at SRA Code of Conduct for Solicitors, RELs and RFLs para.6.3 (repeated at SRA Code of Conduct for Firms para.6.3 and therefore applicable to everyone in the firm): 'You keep the affairs of current and former clients confidential unless disclosure is required or permitted by law or the client consents.'

Information which you receive in the context of a joint retainer (e.g. when acting for two co-owners of a property on a sale, when acting for several family members in a trust or similar matter, shareholders in a corporate matter, etc.) must be available to share with the complete client base. If one client forbids disclosure to the other client, this triggers a need to consider whether you have a conflict of duties (i.e. a conflict between the duty of confidentiality owed to one client but the duty of disclosure of material information owed to another client) and would need to consider whether you could continue to act for both.

All clients must give their informed consent to disclosure of any confidential information to a third party regardless of who might have been the original source of such confidential information.

What are the compliance challenges?

- Remember that this duty applies to all clients who have retained you, even in circumstances where you take your instructions predominantly from one of them only.

What resources will help?

- SRA materials:
  - SRA Principles (**www.sra.org.uk/solicitors/standards-regulations/principles/**);
  - SRA Codes of Conduct: SRA Codes of Conduct: SRA Code of Conduct for Solicitors, RELs and RFLs (**www.sra.org.uk/solicitors/standards-regulations/code-conduct-solicitors/**); SRA Code of Conduct for Firms (**www.sra.org.uk/solicitors/standards-regulations/code-conduct-firms/**);
  - SRA guidance: 'Confidentiality of client information' (updated 5 April 2022, **www.sra.org.uk/solicitors/guidance/confidentiality-client-information/**).

- Law Society Practice Note: Who Owns the File? (9 September 2021, **www.lawsociety.org.uk/en/topics/client-care/who-owns-the-file**).

Compliance tips – how to mitigate the risk of getting it wrong

- Provide appropriate training on this subject.
- Implement a confidentiality policy which includes relevant information about this issue.
- Involve the COLP and/or risk and compliance team if this issue arises.
- Communicate to fee earners/case handlers the requirement to make sufficiently detailed file notes about these types of matters.
- Conduct supervisory oversight.

17.7 Can we disclose a will document to the testator's attorney or another family member?

The testator (i.e. the person who has made the will) is your client and your duties of confidentiality are owed to them during their lifetime. Bear in mind SRA Code of Conduct for Solicitors, RELs and RFLs, para.6.3 (repeated at the same paragraph number in the SRA Code of Conduct for Firms, and therefore relevant to everyone in the firm) which states that: 'You keep the affairs of current and former clients confidential unless disclosure is required or permitted by law or the client consents.'

Where a family member or other associate of the client requests sight of the will – perhaps because they know that they are named as an executor or for another reason – then it is necessary to obtain instructions from the client. SRA Code of Conduct for Solicitors, para.3.1 (repeated in identical form at SRA Code of Conduct for Firms, para.4.1) explains why this is your position:

> You only act for clients on instructions from the client, or from someone properly authorised to provide instructions on their behalf. If you have reason to suspect that the instructions do not represent your client's wishes, you do not act unless you have satisfied yourself that they do. However, in circumstances where you have legal authority to act notwithstanding that it is not possible to obtain or ascertain the instructions of your client, then you are subject to the overriding obligation to protect your client's best interests.

The position might be different in circumstances where a request for disclosure has come from a client's property and financial affairs attorney or in circumstances where a client has lost mental capacity and a deputy has been appointed by the Court of Protection. You are entitled to accept instructions from the attorney or deputy where they have the authority to make such a request on behalf of the client (i.e. where the power is registered or the deputy has been appointed by the court) but it is necessary to remain mindful that a duty of care is owed to the underlying client and you will want to consider whether there is any risk of abuse associated with the request. You will want to have evidence of the appointment rather than rely on what an individual tells you about the circumstances.

For these reasons, it is important to discuss with the client/donor at the time of drafting a lasting power of attorney what their instructions are in respect of the release of their will and other documents and these instructions can be borne in mind when responding to the donee. If this information is not provided, then guidance produced by the Law Society and the SRA is that a full copy of the will can be disclosed to the donee/deputy unless that solicitor has cause for concerns about the individual role-holder and their reason for requesting the document.

What are the compliance challenges?

- Ensure that you understand the legal position – e.g. in respect of the Mental Capacity Act 2005.
- Ensure that fee earners, etc. understanding the need to consider the testator's position.
- Ensure that you have sufficient documentary evidence about the third party.
- Ensure that confidentiality duties are not breached.

What resources will help?

- SRA materials:
  - SRA Codes of Conduct: SRA Code of Conduct for Solicitors, RELs and RFLs (**www.sra.org.uk/solicitors/standards-regulations/code-conduct-solicitors/**); SRA Code of Conduct for Firms (**www.sra.org.uk/solicitors/standards-regulations/code-conduct-firms/**);
  - SRA guidance: 'Access to and disclosure of an incapacitated person's will' (updated 25 November 2019, **www.sra.org.uk/solicitors/guidance/incapacitated-persons/**).
- Law Society materials:
  - Law Society Practice Note: Access and Disclosure of an Incapacitated Person's Will (11 December 2019, **www.lawsociety.org.uk/en/topics/private-client/access-and-disclosure-of-an-incapacitated-persons-will**);
  - Law Society Practice Note: Lasting Powers of Attorney (2 December 2019, **www.lawsociety.org.uk/en/topics/private-client/lasting-powers-of-attorney**).
- Mental Capacity Act 2005 and ancillary guidance.
- Guidance from the Office of the Public Guardian (**www.gov.uk/government/organisations/office-of-the-public-guardian**).

Compliance tips – how to mitigate the risk of getting it wrong

- Provide training on this specific topic.
- Create a procedural checklist to deal with such requests.
- Involve the COLP or risk and compliance team in decision-making.
- Conduct supervisory oversight.

17.8 We have recently hired a solicitor who was acting for our client's opponent whilst employed in their previous law firm. What are the solicitor's and our own ethical duties?

This is a common issue which must always be identified and risk managed in order to avoid a breach of regulatory duties either on the part of the solicitor moving firms or in respect of your own firm's duties to its clients.

The starting point for everyone concerned is the duty of confidentiality which is described in para.6.3 of each of the SRA Codes of Conduct: 'You keep the affairs of current and former clients confidential unless disclosure is required or permitted by law or the client consents.' The duty applies to all former as well as current clients and it is not negated by the fact that an individual moves firms; the duty is portable and is carried forward with the individual.

This duty of confidentiality needs to be reconciled with the duty of disclosure which applies to all current clients of your firm and which is expressed in para.6.4 of each of the SRA Codes of Conduct, where 'you are acting for a client on a matter, you make the client aware of all information material to the matter of which you have knowledge …'

Your challenge, on behalf of your firm, is to ensure that the incoming solicitor does not taint the retainer with their knowledge of the other side's instructions. In practical terms, this will involve the need to isolate the solicitor from the matter in hand by erecting an effective information barrier to protect accidental disclosure of confidential information.

What are the compliance challenges?

- Ensure that you do not misunderstand these duties.
- Ensure that you check with the incoming solicitor whether they have any knowledge of matters.

What resources will help?

- SRA Codes of Conduct: SRA Code of Conduct for Solicitors, RELs and RFLs (**www.sra.org.uk/solicitors/standards-regulations/code-conduct-solicitors/**); SRA Code of Conduct for Firms (**www.sra.org.uk/solicitors/standards-regulations/code-conduct-firms/**).
- SRA guidance: 'Confidentiality of client information' (updated 5 April 2022, **www.sra.org.uk/solicitors/guidance/confidentiality-client-information/**).

Compliance tips – how to mitigate the risk of getting it wrong

- Provide training to all staff on this duty.
- Review an incoming solicitor's portfolio of previous instructions; this should be a relatively straightforward exercise in that your own fee earners will be aware of the solicitors and firms acting on the other side of their matters.

17.9 How does the SRA define 'adverse interests' for the purposes of the conflict of duties and para.6.5 of the SRA Codes?

The SRA does not define this wording, but it is essential that the significance of these words is understood. This is crucial if you are to demonstrate that you are acting correctly in circumstances where a conflict of duties (between the duties of confidentiality and disclosure) is identified.

Paragraph 6.3 of each of the SRA Codes of Conduct describes the duty of confidentiality owed to current and former clients. Paragraph 6.4 of the Codes contains the duty of disclosure of material information owed to current clients.

Paragraph 6.5 of each of the Codes (with slightly different wording) adds to these starting points and describes your further duties where you have identified the existence of each of these duties in the specific circumstances where adversity is present. The SRA Code of Conduct for Solicitors states:

> 6.5 You do not act for a client in a matter where that client has an interest adverse to the interest of another current or former client of you or your business or employer, for whom you or your business or employer holds confidential information which is material to that matter, unless:
>
> (a) effective measures have been taken which result in there being no real risk of disclosure of the confidential information; or
>
> (b) the current or former client whose information you or your business or employer holds has given informed consent, given or evidenced in writing, to you acting, including to any measures taken to protect their information.

An explanation about 'interests adverse' has been provided in earlier regulatory handbooks and in guidance provided by the SRA. It is important to note:

- This requires a consideration of situations where the prospective client has an interest adverse to a current or former client of the firm. This is wider than the duty to consider client conflict of interests which apply only to current clients.
- Whilst adversity is not defined, it has always been the SRA's intention to mirror the common law position. In the Solicitors' Code of Conduct 2007, we were advised:

> Essentially, adversity arises where one party is, or is likely to become, the opposing party on a matter, whether in negotiations or some form of dispute resolution. For example, if your firm acted for a client in a criminal case in which the client was convicted of assault and the client's wife, unaware of the conviction, then wished you to represent her in divorce proceedings you would have to refuse the instructions. The confidential information held about the husband would be material to her case and, if so, her interests would be adverse to his.

What are the compliance challenges?

- Be aware that the conflict between para.6.3 (confidentiality) and para.6.4 (disclosure) arises in circumstances where the respective clients have interests adverse, otherwise the conditions included in para.6.5 in respect of your next steps are not followed.

What resources will help?

- SRA materials:
  - SRA Codes of Conduct: SRA Code of Conduct for Solicitors, RELs and RFLs (**www.sra.org.uk/solicitors/standards-regulations/code-conduct-solicitors/**); SRA Code of Conduct for Firms (**www.sra.org.uk/solicitors/standards-regulations/code-conduct-firms/**);
  - SRA guidance: 'Conflicts of interest' (2 March 2020, **www.sra.org.uk/solicitors/guidance/conflicts-interest/**).
- Case law: *Prince Jeffrey Bolkiah* v. *KPMG* [1998] UKHL 52.
- *Compliance and Ethics in Law Firms*, 2nd edn (Tracey Calvert, Law Society Publishing, 2019).

Compliance tips – how to mitigate the risk of getting it wrong

- Provide training on all the nuances of the confidentiality versus disclosure conflict, including the need to understand and identify adversity.
- Ensure that conflicts checks are suitably thorough to enable a consideration of adversity.
- Include procedures within your confidentiality policy to ensure a consistent approach to para.6.5; maybe this will be a blanket ban on acting when adversity is identified or perhaps it will be a decision which must be made by a head of department, the COLP, or compliance managers.
- Conduct supervisory oversight.

17.10 What policies help us to comply with duties relating to conflicts of interest and conflicts of duties?

There is nothing prescribed in the SRA Standards and Regulations that is an explanation of any mandatory requirements, or best practice suggestions as to how to demonstrate compliance with regulatory duties which arise in connection with conflicts of interest or conflicts of duties.

These regulatory duties are described in section 6 of each of the SRA Codes of Conduct (and as such are relevant to everyone in the law firm) as follows:

- para.6.1 – the duty not to act in circumstances where there is an own interest conflict or a significant risk of this;
- para.6.2 – the duty not to act in circumstances where there is a conflict of interest (i.e. a client conflict of interest) or a significant risk of this except if one of two exceptions can be used;

- para.6.3 – the duty of confidentiality;
- para.6.4 – the duty of disclosure;
- para.6.5 – acting in circumstances where clients have adverse interests.

The SRA is concerned with whether the appropriate objective is met. Its interest in how the objective is achieved is restricted to requirements in terms of compliance and business systems as described in section 2 of the SRA Code of Conduct for Firms and the reference to having 'effective governance structures, arrangements, systems and controls in place' such that these ensure compliance with regulatory and legislative requirements including duties as described in section 6 of both Codes.

A firm with a good compliance culture will see the sense in supporting managers and employees in their understanding of regulatory and professional topics through the development of a series of systems and controls that seek to educate all colleagues and support them in their response. The exact response is a decision based on the circumstances of each firm and the firm's attitude towards risk.

Whatever the firm's starting point, with section 6 duties, it is helpful to share the SRA's requirements and document your position in respect of the following:

- Conflict search requirements – when this will be done, how and where evidence will be retained, next steps in terms of decision-making if conflicts are identified, the format of information which must be given to affected clients.
- Expectations about the recording of own interest decisions and how this supports section 6 compliance.
- Possibly what own interest circumstances must be shared with the managers, COLP or risk and compliance team.
- The firm's expectations if conflicts of interest/significant risk of conflicts of interest are identified; e.g. how these are recorded, who is to be involved in decision-making about next steps, how information will be shared with affected clients.
- The firm's policy on the use of the two exceptions in para.6.2; whether the firm will allow the use of the exceptions; who can make decisions of this type; who needs to be notified internally; what the clients will be told; how evidence of compliance with the conditions will be collected.
- Explanation about the differing type of conflict that arises in connection with confidentiality and disclosure duties (either in a separate internal policy or combined in a policy which also addresses conflicts of interest).
- The extent of the confidentiality duty and the firm's expectations should there be a breach (who should be notified and how).
- The internal procedure and decision-making process should it be necessary to consider circumstances where a legal obligation overrides the duty of confidentiality (ideally this will be a decision made with the knowledge and consent of the COLP and risk and compliance colleagues).
- The internal procedure should it be considered appropriate to ask a client for informed consent for disclosure of confidential information (again, it is pru-

dent that this decision is made with involvement from the COLP and the risk and compliance team).

- A statement about the conflict of duties which arise when confidentiality and disclosure duties cannot be reconciled.
- A process for agreeing and documenting next steps (which again should involve high-level, firm-wide decision-making particularly if information barriers are suggested).
- The internal procedure should it be considered appropriate to seek informed consent to non-disclosure (with the role of the COLP and risk and compliance team explained).
- A statement on the firm's position in circumstances where an adverse interest scenario is detected.
- A reminder about the need for ongoing monitoring of risk decisions made at the beginning of a matter and the steps which must be taken if that initial analysis changes in any way.
- An explanation about the firm's position on commercial issues connected with conflict topics; e.g. whether the firm has made a decision never to act against the interests of particular clients, etc.; specific agreements reached with specific clients, etc.

What are the compliance challenges?

- Whilst it is not a compulsory requirement to roll out a specific internal procedure, it will firstly be difficult to demonstrate the correct response without an appropriate control document but, secondly, it will be necessary to ensure that if the firm has a policy, then this policy is not just a beautifully crafted document but is a working procedure which is appropriate and used by all relevant colleagues. In other words, the SRA will want to be satisfied that the firm has considered how best to express their response to the risk of mismanagement and, if this is with a conflicts policy, that this is both appropriate and applied. A template 'off the shelf' solution is usually not appropriate.
- If you have a policy, do not allow it to gather dust or allow colleagues to act on matters without proper regard for it.
- If you have a policy, ensure that you deliver training on the underlying regulatory and professional duties.
- If you have a policy, ensure that it is adequate and does not jeopardise accreditation scheme membership and similar.

What resources will help?

- SRA materials:
  - SRA Principles (**www.sra.org.uk/solicitors/standards-regulations/principles/**);
  - SRA Codes of Conduct: SRA Code of Conduct for Solicitors, RELs and RFLs (**www.sra.org.uk/solicitors/standards-regulations/code-conduct-solicitors/**); SRA Code of Conduct for Firms (**www.sra.org.uk/solicitors/standards-regulations/code-conduct-firms/**);

  - SRA guidance: 'Conflicts of interest' (2 March 2020, **www.sra.org.uk/solicitors/guidance/conflicts-interest/**).

- Law Society Practice Note: Conflict of Interests (18 October 2021, **www.lawsociety.org.uk/en/topics/client-care/conflict-of-interests**).
- *Compliance and Ethics in Law Firms*, 2nd edn (Tracey Calvert, Law Society Publishing, 2019).

Compliance tips – how to mitigate the risk of getting it wrong

- Obtain agreement by the owners/managers of the firm to the risk decisions that must be made about these topics.
- Provide training on section 6 of the SRA Codes of Conduct.
- Implement a conflicts policy which addresses the regulatory requirements and the firm's response.
- Implement an ancillary (or integral) policy on the noting of personal interests which might trigger conflict issues.
- Create a robust conflict searches procedure.
- Implement a system for the recording of searches and conflict decisions perhaps centrally and on individual files.
- Conduct supervisory oversight.

CHAPTER 18

Acting on a client's matter

18.1 What are the pros and cons of using a limited retainer?

The term 'limited retainer' is used to describe any situation where you restrict your retainer so that the services provided to a client or clients is not what would ordinarily be expected.

Limited retainers can be used to deal with situations such as the following:

- A conflict of interest is identified but clients have a substantially common interest (as described in the Solicitors Regulation Authority (SRA) Codes of Conduct, para.6.2) and a limited retainer is agreed so that the clients do not receive advice on the conflict point but that you continue to act and aim to achieve their overriding common objective.
- You are asked to prepare a legal document for two parties but you are not being asked to give advice about the terms or their respective positions.
- You are unable to fulfil your duty of full disclosure to a client (SRA Codes, para.6.4) and the client agrees to waive their right to this information.
- You are asked to provide an unbundled service to the client so that you are instructed in parts of a transaction.

What are the compliance challenges?

- The client(s) must understand the effect of the limited retainer; i.e. what you will, and just as importantly, will not be doing if you provide legal services.
- You should be able to justify that it is reasonable to suggest this format to the clients. Is a limited retainer being suggested for the benefit of the firm, or can it be shown that it is in each client's best interests to agree to this?
- You should consider the merits of advising each client to take independent advice on limitations.
- What is the position of each client? Any issues connected with vulnerability, imbalance of bargaining position, or other signs of weakness should be taken into account when deciding whether each client would be better protected with a

full-service retainer and therefore continuing to act but with limitations is a high-risk strategy.
- The limited retainer should be evidenced in writing.

What resources will help?

- SRA materials:
  - SRA Principles (**www.sra.org.uk/solicitors/standards-regulations/principles/**);
  - SRA Codes of Conduct: SRA Code of Conduct for Solicitors, RELs and RFLs (**www.sra.org.uk/solicitors/standards-regulations/code-conduct-solicitors/**); SRA Code of Conduct for Firms (**www.sra.org.uk/solicitors/standards-regulations/code-conduct-firms/**);
  - SRA guidance: 'Conflicts of interest' (2 March 2020, **www.sra.org.uk/solicitors/guidance/conflicts-interest/**).
- Law Society Practice Note: Client Information Requirements (8 September 2021, **www.lawsociety.org.uk/en/topics/client-care/client-information-requirements**).

Compliance tips – how to mitigate the risk of getting it wrong

- Provide training on retainer drafting.
- Create a client care statement and conflicts policy which explain the firm's position on use of limited retainer.
- Ensure compliance team involvement in all decisions based on a limitation.
- Conduct supervisory review of whether retainer documents are sufficiently clear as to what services will be provided.

18.2 What are the risks when supporting a client with unbundled legal services and how do we manage them?

Unbundling is becoming more popular and you will want to be satisfied that you have firstly considered whether this is an activity you wish to engage in; and, secondly, that if you do, you have managed the risks associated with the activity.

Unbundling describes the process when the legal activities that would normally be part of your instructions are instead carved out and performed by the client themselves. For example, in family law, it is not uncommon for the client to complete some of the legal paperwork themselves and/or attend court hearings by themselves. Often unbundling is helpful for clients with limited means.

This is not a light touch arrangement insofar as regulation and compliance is concerned, and you will want to ensure appropriate risk management. You will want to be satisfied on the following points:

- Whether it is appropriate to agree to an unbundled service. It might be inappropriate because of, for example, the complexity of the matter, or the vulnerability of the client.

- You have onboarded the client in the same way as any client receiving a full service – conflict checks have been performed, identification requirements satisfied, etc.
- You have managed the client's expectations about what you will, and will not, be doing for them and what they will need to do themselves to protect their position.
- You will need to ensure that costs information is clear, taking into account requirements under the SRA Transparency Rules where relevant.
- You will have responsibilities to ensure that the unbundling does not leave gaps in the legal process and what has to be done to achieve the client's objectives.
- You will need to ensure clients are given a degree of 'hand-holding' in respect of those activities which they will be doing. Do they need to be advised on key dates, etc.?
- You will want to ensure proper file record-keeping so that you have evidence that the client was provided with an adequate service.

What are the compliance challenges?

- Ensure that there is no lack of supporting documentation – client care and terms of business documentation which is appropriately worded – and file-based evidenced of the solicitor–client relationship.
- Ensure that the client's position is protected – if the client's position is not protected, this could lead to complaints of an inadequate service (for the attention of the Legal Ombudsman) or misconduct (for the SRA's attention).
- Ensure that unbundled services are not being provided without the knowledge of your indemnity insurer, as this could create difficulties with their coverage of any claims.

What resources will help?

- SRA materials:
  - SRA Principles (**www.sra.org.uk/solicitors/standards-regulations/principles/**);
  - SRA Codes of Conduct: SRA Code of Conduct for Solicitors, RELs and RFLs (**www.sra.org.uk/solicitors/standards-regulations/code-conduct-solicitors/**); SRA Code of Conduct for Firms (**www.sra.org.uk/solicitors/standards-regulations/code-conduct-firms/**);
  - SRA Transparency Rules (**www.sra.org.uk/solicitors/standards-regulations/transparency-rules/**);
  - SRA risk report: 'Providing services to people who are vulnerable' (15 March 2016, **www.sra.org.uk/sra/research-publications/vulnerable-people/**).
- Law Society Practice Note: Unbundling Civil Legal Services (13 April 2022, **www.lawsociety.org.uk/en/topics/civil-litigation/unbundling-civil-legal-services**).

Compliance tips – how to mitigate the risk of getting it wrong

- Agree a firm-wide policy on providing unbundled services which is communicated to relevant staff.
- Develop a selection procedure to decide whether use of unbundled services is appropriate in specific circumstances.
- Create template documentation to deal with retainer and other information.
- Conduct supervisory oversight to check that files are appropriately maintained.

18.3 Is it unethical to contact another lawyer's client directly?

Usually yes.

Your default position is that it is unprofessional to contact another party to a matter if you know that they are represented by a lawyer (e.g. by a solicitor, an authorised law firm, by a licensed conveyancer or similar). Not only will this be viewed as a discourtesy, there is a risk that you might be accused of taking unfair advantage of the other party and be in breach of SRA Code of Conduct for Solicitors, RELs and RFLs, para.1.2 (repeated in identical form in the SRA Code of Conduct for Firms) which is the duty that: 'You do not abuse your position by taking unfair advantage of clients or others.'

However, it is not necessarily unprofessional to contact a person/entity on the other side of a matter in the following circumstances:

- to establish whether they have legal representation and to ask, if this is the case, that your letter is forwarded to their lawyer;
- if you consider that the other lawyer is not taking instructions from their client and/or failing to share your correspondence with their client (having given the lawyer advance warning of your intention to contact their client and the reason why you consider this to be a necessary step to protect your own client's best interests).

Also, it is not necessarily unprofessional to suggest that your client speaks directly with the other lawyer's client and this might be a pragmatic way to resolve any stalemate situation.

What are the compliance challenges?

- Be alive to the potential for misunderstandings about relationships with other lawyers.
- Be alert to the potential for being put under pressure by a client to breach your professional duties by contacting the other side.
- It may be difficult to have sufficient evidence to justify such an approach.

What resources will help?

- SRA Codes of Conduct: SRA Code of Conduct for Solicitors, RELs and RFLs (**www.sra.org.uk/solicitors/standards-regulations/code-conduct-solicitors/**); SRA Code of Conduct for Firms (**www.sra.org.uk/solicitors/standards-regulations/code-conduct-firms/**).

Compliance tips – how to mitigate the risk of getting it wrong

- Provide training on professional duties and relationships with the other party and their lawyers.
- When considering this because of lack of communication with the other side's lawyer, involve the compliance officer for legal practice (COLP) and risk and compliance team in your next steps to ensure that these are justified and that there is sufficient evidence to support your decision.
- Conduct supervisory oversight.

18.4 We are acting for a client and the other side is unrepresented. Do we have a duty to help the other side?

No, however the fact that the other side is unrepresented is a significant factor in how you provide legal services to your client and this fact triggers the need for risk management on the part of you and your firm.

SRA Principle 2 is relevant: 'You act in a way that upholds public trust and confidence in the solicitors' profession and in legal services provided by authorised persons'; as are SRA Principle 5 'You act with integrity' and Principle 7's duty that 'You act in the best interests of each client'.

SRA Code of Conduct for Solicitors, RELs and RFLs, para.1.2 (which is repeated at SRA Code of Conduct for Firms, para.1.2) is also relevant: 'You do not abuse your position by taking unfair advantage of clients or others.'

These principles mean that nothing about the fact that the other side is unrepresented should enable you or your client to have an unfair advantage. This would be damaging to the individual fee earner's and the firm's reputations and would be evidence that integrity (doing the right thing) has not been demonstrated. In addition, and whilst your client might wish you to take advantage of the imbalance of legal support, this is not ultimately in their best interests and it would be unethical for you to act in a way that exploits this dynamic. It would be prudent to make these points clearly to your client with, if necessary, a reminder to them that you cannot be in breach of your personal professional duties even if this is, in effect, their instructions to you.

It is also prudent – not only in the interest of trust and confidence values but also for your client's best interests – that it is made clear to the other side that you do not represent their interests and that they are advised to take independent legal advice.

What are the compliance challenges?

- Be aware of the potential for pressure from the client to take advantage of this situation.
- Be aware of the potential for pressures from the other side to give them legal advice.
- Be clear about the role of legal representation.
- Be aware that you would not be acting in your client's best interests by negotiating onerous or similar terms without suggesting that the other side takes legal advice.

What resources will help?

- SRA Principles (**www.sra.org.uk/solicitors/standards-regulations/principles/**).
- SRA Code of Conduct for Solicitors, RELs and RFLs (**www.sra.org.uk/solicitors/standards-regulations/code-conduct-solicitors/**); SRA Code of Conduct for Firms (**www.sra.org.uk/solicitors/standards-regulations/code-conduct-firms/**).
- SRA Guidance – 'Public trust and confidence' (25 November 2019, **www.sra.org.uk/solicitors/guidance/public-trust-confidence/**).

Compliance tips – how to mitigate the risk of getting it wrong

- Provide training.
- Create a template wording to address the risks that either the client or the other side misunderstand your role.
- Pay careful attention to the file notes and other evidence that should be added to the file to demonstrate compliance with your personal ethical duties.
- Conduct supervisory oversight.

18.5 We are an authorised law firm. The solicitor on the other side of a matter describes themselves as a freelancer. Should we deal with them in the same way as we would with a recognised sole practitioner or a solicitor employed in private practice?

Subject to your due diligence (which you are advised to undertake in respect of all lawyers), then there is no reason not to correspond with a freelance solicitor and, in fact, it may be deemed unprofessional not to correspond with them.

However, it is important to reflect on the restrictions of freelance practice – for example, freelancers cannot hold client money except money on account of their costs and they can only provide reserved legal activities in specific circumstances. Do these restrictions create any obstacles in connection with your client's matter?

Remember that you are required to comply with the SRA Principles and you have a duty to 'act in the best interests of each client' (Principle 7). You would be expected to reflect on whether this overarching duty can be reconciled with the specific circumstances and, if appropriate, it might be necessary to have conversations about restrictions and conditions of practice with the freelancer and with your client.

What are the compliance challenges?

- Ensure that you do not fail to treat the freelancer in an appropriately courteous manner because of confusion about their status and your professional duties.
- Equally, ensure that you consider the circumstances of the freelancer's practice, and the interests of your client, in an appropriate way.

What resources will help?

- SRA materials:
  - SRA Principles (**www.sra.org.uk/solicitors/standards-regulations/principles/**);
  - SRA Code of Conduct for Solicitors, RELs and RFLs (**www.sra.org.uk/solicitors/standards-regulations/code-conduct-solicitors/**);
  - SRA Accounts Rules (**www.sra.org.uk/solicitors/standards-regulations/accounts-rules/**);
  - SRA Authorisation of Individuals Regulations (**www.sra.org.uk/solicitors/standards-regulations/authorisation-individuals-regulations/**);
  - SRA guidance: 'Preparing to become a sole practitioner or an SRA-regulated freelance solicitor' (updated 25 November 2019, **www.sra.org.uk/solicitors/guidance/preparing-sole-practitioner-regulated-independent-solicitor/**).
- Law Society Practice Note: Freelance Solicitors (13 July 2021, **www.lawsociety.org.uk/en/topics/regulation/freelance-solicitors**).

Compliance tips – how to mitigate the risk of getting it wrong

- Always undertake appropriate checks on lawyers acting for other parties to understand their regulated status.
- Ensure that the COLP and compliance team can assist with decisions that might need to be made about specific issues that arise, e.g. in terms of reliance on financial undertakings, client money issues more generally, etc.
- Raise awareness of this newer type of practice with colleagues and be clear about your risk and compliance expectations.

18.6 The solicitor on the other side of a matter works in an unauthorised business. Can we correspond with them?

In-house solicitors (i.e. solicitors employed in non SRA-authorised law firms or otherwise working as a solicitor in unauthorised employment) are able to provide legal services to their employer and, subject to certain restrictions, also members of the public. They are subject to the relevant sections of the SRA Standards and Regulations which include:

- SRA Principles;
- SRA Code of Conduct for Solicitors, RELs and RFLs;
- SRA Authorisation of Individuals Regulations.

You may need to correspond with an in-house solicitor when providing services to your clients. This is permitted and, in fact, it would be unprofessional not to do so, but bear in mind the following points:

- generally, in-house solicitors are not allowed to operate a client account;
- an in-house solicitor can give an undertaking and will be bound to honour it, but it does not bind their employer.

What are the compliance challenges?

- Ensure that you don't misunderstand the position of an in-house solicitor and breach duties to your client and/or to another member of the profession.

What resources will help?

- SRA materials:
  - SRA Principles (**www.sra.org.uk/solicitors/standards-regulations/principles/**);
  - SRA Code of Conduct for Solicitors, RELs and RFLs (**www.sra.org.uk/solicitors/standards-regulations/code-conduct-solicitors/**);
  - SRA Authorisation of Individuals Regulations (**www.sra.org.uk/solicitors/standards-regulations/authorisation-individuals-regulations/**);
  - SRA guidance: 'Unregulated organisations for employers of SRA regulated lawyers' (updated 25 November 2019, **www.sra.org.uk/solicitors/guidance/unregulated-organisations-employers-sra-regulated-lawyers/**);
  - SRA guidance: 'Not for profit sector: summary' (updated 25 November 2019, **www.sra.org.uk/solicitors/guidance/not-for-profit-sector---summary/**);
  - SRA case study: 'Complaints about solicitors working outside SRA-regulated firms' (25 November 2019, **www.sra.org.uk/solicitors/guidance/complaints-solicitors-working-outside-sra-regulated-firms/**).
- Law Society Practice Note: Solicitors Offering Legal Services to the Public from Unregulated Entities (13 July 2021, **www.lawsociety.org.uk/en/topics/business-management/solicitors-offering-legal-services-to-the-public-from-unregulated-entities**).

Compliance tips – how to mitigate the risk of getting it wrong

- Ensure that relevant colleagues have necessary information about this style of practice.
- Ensure that the COLP and compliance team can assist with decisions that might need to be made about specific issues that arise, e.g. in terms of reliance on financial undertakings, client money issues more generally, etc.
- Conduct supervisory oversight.

Related questions/issues

- Can an in-house solicitor hold client money?

18.7 Our client has misled the court – what must we do?

This situation creates an ethical conflict between your duties to the court and duties to your client.

Your duties to the court take precedence.

This is because SRA Principle 1 states that we have a duty to act 'in a way that upholds the constitutional principle of the rule of law, and the proper administration of justice', and this is a public interest duty. This means that if we know that our client has misled the court, our duty to the court and to the rule of law will take precedence over the individual client's interests.

To continue to act in circumstances where the client has misled the court will place you in breach of SRA Code of Conduct for Solicitors, RELs and RFLs, para.1.4 or the identical para.1.4 of the SRA Code of Conduct for Firms which states: 'You do not mislead or attempt to mislead your clients, the court or others, either by your own acts or omissions or allowing or being complicit in the acts or omissions of others (including your client).'

Notwithstanding that the client is misleading the court, the client is still owed a duty of confidentiality from you, and therefore the practical steps to resolve the ethical conflict would be:

1. Discuss the issue with your client and ask them to correct their misleading behaviour.
2. If they refuse to do this, then remove yourself from the record and terminate your instructions. It would be improper to continue to act in circumstances where the client's behaviour is placing you in breach of SRA Principle 1 and SRA Codes, para.1.4.
3. If your retainer is terminated, you will no longer have a duty to the court in the matter and you will be able to maintain your duty of confidentiality to the now former client.

What are the compliance challenges?

- Be alive to potential misunderstandings about your priorities about ethical behaviours and potential assumption that your duties to the client are more important than duties to the court and in respect of the rule of law.
- Be aware of the potential for client pressures or commercial pressures triggering unethical behaviour.

What resources will help?

- SRA Principles (**www.sra.org.uk/solicitors/standards-regulations/principles/**).
- SRA Codes of Conduct: SRA Code of Conduct for Solicitors, RELs and RFLs (**www.sra.org.uk/solicitors/standards-regulations/code-conduct-solicitors/**); SRA Code of Conduct for Firms (**www.sra.org.uk/solicitors/standards-regulations/code-conduct-firms/**).
- SRA topic guide: 'A guide to the application of Principle 1' (updated 25 November 2019, **www.sra.org.uk/sra/corporate-strategy/sra-enforcement-strategy/enforcement-practice/guide-application-principle-1/**).
- SRA risk report: 'Balancing duties in litigation' (27 November 2018, **www.sra.org.uk/sra/research-publications/balancing-duties-litigation/**).
- SRA guidance: 'Conduct in disputes' (4 March 2022, **www.sra.org.uk/solicitors/guidance/conduct-disputes/**).

Compliance tips – how to mitigate the risk of getting it wrong

- Deliver the right communication strategy about adherence to professional duties to colleagues by the owners and managers.
- Conduct effective supervision of colleagues involved in litigation.
- Provide training on ethical duties.
- Give clarity about the firm's support of ethical behaviour and support available to fee earners facing these dilemmas.

CHAPTER 19

Client care

19.1 What are the dos and don'ts of contacting prospective clients?

This is a discussion about publicity and the types of publicity which are sanctioned by the Solicitors Regulation Authority (SRA).

As your starting point, there are legal considerations which must be taken into account when advertising to the public, and the SRA might consider disciplinary action if an individual or a firm is found to be in breach of a legal duty – see SRA Code of Conduct for Firms, para.4.3: 'You ensure that your managers and employees are competent to carry out their role, and keep their professional knowledge and skills, as well as understanding of their legal, ethical and regulatory obligations, up to date.'

You will want to be satisfied that the firm, and relevant employees (which would include anyone involved in marketing and promotional activities) has identified and understood the relevant legislation.

However, legislation sets the minimum standards of behaviour only, and you will also be expected to comply with higher regulatory standards as specifically described in the SRA Principles and SRA Codes of Conduct:

- SRA Principle 2 – trust and confidence;
- SRA Principle 4 – honesty;
- SRA Principle 5 – integrity;
- SRA Code of Conduct for Solicitors, RELs and RFLs, para.8.9 (repeated at SRA Code of Conduct for Firms, para.7.1(c) and therefore relevant to all people who own or are otherwise employed in the firm): 'You do not make unsolicited approaches to members of the public, with the exception of current or former clients, in order to advertise legal services provided by you, or your business or employer.'

It is 'unsolicited approaches' which are prohibited by the SRA.

The SRA has chosen not to define this phrase in the SRA Glossary, but in previous versions of regulatory duties, and in current guidance, we have been given guidance as to what is meant and the prohibition is designed to forbid cold-calling or any other type of direct or specifically targeted approach to members of the public in person, by phone, or other form of individual and targeted approach.

Examples of publicity which is *unlikely* to be regarded as an unsolicited approach include:

- television, radio or print media adverts;
- billboard advertising;
- online or social media advertising;
- sending leaflets to postal addresses in circumstances where this is not targeted to a specifically identified audience.

Examples of publicity which is *likely* to be regarded as an unsolicited approach include:

- telephone calls;
- sending a leaflet, a letter or an email to an individual who has been identified as a prospective client and deliberately targeted as a consequence;
- approaching people in the street, at hospitals, in police stations and similar and inviting them to instruct you or the firm.

What are the compliance challenges?

- Do not turn a blind eye to third parties who are conducting publicity on behalf of the firm which amount to unsolicited approaches on your behalf. The SRA would regard the third party's improper means of contact as a breach by you.
- Ensure that you check how clients have been contacted.
- Ensure that you understand the breadth of the prohibition, which now extends to written contact as well as face-to-face and telephone contact.

What resources will help?

- SRA materials:
  - SRA Codes of Conduct: SRA Code of Conduct for Solicitors, RELs and RFLs (**www.sra.org.uk/solicitors/standards-regulations/code-conduct-solicitors/**); SRA Code of Conduct for Firms (**www.sra.org.uk/solicitors/standards-regulations/code-conduct-firms/**);
  - SRA guidance: 'Unsolicited approaches (advertising) to members of the public' (16 December 2019, **www.sra.org.uk/solicitors/guidance/unsolicited-approaches-advertising/**);
  - SRA guidance: 'Offering inducements to potential clients or clients' (updated 25 November 2019, **www.sra.org.uk/solicitors/guidance/offering-inducements-potential-clients-clients/**);
  - SRA guidance: 'Q&As on the ban of personal injury referral fees' (updated 3 December 2019, **www.sra.org.uk/solicitors/guidance/ban-personal-injury-referral-fees/**).
- Law Society Practice Note: Information on Letterheads, Emails and Websites (26 January 2021, **www.lawsociety.org.uk/en/topics/client-care/information-on-letterheads-emails-and-websites**).

Compliance tips – how to mitigate the risk of getting it wrong

- Provide training (including anyone involved in marketing employed by the firm).
- Conduct thorough vetting of third parties, including those organisations with whom you have referral arrangements.
- Make spot checks of clients to ascertain how they found out about your firm.
- Conduct supervisory oversight.

19.2 What should we tell clients about equality?

Clients of the firm are protected from mistreatment through your need to comply with the following professional duties:

- SRA Principle 2: 'You act in a way that upholds public trust and confidence in the solicitors' profession and in legal services provided by authorised persons.'
- SRA Principle 6: 'You act in a way that encourages equality, diversity and inclusion.'
- SRA Codes of Conduct, para.1.1 of each Code: 'You do not unfairly discriminate by allowing your personal views to affect your professional relationships and the way in which you provide your services.'
- SRA Codes of Conduct, para.1.2 of each Code: 'You do not abuse your position by taking unfair advantage of clients or others.'

The values of equality, diversity and inclusivity can be demonstrated through your focus on appropriate client communication, which takes into account the needs and attributes of individual clients (as expressed in para.3.4 of the SRA Code of Conduct for Solicitors, RELs and RFLs and para.4.2 of the SRA Code of Conduct for Firms). The client's attributes will include any vulnerabilities which they display. You will also be expected to ensure that any decision not to accept instructions is not based on discriminatory grounds.

It is important that clients understand that they can raise a complaint with you if they feel that they have been treated unfairly. How this information is delivered to the client is not prescribed and will be a matter to be decided by you.

Firms will often include a statement about their equality values on the website and/or in the terms of business, together with their complaints procedure (noting that the latter must be included on the firm's website in order to comply with the SRA Transparency Rules). Many firms add an equality policy to these materials or otherwise make it clear that this is available on request. Having said that, it is not mandatory to have a documented policy, although this is surely best practice and will support compliance with the standards described earlier in this section, and also SRA Code of Conduct for Solicitors, RELs and RFLs, para.8.5 (repeated in the SRA Code of Conduct for Firms) which is the duty that: 'You ensure that complaints are dealt with promptly, fairly, and free of charge.'

What are the compliance challenges?

- Handling these complaints improperly, or not all, could mean facing legal and regulatory repercussions as a consequence.
- Ensure that complaints are brought to the attention of the compliance officer for legal practice (COLP), anyone with responsibilities for complaints handling, or the risk and compliance team.
- Do not 'make the issue go away' through improper means such as the improper use of a non-disclosure agreement.

What resources will help?

- SRA Principles (**www.sra.org.uk/solicitors/standards-regulations/principles/**).
- SRA Codes of Conduct: SRA Code of Conduct for Solicitors, RELs and RFLs (**www.sra.org.uk/solicitors/standards-regulations/code-conduct-solicitors/**); SRA Code of Conduct for Firms (**www.sra.org.uk/solicitors/standards-regulations/code-conduct-firms/**).
- SRA Transparency Rules (**www.sra.org.uk/solicitors/standards-regulations/transparency-rules/**).
- SRA guidance: 'Reporting and notification obligations' (25 November 2019, **www.sra.org.uk/solicitors/guidance/reporting-notification-obligations/**).
- SRA guidance: 'The SRA's approach to equality, diversity and inclusion' (updated 25 November 2019, **www.sra.org.uk/solicitors/guidance/sra-approach-equality-diversity-inclusion/**).
- SRA report: 'Providing services to people who are vulnerable' (15 March 2016, **www.sra.org.uk/sra/research-publications/vulnerable-people/**).
- SRA guidance: 'Client care letters' (updated 25 November 2019, **www.sra.org.uk/solicitors/guidance/client-care-letters/**).
- SRA case study: 'Sexual harassment' (23 July 2019, **www.sra.org.uk/solicitors/guidance/sexual-harassment/**).
- SRA collection of guidance and resources: 'Sexual harassment and the law' (**www.sra.org.uk/solicitors/resources/diversity-toolkit/sexual-harassment/**).
- SRA warning notice: 'Use of non disclosure agreements (NDAs)' (updated 12 November 2020, **www.sra.org.uk/solicitors/guidance/non-disclosure-agreements-ndas/**).
- SRA collection of resources: 'Encouraging equality, diversity and inclusion' (**www.sra.org.uk/solicitors/resources/diversity-toolkit/**).

Compliance tips – how to mitigate the risk of getting it wrong

- Provide training on legislation, regulation and the firm's systems and controls.
- Implement an equality policy.
- Make reference to your equality policy in your terms of business, website, etc.
- Implement a complaints procedure which can be used for dealing with equality issues.
- Conduct supervisory oversight of this topic – are we treating our clients fairly?

19.3 Do we need to send client care/terms of engagement literature when acting on repeat instructions for a regular client?

It is not necessary to send client care letters at all, let alone to established clients for whom the firm does regular work of a repetitive nature (e.g. debt collection work for a corporate client and similar).

However, in any circumstances where new instructions do not trigger a client care letter as part of the file opening procedure, there is a risk that there will be an inadvertent breach of client care and service standard regulatory duties. In addition lack of documentary evidence about coverage of these topics is likely to compromise the firm's position should there be a regulatory or service-type complaint under consideration by either the SRA or the Legal Ombudsman.

The client care and service information which must be considered is described in full in SRA Code of Conduct for Solicitors, sections 3 and 8 and repeated in the SRA Code of Conduct for Firms (so applies to everyone in the firm):

- para.3.1: the duty to act on instructions either directly from the client or otherwise from someone properly authorised to provide instructions on their behalf;
- para.3.4: the need to consider and take account of your client's attributes, needs and circumstances;
- para.8.3: clients are informed in writing at the time of engagement about their right to complain; your complaints procedure; information about the Legal Ombudsman;
- para.8.6: you ensure that clients are in a position to make informed decisions about the services which they need, how their matter will be handled, and the options available to them;
- para.8.7: you ensure clients receive the best possible information about how their matter will be priced, and about the likely overall cost of the matter and any costs incurred.

What are the compliance challenges?

- Be aware of the risk of compliance fatigue or complacency caused by overfamiliarity with a particular client.
- Be aware of the potential for providing services to a regular client but where these are not of a repetitive nature and therefore the service standards/client care expectations are different.
- Be aware of situations where services are being provided by a different individual, or an individual whose hourly rate has increased, so that the agreement on which the client is relying is no longer appropriate.
- In particular, ensure that you are managing costs issues so that financial issues (your fees, any annual increase in your fees, the disbursements, liability to other parties, etc.) are not a surprise.

- Ensure that – in respect of clients and services to which the SRA Transparency Rules apply or you otherwise publish client care/costs information on your website – information provided to such clients is consistent with this publicity.

What resources will help?

- SRA materials:
  - SRA Principles (**www.sra.org.uk/solicitors/standards-regulations/principles/**);
  - SRA Codes of Conduct: SRA Code of Conduct for Solicitors, RELs and RFLs (**www.sra.org.uk/solicitors/standards-regulations/code-conduct-solicitors/**); SRA Code of Conduct for Firms (**www.sra.org.uk/solicitors/standards-regulations/code-conduct-firms/**);
  - SRA Transparency Rules (**www.sra.org.uk/solicitors/standards-regulations/transparency-rules/**);
  - SRA guidance: 'Transparency in price and service' (updated 3 August 2021, **www.sra.org.uk/solicitors/guidance/transparency-in-price-and-service/**);
  - SRA guidance: 'Client care letters' (updated 25 November 2019, **www.sra.org.uk/solicitors/guidance/client-care-letters/**);
  - SRA risk report: 'Maintaining standards of service and reducing complaints' (1 July 2019, **www.sra.org.uk/sra/research-publications/maintaining-standards-service-reducing-complaints/**).
- Law Society Practice Note: Client Information Requirements (8 September 2021, **www.lawsociety.org.uk/en/topics/client-care/client-information-requirements**).

Compliance tips – how to mitigate the risk of getting it wrong

- Maintain centralised risk management of relationships with longstanding clients.
- Where relevant, obtain written agreement to provide repetitive work for a fixed period of time and in agreed conditions.
- Establish an onboarding process for each new matter for longstanding clients and/or where subject to a written agreement for services to include reference to terms which have previously been agreed.
- With longstanding relationships and written agreements, establish a review cycle to ensure that (at least annually) terms are reviewed and, if necessary updated.

19.4 Do we need to include a detailed description of the legal services we are providing in our client care letter?

The SRA Standards and Regulations are silent on this point, but it is sensible (and best practice) to include a description of the instructions which you are acting on in order to support compliance with the following paragraphs of the SRA Code of Conduct for Solicitors, RELs and RFLs (and repeated in the SRA Code of Conduct for Firms, and in this way applicable to everyone in the firm):

- para.3.1: 'You only act for clients on instructions from the client, or from someone properly authorised to provide instructions on their behalf . . .'

- para.3.4: 'You consider and take account of your client's attributes, needs and circumstances.'
- para.8.6: 'You give clients information in a way they can understand. You ensure they are in a position to make informed decisions about the services they need, how their matter will be handled and the options available to them.'

In other words, it is sensible to ensure that the client understands what steps are necessary in order to understand the scope of their instructions. It is best practice (but not a mandatory requirement) to provide information about major steps in the process. Not only does this support management of client expectations about what you will, and just as importantly, won't be doing for them, it also ensures that the client is in a position to make informed decisions about their matter when giving instructions to you.

In any event, this type of detail and description mirrors the requirements contained in the SRA Transparency Rules at rule 1.5(f). which states that costs information must include 'details of what services are included in the price displayed, including the key stages of the matter and likely timescales for each stage, and details of any services that might reasonably be expected to be included in the price displayed but are not'. Whilst the Transparency Rules apply to the information we provide to clients and potential clients, it makes sense to include similar levels of information once instructed. It also helps to have this evidence should the client raise a complaint about service standards.

What are the compliance challenges?

- Ensure that you are using template wording which is accurate, so that the client is given accurate information.
- Avoid using language and wording which is unsuitable because of the individual client's needs and attributes.
- Where there is a change of instructions meaning that the original information is no longer correct, ensure that it is revised and the client's expectations are managed properly as a consequence.

What resources will help?

- SRA materials:
  - SRA Principles (**www.sra.org.uk/solicitors/standards-regulations/principles/**);
  - SRA Codes of Conduct: SRA Code of Conduct for Solicitors, RELs and RFLs (**www.sra.org.uk/solicitors/standards-regulations/code-conduct-solicitors/**); SRA Code of Conduct for Firms (**www.sra.org.uk/solicitors/standards-regulations/code-conduct-firms/**);
  - SRA Transparency Rules (**www.sra.org.uk/solicitors/standards-regulations/transparency-rules/**);
  - SRA guidance: (updated 3 August 2021, **www.sra.org.uk/solicitors/guidance/transparency-in-price-and-service/**);

  - SRA guidance: 'Client care letters' (updated 25 November 2019, **www.sra.org.uk/solicitors/guidance/client-care-letters/**);
  - SRA risk report: 'Maintaining standards of service and reducing complaints' (1 July 2019, **www.sra.org.uk/sra/research-publications/maintaining-standards-service-reducing-complaints/**);
  - SRA report: 'Providing services to people who are vulnerable' (15 March 2016, **www.sra.org.uk/sra/research-publications/vulnerable-people/**).
- Law Society Practice Note: Client Information Requirements (8 September 2021, **www.lawsociety.org.uk/en/topics/client-care/client-information-requirements**).

Compliance tips – how to mitigate the risk of getting it wrong

- Ask fee earners to draft this part of the client care literature themselves rather than use a standard document or a template which is not modified.
- Conduct checks to ensure that language and style are appropriate.
- Conduct supervisory checks to ensure that accurate information has been provided.

19.5 Who is our client?

This is not as silly a question as it seems. It is important to identify the client correctly but sometimes it is hard to identify the client on whose behalf you are acting.

The SRA Glossary defines the client as 'the person for whom you act and, where the context permits, includes prospective and former clients'. This can also be described as the individual or entity whose interests you are protecting, promoting or otherwise altering because of the provision of legal services. This may not necessarily be the same person or entity which provides you with instructions.

Establishing the identity of the correct client, and being clear about the role of non-clients, is essential if you are to comply with your professional duties. For example, SRA Code of Conduct for Solicitors, RELs and RFLs, para.3.1 (repeated at SRA Code of Conduct for Firms, para.4.1, and therefore relevant to everyone employed on the firm) states: 'You only act for clients on instructions from the client, or from someone properly authorised to provide instructions on their behalf'.

Other service and competence duties are in SRA Code of Conduct for Solicitors, section 3 and repeated in the Code for Firms, section 4, and are drafted to strengthen the relationship with your correctly identified client. These duties support the SRA Principles, particularly Principle 7 and the duty to act in the best interests of each client. For example:

- SRA Code of Conduct for Solicitors, para.3.2 (Code for Firms, para.4.2): the service you provide to clients is competent and delivered in a timely manner;

- SRA Code of Conduct for Solicitors, para.3.4 (Code for Firms, para.4.4): you consider and take account of your client's attributes, needs and circumstances.

In addition, it is essential to identify the client correctly so that duties relating to clients described in various sections of the SRA Standards and Regulations are met. Bear in mind that duties to identify conflicts of interest (section 6 of both SRA Codes of Conduct) attach to current clients only; duties of confidentiality (also section 6) are owed to current and former clients only, and your duty of disclosure (again section 6) applies to current clients only.

Also, in SRA Code of Conduct for Solicitors, section 8 (and again repeated in the SRA Code of Conduct for Firms), there are client-specific duties such as:

- para.8.1: you identify who you are acting for in relation to any matter;
- paras.8.3–8.4: complaints handing information is delivered to the client;
- para.8.6: clients are given information in a way they can understand and 'you ensure they are in a position to make informed decisions about the services they need, how their matter will be handled and the options available to them';
- para.8.7: you ensure that clients receive the best possible information about how their matter will be priced, etc.

Hotspots and confusion can easily arise when acting for corporate clients and taking instructions from directors who might imagine that duties are owed to them personally; when acting in probate matters when beneficiaries might assume that they can give instructions to you (particularly in the absence of lay executors) and in all circumstances where instructions are provided by third parties.

What are the compliance challenges?

- Ensure that you understand the importance of this identification process.
- Ensure that you satisfy yourself on capacity or duress issues.
- Ensure that you satisfy yourself that you can act on third party instructions.

What resources will help?

- SRA Principles (**www.sra.org.uk/solicitors/standards-regulations/principles/**).
- SRA Codes of Conduct: SRA Code of Conduct for Solicitors, RELs and RFLs (**www.sra.org.uk/solicitors/standards-regulations/code-conduct-solicitors/**); SRA Code of Conduct for Firms (**www.sra.org.uk/solicitors/standards-regulations/code-conduct-firms/**).
- SRA report: 'Providing services to people who are vulnerable' (15 March 2016, **www.sra.org.uk/sra/research-publications/vulnerable-people/**).
- SRA guidance: 'Identifying your client' (25 November 2019, **www.sra.org.uk/solicitors/guidance/identifying-client/**).

Compliance tips – how to mitigate the risk of getting it wrong

- Have an onboarding checklist which requires the fee earner to identify the client and answer questions about their authority to act on instructions.
- Create template wording to explain to third parties the nature of our relationship with them, duties to the client, matters arising in respect of confidentiality.
- When dealing with a third party, obtain authority to discuss matters with them.
- Conduct ongoing monitoring of initial onboarding decisions.
- Conduct supervisory oversight.

19.6 Can we open a general file to deal with a particular client's matters?

The description 'general file' is used to explain the circumstances where a fee earner, or a legal team, might deal with a series of (usually small) legal queries for the same client and rather than open a new file with a unique file reference number for each piece of advice, but wanting to bill for time spent on dealing with the issue, will add time recording to one reference – hence this becomes a general file.

There is no regulatory prohibition that would restrict the use of a general file, but it does create compliance challenges if the firm does not identify when they are being used and addresses all the regulatory and ethical issues, not least the following:

- appropriate client care and service information is not provided;
- misunderstandings arise which lead to client complaints;
- lack of effective supervision as a consequence of the use of a general file.

What are the compliance challenges?

- Ensure that fee earners are not using a general file which has been set up inappropriately to avoid dealing with client care and other onboarding requirements.
- Combat compliance fatigue or complacency, which could result in a general file being used inappropriately.
- Be aware of the risk of smaller matters becoming larger, warranting an individual file and file reference number, and because of the response to the initial enquiry there is a lack of proper onboarding process which is not remedied.
- Ensure that matters to which the Money Laundering, Terrorist Financing and Transfer of Funds (Information on the Payer) Regulations 2017, SI 2017/692 (AML Regulations) apply are onboarded and monitored in a way that demonstrates compliance with legal duties relating to customer due diligence (CDD) and matter risk assessment.
- More generally, ensure that risk assessment is considered.
- Put in place procedures to combat lack of attention to other compliance duties; for example, conflict checks, consideration of conflict of duties (i.e. confidentiality duties creating a difficulty with duty of disclosure) on each new matter.

What resources will help?

- SRA materials:
  - SRA Codes of Conduct: SRA Code of Conduct for Solicitors, RELs and RFLs (**www.sra.org.uk/solicitors/standards-regulations/code-conduct-solicitors/**); SRA Code of Conduct for Firms (**www.sra.org.uk/solicitors/standards-regulations/code-conduct-firms/**);
  - SRA guidance: 'Client care letters' (updated 25 November 2019, **www.sra.org.uk/solicitors/guidance/client-care-letters/**);
  - SRA guidance: 'Conflicts of interest' (updated 2 March 2020, **www.sra.org.uk/solicitors/guidance/conflicts-interest/**).
- Law Society Practice Note: Conflicts of Interests (18 October 2021, **www.lawsociety.org.uk/en/topics/client-care/conflict-of-interests**).

Compliance tips – how to mitigate the risk of getting it wrong

- Consider a prohibition on the use of general files.
- Or, allow general files, but with a procedure overseen by the risk and compliance team.
- Conduct supervisory oversight.

19.7 Can we enter into a long-term service agreement with our clients?

There is no limit on the length of a retainer and it is common to have fixed long-term service agreements for some workstreams – notably when providing employment services to corporate clients so that they receive helpline-type legal services.

It is important to ensure that notwithstanding the length of any agreement, or the familiarity with a client which is generated through a good relationship, that you are still able to comply with the following paragraphs in the SRA Code of Conduct for Solicitors, RELs and RFLs (and repeated in the SRA Code of Conduct for Firms, and therefore applicable to everyone in the firm):

- para.3.1: 'You only act for clients on instructions from the client, or from someone properly authorised to provide instructions on their behalf . . . ';
- paras.8.6 and 8.7: client information.

What are the compliance challenges?

- Ensure that you have an adequate service agreement so that the extent of the legal services being provided is clear.
- Avoid providing a less than competent service because costs have been calculated incorrectly.
- Do not take instructions from someone without proper authority.
- Ensure that you undertake conflict checks and consider other ethical issues such as confidentiality and disclosure duties, etc. when dealing with new topics.

What resources will help?

- SRA materials:
  - SRA Principles (**www.sra.org.uk/solicitors/standards-regulations/principles/**);
  - SRA Codes of Conduct: SRA Code of Conduct for Solicitors, RELs and RFLs (**www.sra.org.uk/solicitors/standards-regulations/code-conduct-solicitors/**); SRA Code of Conduct for Firms (**www.sra.org.uk/solicitors/standards-regulations/code-conduct-firms/**);
  - SRA Transparency Rules (**www.sra.org.uk/solicitors/standards-regulations/transparency-rules/**);
  - SRA guidance: 'Client care letters' (updated 25 November 2019, **www.sra.org.uk/solicitors/guidance/client-care-letters/**).
- Law Society Practice Note: Client Information Requirements (8 September 2021, **www.lawsociety.org.uk/en/topics/client-care/client-information-requirements**).

Compliance tips – how to mitigate the risk of getting it wrong

- Ensure that agreements of this type are properly documented and signed-off by the COLP and/or the compliance team.
- Provide training on the service agreement to all fee earners and other staff who may be called upon to provide services.
- Draft a compliance checklist to ensure that all regulatory and ethical considerations are taken into account on each new matter.
- Create a template to ensure that all advice is documented to produce a proper audit trail.

19.8 Do we have to accept all new instructions?

No. Solicitors and law firms are not obliged to accept every request for representation.

Provided that this decision is not based on any consideration that places the individual and the firm in breach of the Equality Act 2010, there is no ethical or regulatory obligation to act.

In fact, there are a number of legal, regulatory and ethical considerations which must be considered before instructions are accepted, which include the following:

- Can we comply with the AML Regulations (if appropriate) and undertake appropriate client due diligence and risk assessment measures?
- Do we have the competence (e.g. the time, the resources and the necessary skill sets and legal knowledge) to provide a proper standard of service to the client?
- Does a conflict of interests or conflict of duties prevent us from accepting instructions?

What are the compliance challenges?

- An individual or entity who is refused legal services can complain about this to the Legal Ombudsman, so it is essential that there are records of why instructions were refused.
- Ensure that you do not misunderstand this position and accept instructions which place the individual or the firm in breach of regulatory and ethical duties.

What resources will help?

- SRA Principles (**www.sra.org.uk/solicitors/standards-regulations/principles/**).
- SRA Codes of Conduct: SRA Code of Conduct for Solicitors, RELs and RFLs (**www.sra.org.uk/solicitors/standards-regulations/code-conduct-solicitors/**); SRA Code of Conduct for Firms (**www.sra.org.uk/solicitors/standards-regulations/code-conduct-firms/**).
- SRA guidance: 'The SRA's approach to equality, diversity and inclusion' (updated 25 November 2019, **www.sra.org.uk/solicitors/guidance/sra-approach-equality-diversity-inclusion/**).

Compliance tips – how to mitigate the risk of getting it wrong

- Provide training on the regulatory and ethical position.
- Implement an internal procedure so that there is evidence to show why instructions are refused.
- Create a template letter to explain to the individual/entity why the firm will not act.

CHAPTER 20

Running a law firm – compliance questions

20.1 What job titles should we avoid and why?

A job title is a form of publicity, so there are a number of regulatory, and sometimes also legal, issues if your title is misleading.

There are a number of risks associated with job titles, some of which can have regulatory consequences because the wrong title might be seen as misleading publicity in breach of Solicitors Regulation Authority (SRA) Code of Conduct for Solicitors, registered European lawyers (RELs) and registered foreign lawyers (RFLs), para.8.8 (repeated in the SRA Code of Conduct for Firms, and therefore of relevance to everyone in your firm): 'You ensure that any publicity in relation to your practice is accurate and not misleading . . . '

Important points to bear in mind:

- It is a criminal offence to call yourself a 'solicitor' unless you are on the roll of solicitors. The SRA has powers to prosecute 'bogus solicitors'.
- It would be prudent for a solicitor from another jurisdiction (e.g. a solicitor qualified in New South Wales and other Australian states) to make reference to this when describing themselves and in letterheads, business cards, etc.
- Take care if describing yourself as a 'lawyer'. This word is a defined term in the SRA Glossary which is part of the SRA Standards and Regulations:

  > . . . a member of one of the following professions, entitled to practise as such:
  >
  > (a) the profession of solicitor, barrister or advocate of the UK;
  > (b) an authorised person other than one authorised by the SRA;
  > (c) any profession approved by the SRA for RFL status; and
  > (d) any other regulated legal profession specified by the SRA for the purpose of this definition

- More specifically, 'lawyer of England and Wales' is also a Glossary term and means:

  > (a) a solicitor; or
  > (b) an individual who is authorised to carry on legal activities in England and Wales by an approved regulator other than the SRA, but excludes an indivi-

dual registered with the Bar Standards Board under the European Communities (Lawyer's Practice) Regulations 2000.

- Only Fellows of the Chartered Institute of Legal Executives can call themselves Chartered Legal Executives or lawyers – it should be noted that any member of this Institute is accountable to this approved regulator as well as the SRA, and any misuse of this title is likely to be investigated as a breach of the rules of this organisation as well.
- Only the European and foreign lawyers who are currently registered with the SRA can use the prefix 'registered'.
- 'Counsel', 'attorney' and 'legal practitioner' imply a professional qualification as a lawyer, so should not be used by a non-lawyer.

What are the compliance challenges?

- Ensure that you correct the assumptions of clients or others about your legal qualification, or status.
- Do not allow unqualified individuals to use titles that directly or indirectly imply that they are legally qualified.
- Do not assume that a solicitor on the roll of solicitors can use a title to imply that they are non-practising or non-legally qualified as a way to avoid a breach of the Solicitors Act 1974 and the requirement to hold a practising certificate when providing legal services.
- Do not allow misleading publicity about status to be included on your website, promotional materials and on letterheads, etc.

What resources will help?

- SRA Codes of Conduct: SRA Code of Conduct for Solicitors, RELs and RFLs (**www.sra.org.uk/solicitors/standards-regulations/code-conduct-solicitors/**); SRA Code of Conduct for Firms (**www.sra.org.uk/solicitors/standards-regulations/code-conduct-firms/**).
- Law Society Practice Note: Information on Letterheads, Emails and Websites (26 January 2021, **www.lawsociety.org.uk/en/topics/client-care/information-on-letterheads-emails-and-websites**).

Compliance tips – how to mitigate the risk of getting it wrong

- Provide training on this issue.
- Ensure that colleagues with responsibilities for marketing or with HR roles understand the need to be meticulous in terms of the descriptions used by colleagues.

20.2 The SRA talks about 'effective supervision'. What does this mean?

The SRA Standards and Regulations contain two explicit references to effective supervision, as follows:

1. SRA Code of Conduct for Solicitors, RELs and RFLs, para.3.5, which describes the individual responsibilities of supervisory solicitors, etc. as follows:

   > Where you supervise or manage others providing legal services:
   >
   > (a) you remain accountable for the work carried out through them; and
   > (b) you effectively supervise work being done for clients.

2. SRA Code of Conduct for Firms, para.4.4:

   > You have an effective system for supervising clients' matters.

In addition, the expectation that there is effective supervision is implied by reference to the requirements in SRA Code of Conduct for Firms, section 2 which describes the SRA's requirements about compliance and business systems in authorised law firms.

However, notwithstanding the copious uses of the word 'effective', the SRA use this term without explaining how we can meet this requirement and what they expect to see in practice. This is intentional. Supervision must ensure that competent (i.e. services of the right standard in terms of the relevant law and standards of service) and ethical legal services are provided. Each law firm is asked to consider what oversight is necessary to ensure that competence and ethical behaviour is supported in that specific environment, taking into account the type of staff employed, their qualifications, the roles of support staff, the types of services provided, the needs of the client base, how services are provided, and the physical circumstances (i.e. is the firm based in one or several offices, what remote/hybrid working needs to be considered, etc).

It should also be remembered that supervision is also checked and assessed in connection with certain accreditations.

What are the compliance challenges?

- Do not allow any colleague to escape your supervisory coverage; for example, whilst senior and more experienced lawyers and/or the owners of the firm will not need the same type of supervision as someone in a different position, there will nonetheless be the need to ensure appropriate supervision to meet the needs of evidencing that consideration has been given to competency, etc.
- Ensure that supervisors have the right skillsets to be effective. It is essential that they are effective communicators, able to empathise with those whom they supervise but also able to sometimes deliver tough measures about the firm's expectations.

- Ensure that supervisors have sufficient time to fulfil their supervisory function. Done in a meaningful way, supervision is as important a part of the individual's job description as the legal services which they might also be performing.
- Ensure that supervisors have sufficient support. Insufficient support places them in a perilous regulatory position; solicitor-supervisors must bear in mind their individual accountability to the SRA as described in para.3.5, and this expectation is inferred on all solicitors by the requirements in the SRA Code of Conduct for Firms.

What resources will help?

- SRA materials:
  - SRA Codes of Conduct: SRA Code of Conduct for Solicitors, RELs and RFLs (**www.sra.org.uk/solicitors/standards-regulations/code-conduct-solicitors/**); SRA Code of Conduct for Firms (**www.sra.org.uk/solicitors/standards-regulations/code-conduct-firms/**);
  - SRA guidance: 'Workplace environment: risks of failing to protect and support colleagues' (7 February 2022, **www.sra.org.uk/solicitors/guidance/workplace-environment/**).
- Law Society Practice Note: Supervision (29 July 2021, **www.lawsociety.org.uk/en/topics/hr-and-people-management/supervision**).
- *Compliance and Ethics in Law Firms*, 2nd edn (Tracey Calvert, Law Society Publishing, 2019).

Compliance tips – how to mitigate the risk of getting it wrong

- Implement a supervision policy – explaining the purpose of supervision and how supervision will be performed.
- Ensure that procedures enable supervisors to assess compliance with SRA expectations as well as file auditing for more usual reasons.
- Provide job descriptions for supervisors which include training on skills needed, acknowledgment of time and resources allotted to the task, record-keeping, etc.
- Monitor the supervision process – ask for feedback from those who are supervisors and, as importantly, those who are subject to supervision.
- Use information gathered through supervision to support compliance strategies, training delivery, etc.

20.3 What compliance response supports effective supervision and risk management?

As a firm you must be able to demonstrate an appropriate response to the SRA's requirement that you have an effective system for supervising clients' matters (as described in SRA Code of Conduct for Firms, para.4.4). Your failure to demonstrate this is likely to create difficulties in demonstrating to the SRA that you are a well-run firm with appropriate compliance and business systems.

As a firm, you will also want to support your supervisors to fulfil their supervisory responsibilities. For solicitors, RELs and RFLs, you will want to support them to comply with SRA Code of Conduct for Solicitors, para.3.5 which makes them personally accountable in the following circumstances:

> Where you supervise or manage others providing legal services:
>
> (a) you remain accountable for the work carried out through them; and
> (b) you effectively supervise work being done for clients.

By implication, a similar expectation about accountability will apply to those supervisors employed in your firm who are not subject to this code but are nonetheless subject to regulatory oversight because they are employed in an authorised law firm and subject to compliance with the SRA Code of Conduct for Firms.

When done well, supervision will deliver a number of positive results:

- it supports the delivery of ethical legal services;
- it supports compliance with individual and firmwide regulatory obligations;
- it supports the ongoing authorisation of your law firm;
- it is part of your risk management response;
- it ensures that training will be delivered to those who need it;
- it provides oversight of the working of the firm's compliance strategies and manages the risks that come if competency standards are not met; and
- it improves and strengthens the firm's one voice culture and branding.

Doing supervision effectively means that it is treated as a real, important and discrete task which requires continual communication between the owners/managers and supervisors and those who are supervised. Openness and accountability support effective supervision, and regular person and work review and documented evidence of supervision in practice events are best practice.

Unfortunately, none of this is described by the SRA, and firms must consider and roll-out their own solution. The solutions will be formulated through appropriate leadership from the compliance officers and the firm's risk and compliance professionals. Much of the SRA's expectations about the outcomes which they expect us to achieve relate to regulatory and ethical standards. The compliance function can support others in this by:

- being accessible to all members of the firm and providing first, or sometimes, second, decisions on compliance issues;
- providing training to supervisors on SRA Standard and Regulations;
- being involved in developing review evidence (such as file review checklists in respect of regulatory topics) or even being part of the supervisory process themselves; and
- by having a more frontline role in this process.

What are the compliance challenges?

- Ensure that the purpose of supervision is being effectively communicated to supervisors, and also those whom they supervise.
- Ensure that supervision objectives incorporate regulatory and ethics assessments.
- Ensure that supervision is not being bolted-on to the supervisors' day jobs and performed in an ad hoc and undisciplined way.
- Ensure that supervision adapts to the needs of those who are supervised and to accommodate how they work.
- Ensure that there is ongoing, continuous, mentoring and support so that the process facilitates personal development (this being good for the individual and good for the firm).
- Ensure that supervisors are being supported in their role.
- Ensure that the risk and compliance team is included in the supervisory process.

What resources will help?

- SRA materials:
  - SRA Standards and Regulations (**www.sra.org.uk/solicitors/standards-regulations/**);
  - SRA guidance: 'Responsibilities of COLPs and COFAs' (25 November 2019, **www.sra.org.uk/solicitors/guidance/responsibilities-of-colps-and-cofas/**);
  - SRA guidance: 'Workplace environment: risks of failing to protect and support colleagues' (7 February 2022, **www.sra.org.uk/solicitors/guidance/workplace-environment/**).
- Law Society materials:
  - Law Society Practice Note: Compliance Officers (14 September 2021, **www.lawsociety.org.uk/en/topics/business-management/compliance-officers**);
  - Law Society Practice Note: Supervision (29 July 2021, **www.lawsociety.org.uk/en/topics/hr-and-people-management/supervision**).
- *Compliance and Ethics in Law Firms*, 2nd edn (Tracey Calvert, Law Society Publishing, 2019).

Compliance tips – how to mitigate the risk of getting it wrong

- Develop an appropriate culture in which supervision is treated as a significant task supporting individuals and supporting the longevity of the firm.
- Provide training on the purpose of supervision to manager/owners, supervisors and those who are supervised.
- Implement an internal supervision policy.
- Prepare review process templates to evidence checks made and results found.
- Analyse supervisory findings by the compliance team to check for training needs and whether changes need to be made to processes, etc.

20.4 How do we deal with a complaint of discrimination raised by a member of staff?

Any compliant of discrimination, or more generally of unfair treatment, is not only a serious matter to be considered in your capacity as employer, but is also of significance when considering the SRA's regulatory expectations.

The relevant regulatory requirements in respect of the firm and the behaviours of the owner/managers and employees are found in the following locations:

- SRA Principle 2: 'You act in a way that upholds public trust and confidence in the solicitors' profession and in legal services provided by authorised persons.'
- SRA Principle 6: 'You act in a way that encourages equality, diversity and inclusion.'
- SRA Codes of Conduct, para.1.1 of each Code – 'You do not unfairly discriminate by allowing your personal views to affect your professional relationships and the way in which you provide your services.'
- SRA Codes of Conduct, para.1.2 of each Code: 'You do not abuse your position by taking unfair advantage of clients or others.'
- SRA Code of Conduct for Firms, section 2 'Compliance and business systems', for example, para.2.1(b): 'You have effective governance structures, arrangements, systems and controls in place that ensure ... your managers and employees comply with the SRA's regulatory arrangements which apply to them ...'
- SRA Code of Conduct for Firms, para.3.9: 'You report promptly to the SRA, or another approved regulator, as appropriate, any facts or matters that you reasonably believe are capable of amounting to a serious breach of their regulatory arrangements by any person regulated by them (including you) of which you are aware. If requested to do so by the SRA, you investigate whether there have been any serious breaches that should be reported to the SRA.'
- SRA Code of Conduct for Firms, para.3.10: 'Notwithstanding paragraph 3.9, you inform the SRA promptly of any facts or matters that you reasonably believe should be brought to its attention in order that it may investigate whether a serious breach of its regulatory arrangements has occurred or otherwise exercise its regulatory powers.'
- SRA Code of Conduct for Firms, para.9.1(d): 'If you are a COLP you must take all reasonable steps to ... (d) ensure that a prompt report is made to the SRA of any facts or matters that you reasonably believe are capable of amounting to a serious breach of the terms and conditions of your firm's authorisation, or the SRA's regulatory arrangements which apply to your firm, managers or employees ...'

For all these reasons, it is essential that complaints of discrimination are handled swiftly and with appropriate attention to demonstrating a fair and consistent process has been applied.

What are the compliance challenges?

- Ensure that the culture in your firm does not discourage openness or, alternatively, enable the wrong behaviours to be practised.
- Prevent an incorrect response to a complaint of discrimination occurring perhaps because of the respective roles of the individuals concerned, their respective contributions to the firm, etc.
- Avoid the resolution of a discrimination complaint without considering the regulatory consequences and whether a report must be made to the SRA.
- Avoid the resolution of a discrimination complaint by means that the SRA would discourage, e.g. through the use of a non-disclosure agreement prohibiting an individual from continuing with their complaint.
- Avoid complaints being handled by your HR department and without a consideration of the regulatory issues or the appropriate involvement of the firm's owners/managers and risk and compliance professionals.

What resources will help?

- SRA materials:
  - SRA Principles (**www.sra.org.uk/solicitors/standards-regulations/principles/**);
  - SRA Codes of Conduct: SRA Code of Conduct for Solicitors, RELs and RFLs (**www.sra.org.uk/solicitors/standards-regulations/code-conduct-solicitors/**); SRA Code of Conduct for Firms (**www.sra.org.uk/solicitors/standards-regulations/code-conduct-firms/**);
  - SRA guidance: 'Reporting and notification obligations' (25 November 2019, **www.sra.org.uk/solicitors/guidance/reporting-notification-obligations/**),
  - SRA guidance: 'The SRA's approach to equality, diversity and inclusion' (updated 25 November 2019, **www.sra.org.uk/solicitors/guidance/sra-approach-equality-diversity-inclusion/**);
  - SRA case study: 'Sexual harassment' (23 July 2019, **www.sra.org.uk/solicitors/guidance/sexual-harassment/**);
  - SRA collection of guidance and resources: 'Sexual harassment and the law' (**www.sra.org.uk/solicitors/resources/diversity-toolkit/sexual-harassment/**);
  - SRA warning notice: 'Use of non disclosure agreements (NDAs)' (updated 12 November 2020, **www.sra.org.uk/solicitors/guidance/non-disclosure-agreements-ndas/**);
  - SRA case study: 'Unfair discrimination' (23 July 2019, **www.sra.org.uk/solicitors/guidance/unfair-discrimination/**);
  - SRA collection of resources: 'Encouraging equality, diversity and inclusion' (**www.sra.org.uk/solicitors/resources/diversity-toolkit/**);
  - SRA guidance: 'Workplace environment: risks of failing to protect and support colleagues' (7 February 2022, **www.sra.org.uk/solicitors/guidance/workplace-environment/**);

- SRA case study: 'Workplace environment: risks of failing to protect and support colleagues' (7 February 2022, **www.sra.org.uk/solicitors/guidance/workplace-environment-case-studies/**).

- Law Society materials:
  - Law Society Practice Note: Implementing Whistleblowing Arrangements (22 November 2019, **www.lawsociety.org.uk/en/topics/regulation/implementing-whistleblowing-arrangements**);
  - Law Society Practice Note: Raising Concerns and Whistleblowing – Guidance for Staff (22 November 2019, **www.lawsociety.org.uk/en/topics/hr-and-people-management/raising-concerns-and-whistleblowing-guidance-for-staff**).

Compliance tips – how to mitigate the risk of getting it wrong

- Provide training on legal and regulatory duties.
- Develop a compliance culture which fosters behaviours that support the fair treatment of others; this message should be delivered by the owners/managers to all others.
- Implement an equality policy addressed to managers and employees.
- Implement a procedure for internal reporting and/or a whistleblowing policy.
- Implement a procedure to ensure a consistent approach to internal complaints.
- Provide specialist training for HR colleagues so that they are familiar with the SRA's position.
- Implement a method to ensure that intelligence is shared securely with relevant colleagues, e.g. the owners/managers, the compliance officer for legal practice (COLP), etc.

20.5 We are acting for a client or manager/employee seeking reasonable adjustments. What is the correct compliance response?

The law provides for reasonable adjustments to ensure that someone with disabilities, or physical or mental health conditions, are not substantially disadvantaged.

In your law firm, you will want to ensure compliance with your legal obligations not only as a service provider and in respect of your clients, but also as an employer and in respect of all managers and employees.

The duty to comply with the law is of interest to the SRA. Not only is this because of SRA Principle 1 and the duty to uphold the rule of law, but also because of your professional conduct duty – expressed in SRA Code of Conduct for Firms, para.3.1 – to 'keep up to date with and follow the law and regulation governing the way you work'.

The correct compliance response is therefore straightforward and will involve an analysis of the legislation and an assessment of what would be a reasonable adjustment in the circumstances. The fact that the wrong decision might have legal and regulatory consequences means that it is best practice to involve risk and compliance colleagues in decision-making and keep an effective audit trail with which to justify your decision-making.

What are the compliance challenges?

- Prevent decisions being made which are not compatible with legal requirements.
- Prevent decisions being made without the involvement of appropriate colleagues; this is not just an HR decision, but one that requires the input of the COLP and compliance team.

What resources will help?

- SRA Principles (**www.sra.org.uk/solicitors/standards-regulations/principles/**).
- SRA Codes of Conduct: SRA Code of Conduct for Solicitors, RELs and RFLs (**www.sra.org.uk/solicitors/standards-regulations/code-conduct-solicitors/**); SRA Code of Conduct for Firms (**www.sra.org.uk/solicitors/standards-regulations/code-conduct-firms/**).
- SRA guidance: 'The SRA's approach to equality, diversity and inclusion' (updated 25 November 2019, **www.sra.org.uk/solicitors/guidance/sra-approach-equality-diversity-inclusion/**).
- SRA report: 'Providing services to people who are vulnerable' (15 March 2016, **www.sra.org.uk/sra/research-publications/vulnerable-people/**).
- SRA report – 'Reasonable adjustments in the provision of legal services' (10 October 2019, **www.sra.org.uk/sra/research-publications/reasonable-adjustments/**).
- SRA guidance: 'Workplace environment: risks of failing to protect and support colleagues' (7 February 2022, **www.sra.org.uk/solicitors/guidance/workplace-environment/**).
- SRA case study: 'Workplace environment: risks of failing to protect and support colleagues' (7 February 2022, **www.sra.org.uk/solicitors/guidance/workplace-environment-case-studies/**).

Compliance tips – how to mitigate the risk of getting it wrong

- Provide training on the legislation and regulation to decision-makers (including fee earners for client matters) and also HR, heads of departments, etc. for employee requests.
- Implement an equality policy which includes a procedure for reasonable adjustment requests.
- Create a notification procedure so that the COLP and risk and compliance team are involved in decision making.

20.6 Must undertakings be in writing?

No, but the risks associated with undertakings are magnified when an undertaking is not provided in written and documented form.

An undertaking is defined as 'a statement, given orally or in writing, whether or not it includes the word "undertake" or "undertaking", to someone who reasonably places reliance on it, that you or a third party will do something or cause something to be done, or refrain from doing something' (SRA Glossary).

SRA Code of Conduct for Solicitors, RELs and RFLs, para.1.3 (repeated in identical form in the SRA Code of Conduct for Firms and therefore applicable to everyone in the firm) states: 'You perform all undertakings given by you, and do so within an agreed timescale or if no timescale has been agreed then within a reasonable amount of time.'

What are the compliance challenges?

- Preventing manager/employees making statements which are treated as undertakings when this was not their intention.
- Do not give or receive undertakings without having appropriate evidence.
- Do not make an ambiguous statement which is subsequently treated as an undertaking.

What resources will help?

- SRA Codes of Conduct: SRA Code of Conduct for Solicitors, RELs and RFLs (**www.sra.org.uk/solicitors/standards-regulations/code-conduct-solicitors/**); SRA Code of Conduct for Firms (**www.sra.org.uk/solicitors/standards-regulations/code-conduct-firms/**).

Compliance tips – how to mitigate the risk of getting it wrong

- Implement an undertakings policy – explaining what an undertaking is, the regulatory duties, the firm's expectations about who can give and receive undertakings, how they will be recorded, etc.
- Provide training on regulation and the firm's procedure.
- Conduct checking for compliance through supervisory process.

20.7 What should our firm's risk management manual contain and why?

The firm must have compliance and business systems in accordance with SRA Code of Conduct for Firms, section 2.

Included in this section is para.2.5: 'You identify, monitor and manage all material risks to your business, including those which may arise from your connected practices.' And para.2.2: 'You keep and maintain records to demonstrate compliance with your obligations under the SRA's regulatory arrangements.'

By implication, the SRA requires authorised firms to maintain accurate records and similar to demonstrate their risk management and risk response, including a record of breaches of regulatory requirements. The format is not prescribed, but firms will struggle to manage their relationship with the SRA, and duties in respect of being open and accountable and making timely notification, without putting into practice some form of record keeping. For this reason, many firms choose to operate a risk management manual. This can contain records of the following:

- the firm's risk management strategy;
- risk analysis evidence;
- relevant policies that support risk management practice;
- high-risk decisions – e.g. acting in a client conflict using an exception, erection of information barriers, etc.;
- own interest declarations;
- undertakings;
- notifications to the COLP or compliance officer for finance and administration (COFA) and evidence of their risk analysis;
- breaches records more generally;
- records of breaches reported to the SRA;
- training records.

What are the compliance challenges?

- Prevent inadequate responses from the owners/managers and employees to the duty to support the maintenance of these records.
- Ensure that records are accurate.
- Ensure that information from breach reporting is analysed or shared with senior management.

What resources will help?

- SRA materials:
  - SRA Code of Conduct for Firms (**www.sra.org.uk/solicitors/standards-regulations/code-conduct-firms/**);
  - SRA guidance: 'Responsibilities of COLPs and COFAs' (25 November 2019, **www.sra.org.uk/solicitors/guidance/responsibilities-of-colps-and-cofas/**).
- *Compliance and Ethics in Law Firms*, 2nd edn (Tracey Calvert, Law Society Publishing, 2019).

Compliance tips – how to mitigate the risk of getting it wrong

- Ensure effective communication from owner/managers about their risk management expectations.
- Ensure clarity about information that must be provided, and to whom, in respect of the maintenance of these records.
- Conduct supervisory oversight of compliance with this requirement.
- Obtain assistance from the risk and compliance team in terms of the management and monitoring of these records.
- Provide regular reports of risk position to the owners/managers.

20.8 How do we manage referral and introductions effectively?

Referral arrangements create a number of potentially serious legal and regulatory issues if they are not managed correctly. For this reason, it is essential that there is adequate compliance oversight of all arrangements with third parties which relate to the referral of your clients to them or the introduction of individuals to you.

Points to be satisfied on include:

- Are you complying with the Legal Aid Sentencing and Punishment of Offenders Act 2012 (LASPO 2012) and the restrictions that apply in respect of payments that are connected with personal injury matters (as described in LASPO 2012, s.56)?
- Are you complying with the SRA Principles? In particular, think about duties connected with upholding trust and confidence in the profession (Principle 2), your independence and this not being compromised by your relationship with third parties (Principle 3) and making sure that whatever you do does not compromise your duty to act in each client's best interests (Principle 7).
- In more detail, are you complying with the regulatory and professional duties in SRA Code of Conduct for Solicitors, RELs and RFLs, section 5 (and repeated in the SRA Code of Conduct for Firms)? These include:
  - the need to tell clients relevant information about the arrangement, including any payments you may make or receive (SRA Code of Conduct for Solicitors, para.5.1(a));
  - fee-sharing agreements are disclosed to the client and they are in writing (paras.5.1(b) and (c)); and
  - that you are satisfied that the client has not been acquired by the third party by any publicity that would be in breach of the Codes if undertaken by you (para.5.1 (e)).

Suggestions to support effective management of all such arrangements include:

- vetting of new arrangements as a centralised role in the firm for consistency purposes;
- undertaking thorough due diligence of business associates;
- offering training to them on your legal and regulatory duties so that they understand your concerns;
- all agreements to be in writing;
- monitoring and spot checks for compliance;
- training of your staff as to the law, their regulatory duties and your internal procedures;
- template letters, etc. to ensure clients receive the correct information.

What are the compliance challenges?

- Ensure that there is no lack of awareness of all the arrangements which exist in your firm.
- Ensure that there is no lack of consideration of duties to clients because of a good relationship with a third party.
- Ensure that you put the interests of the client before your own commercial interests or the interests of the third party.
- Do not agree terms with a third party which fall short of the regulatory duties.

What resources will help?

- SRA Principles (**www.sra.org.uk/solicitors/standards-regulations/principles/**).
- SRA Codes of Conduct: SRA Code of Conduct for Solicitors, RELs and RFLs (**www.sra.org.uk/solicitors/standards-regulations/code-conduct-solicitors/**); SRA Code of Conduct for Firms (**www.sra.org.uk/solicitors/standards-regulations/code-conduct-firms/**).
- SRA case study: 'Lack of independence' (updated 25 November 2019, **www.sra.org.uk/solicitors/guidance/lack-independence/**).
- SRA warning notice: 'Referral fees LASPO and SRA Principles' (updated 25 November 2019, **www.sra.org.uk/solicitors/guidance/referral-fees-laspo-sra-principles/**).

Compliance tips – how to mitigate the risk of getting it wrong

- Implement an introduction and referrals policy which provides a firm-wide consistent strategy on arrangements with third parties.
- Create a central role for the COLP and/or the risk and compliance team in establishing agreements and negotiating terms.
- Provide training to relevant staff on relevant legislation, regulation and your internal procedures.
- Create a suite of template documents to support communications of all relevant information to clients.
- Conduct supervisory oversight.

20.9 What services can we outsource to third parties and what are the risk and compliance challenges?

You can outsource a number of different activities to third parties – but you need to manage the risks associated with this and comply with legal restrictions and regulatory duties. These include:

- The legal restriction on providing reserved legal services which is contained in Legal Services Act 2007, s.12. For example, it would be wrong to outsource your probate activities to another business unless it was an authorised body as described in the Act.
- SRA Code of Conduct for Firms, section 2 describes the compliance and business systems which must be implemented by all SRA-authorised law

firms. Bear in mind para.2.3 which states: 'You remain accountable for compliance with the SRA's regulatory arrangements where your work is carried out through others, including your managers and those you employ or contract with.'

- The need to comply with other regulatory and professional duties, including duties of confidentiality in the SRA Codes and the duty to act in each client's best interests (SRA Principle 1).

What are the compliance challenges?

- Ensure that you understand what can – and more importantly, cannot – be outsourced to unauthorised external businesses.
- Provide sufficient oversight of how these businesses are performing services on your behalf.

What resources will help?

- SRA materials:
  - SRA Principles (**www.sra.org.uk/solicitors/standards-regulations/principles/**);
  - SRA Codes of Conduct: SRA Code of Conduct for Solicitors, RELs and RFLs (**www.sra.org.uk/solicitors/standards-regulations/code-conduct-solicitors/**); SRA Code of Conduct for Firms (**www.sra.org.uk/solicitors/standards-regulations/code-conduct-firms/**);
  - SRA guidance: 'Confidentiality of client information' (updated 5 April 2022);
- Law Society Practice Note: Outsourcing (9 September 2021, **www.lawsociety.org.uk/en/topics/business-management/outsourcing**).

Compliance tips – how to mitigate the risk of getting it wrong

- Implement a proper procurement processes with spot checks, service arrangements, etc.
- Provide training on risk and compliance issues for those involved in your procurement processes.
- Ask third parties to enter into a confidentiality agreement.

20.10 What documented procedures and policies will help us to demonstrate effective governance of regulatory requirements?

Even in the smallest of law firms, there is sense in documenting your response to the SRA Standards and Regulations. This is because:

- Documented processes will help to provide assurances to the SRA, and other bodies which have a role in overseeing your provision of legal services, that you have attempted to 'create and maintain the right culture and environment for the delivery of competent and ethical legal services to clients' as described in the introduction to the SRA Code of Conduct for Firms.

- Documented processes will help to deliver the correct message to all the managers and employees about the firm's attitudes and expectations; it is important that the firm's expectations and tolerance levels are unambiguously and clearly stated.
- Documented statements provide benchmarking tools with which to test individual compliance and, overall, the effectiveness of the firm's response.
- Documentation avoids any misunderstandings that might otherwise arise if other forms of communication are used.
- Documentation will also help the firm demonstrate that accreditation scheme standards are being met.

To be clear, there is no list of policies and procedures which the SRA share with us and which they insist that we create. This is because all authorised law firms are required to comply with the previously mentioned SRA Code of Conduct for Firms, which sets out an obligation in section 2 ('Compliance and business systems') for you to have 'effective governance structures, arrangements, systems and controls in place' to ensure firmwide and individual compliance with regulatory arrangements (para.2.1).

The formula for, and content of, your own documented policies will come about through a reflection on what regulatory and ethical issues are relevant to your type of practice (for example, if the firm does not have any referral arrangements, there is little or no need to have a documented policy to deal with this particular topic). The style and tone can be decided to reflect the needs of your own audience (for example, a smaller firm with one office might not need to express supervision expectations in the same way as a firm with multiple offices or remote working arrangements). In other words, it is important that the SRA can see that what has been produced is effective to meet the needs of your environment.

In terms of demonstrating compliance with the content of the SRA Standards and Regulations, consider having documents, systems and controls such as:

- A statement about the SRA Principles – what they are, who they apply to, the firm's expectations about adherence to them.
- Client care policy – which includes the need to identify clients correctly; to consider how to take instructions properly, considering clients attributes; how to deal with vulnerabilities; information about services, costs, retainer information, file closure expectations, etc.
- Complaints policy – the procedure and reference to the role of the Legal Ombudsman.
- Conflicts policy.
- Confidentiality policy (combined with conflicts policy or a separate document).

- Social media policy – explain SRA position on offensive communications, regulatory reach to personal social media use, confidentiality issues, etc.
- Equality, diversity and inclusion policies – both client-facing and relating to provision of services to clients and treatment of third parties and a policy to deal with employer-employee issues, and in both cases how complaints of discrimination will be handled.
- Supervision policy – to demonstrate firm's objectives in terms of ensuring effective supervision, and the roles and expectations in respect of supervisors and those who are being supervised.
- Training policy – to explain the training commitment of the firm, the competency objectives, the responsibilities of managers/employees to attend and record training.
- Undertakings policy – what an undertaking is, who can give and receive an undertaking, how they are recorded.
- Remote/hybrid working policy – how this will operate, consideration of duties to clients, supervisory expectations, the handling of regulatory and ethical duties such as conflicts identification, confidentiality risk management, etc.
- Client money policies – to deal with high-risk compliance issues such as the need to deal with money in accordance with your firm's and the SRA's promptness requirements, explaining what the timing requirements are, dealing with approved signatory issues, interest payments, dealing with balances at the end of the matter, clarity on the banking prohibition.
- Whistleblowing policy – a declaration to provide confidence to anyone who might have concerns or wish to challenge inappropriate behaviours.
- Internal reporting and notification process – to support compliance with individual and firm-based reporting duties.
- Statements about the firm's COLP and COFA (and other compliance colleagues) – how to contact them, the help and support they provide, their roles in decision-making, the breach reporting requirements.

What are the compliance challenges?

- Draft a suite of policies that is truly appropriate to your circumstances.
- If using template materials purchased 'off the shelf', adapt these to meet your firm's needs.
- Ensure that the policies are kept under review so that they remain appropriate.
- Ensure that all managers/employees comply with policies which are relevant to them.
- Ensure that there is suitable visibility of, and support from, the COLP and COFA and compliance professionals.

What resources will help?

- SRA materials:
  - SRA Standards and Regulations (**www.sra.org.uk/solicitors/standards-regulations/**);
  - SRA guidance: 'Reporting and notification obligations' (25 November 2019, **www.sra.org.uk/solicitors/guidance/reporting-notification-obligations/**);
  - SRA guidance: 'Acting with integrity' (updated 25 November 2019, **www.sra.org.uk/solicitors/guidance/acting-with-integrity/**);
  - SRA guidance: 'Workplace environment: risks of failing to protect and support colleagues' (7 February 2022, **www.sra.org.uk/solicitors/guidance/workplace-environment/**).
- *Compliance and Ethics in Law Firms*, 2nd edn (Tracey Calvert, Law Society Publishing, 2019).

Compliance tips – how to mitigate the risk of getting it wrong

- Provide induction training to ensure there is awareness of the firm's compliance attitude.
- Have meetings with the COLP and COFA and the compliance team to facilitate and encourage the communications which are vital if the compliance standards are to be met.
- Engage in ongoing compliance conversations – perhaps at team meetings, in a supervisory environment, through postings on the firm's intranet or through newsletters, etc.
- Diarise review of policies to ensure that they remain appropriate to meet the firm's needs and reflect current regulatory thinking.
- Conduct supervisory oversight.

Index

Accepting new instructions 19.8
Account freezing order 7.3
Accounts rules *see* SRA Accounts Rules
Adverse media checks 3.7
Anti-bribery and corruption officer (ABO) 6.6
Audits 5.9, 5.10
Authorisation of law firms 9.8
- annual renewal exercise 10.3, 10.5
- bulk renewal process 10.3, 10.5

BOOM regime 1.6
Bribery and corruption
- ABO 6.6
- Christmas gifts 6.12
- corporate offence 6.2
- countries with high levels of corruption 6.13, 6.14
- failure to prevent 6.4
- gifts and hospitality 6.8
- grease payments 6.9, 6.15
- offences 6.1
- overseas operations 6.13
- penalties 6.3
- policy 6.5
- privilege 6.11
- risk assessment 6.4
- suspicion 6.11
- third party suppliers 6.10
- training 6.7

Bulk renewal process 10.3, 10.5

Cannabis growing 4.12
Cash payments 3.28
Central onboarding team 3.26
Charities
- donating small client balances 11.6
- due diligence requirement 3.2

China
- transfers of monies from 4.11

Christmas gifts 6.12
Churches 3.2
Client care
- accepting new instructions 19.8
- equality 19.2
- general file 19.6
- identifying the client 19.5
- letter 19.3, 19.4
- literature 19.3
- long-term service agreements 19.7
- unsolicited approaches 19.1

Client due diligence
- adverse media checks 3.7
- charities 3.2
- churches/places of worship 3.2
- client known to partner 3.18
- clubs and associations 3.2
- companies 3.2
- documentation 3.2
- enhanced due diligence 3.9
- failure to undertake 3.5
- funds *see* Source of funds/source of wealth
- government agencies/councils 3.2
- high-risk third countries 3.14
- ID requirements 3.2
  - agents 3.16, 3.17
  - client cannot provide 3.11
  - electronic identification/verification 3.4
  - identity cannot be verified 3.12
  - independent verification 3.3
  - intermediaries 3.16, 3.17
  - representatives 3.16, 3.17
  - working pending verification 3.13
- individuals 3.2
- occasional transactions 3.15
- ongoing monitoring 3.10
- partnerships 3.2
- pension funds 3.2
- people with significant control register 3.19

Client due diligence – *continued*
politically exposed persons 3.6
preliminary work 3.13
records
requirements 3.36
timescale 3.37
referral from another law firm 3.17
reliance on *see* Reliance
requirement to undertake 3.1
sanctions checks 3.7
schools, colleges, universities 3.2
simplified due diligence 3.8
trusts and estate administration 3.2
waiver of process 3.18
well-known entities 3.2
Client and matter risk assessments
client known to partner 3.18
crossover with practice-wide risk assessment 2.7
failure to undertake 2.9
items to take into account 2.6
new matter/during a matter 2.8
requirement to undertake 2.5
reviewing 2.8
Client misleading the court 18.7
Clubs and associations 3.2
Colleges 3.2
COLP/COFA
MLRO/MLCO and 1.9
roles 1.9
Confidentiality/disclosure
adverse interests 17.9
conflicts of duties 17.9, 17.10
conflicts of interest 17.10
email sent to wrong recipient 17.3
end of duty 17.2
incoming solicitor acted for opponent 17.8
information barriers 17.1
informed consent to disclosure 17.4
informed consent to non-disclosure 17.5
joint retainer 17.6
will documents 17.7
Conflicts of interest
acting against interests of former client 16.7
acting for buyer and seller 16.3, 16.4
acting for client after discovering a mistake 16.6
competing for the same objective exception 16.3, 16.5
confidentiality/disclosure 17.10
contract race 16.5
related matter 16.2
significant risk 16.1
substantially common interest exception 16.3, 16.4
Consultants
screening of 5.3
Contacting another lawyer's client directly 18.3
Contacting prospective clients 19.1
Continuing professional development (CPD) 10.4
Conveyancing transactions
price transparency 15.4
Corruption *see* Bribery and corruption
Cryptocurrency 3.24

Data protection
data breach incident 12.4
firm-wide response 12.1
Data protection officer (DPO) 12.2
Data subject access request (DSAR) 12.3
Digital badge 15.3
Disciplinary action 9.4
Disclosure *see* Confidentiality/disclosure
Discrimination
complaint by staff member 20.4
equality 19.2
reasonable adjustments 20.5
Documenting procedures and policies 20.10

Effective supervision 20.2, 20.3
Email sent to wrong recipient 17.3
Employee screening 5.1
adverse result 5.5
agencies 5.3
consultants 5.3
contractors 5.3
options 5.2
outsourcing 5.4
suppliers 5.3
support staff 5.3
Equality, diversity and inclusivity 19.2
see also Discrimination

Financial services 13.1
compliance plans 13.2
insurance distribution officer 13.3
training 13.4

Freelance solicitors 9.11
dealing with 18.5

General file 19.6
Gifts and hospitality 6.8
Christmas gifts 6.12
Grease payments 6.9

High-risk third countries 3.14
Hospitality 6.8

Information barriers 17.1
Insurance distribution officer 13.3
Introductions 20.8

Job titles 20.1
Joint retainer 17.6

Law Society 9.6
Legal advice privilege 4.6
Legal Ombudsman 9.7
Legal Services Board 9.2
Licensed body 9.8
Limited retainer 18.1
Litigation privilege 4.6
Locum support 10.2
Long-term service agreements 19.7

MLCO
appointee 1.8
COLP/COFA and 1.9
role 1.8
training 5.8
MLRO
appointee 1.7
bribery 6.11
COLP/COFA and 1.9
reporting suspicions to 4.2
role 1.7, 4.3
tax evasion 7.10
training 5.8
Modern slavery
annual statement 14.2
compliance plan of action 14.6
failure to publish statement 14.5
offences 14.1
policy 14.3
sanctions for non-compliance 14.5
statement 14.4
Money laundering
appointed officers *see* MLCO; MLRO
audits 5.9, 5.10
BOOM regime 1.6
defences
adequate consideration 1.4
authorised disclosure 1.4
lack of training 1.4
POCA 2002 1.4
privileged circumstances 1.4
reasonable excuse 1.4
definition 1.1
obligations on law firms 1.2
offences
acquisition, use, possession 1.3
arrangements 1.3
concealing 1.3
failure to disclose 1.3
POCA 2002 1.3
prejudicing an investigation 1.3
tipping off 1.3
red flags/warning signs 5.11, 5.12
SRA AML visits 5.13, 5.14, 5.15
tax adviser 1.10, 1.11
terrorist money/property 1.5.1

New partners, directors, members
registration with SRA 9.12

Occasional transactions 3.15
Office of Financial Sanctions Implementation (OFSI) 8.1, 8.6
Office of Foreign Assets Control (OFAC) 8.3
Ongoing monitoring 3.10
Outsourcing
of employee screening 5.4
of services 20.9
Overseas
countries with high levels of corruption 6.13, 6.14
criminal conduct overseas 4.11, 4.12
grease payments 6.15
money transfers from China 4.11
suspicious activity report 4.11, 4.12

Pension funds 3.2
People with significant control register 3.19
Places of worship 3.2
Politically exposed person (PEP) 3.6
Practice-wide risk assessments
contents 2.3
crossover with client and matter risk assessment 2.7

Practice-wide risk assessments – *continued*
format 2.2
implementing PCPs 2.4
obligation to conduct 2.1
reviewing 2.4
Practices, types of 9.10
Practising certificates 10.1
renewal 10.3
retired solicitors 10.2
Price transparency
complaints information 15.2
conveyancing transactions 15.4
digital badge 15.3
requirements 15.1
Privilege
bribery 6.11
money laundering offences 1.4
sanctions 8.7
suspicious activity report 4.6
tax evasion 7.10
Professional ethics
non-solicitors and 9.14
Prospective clients
unsolicited approaches 19.1

Reasonable adjustments 20.5
Recognised body 9.8
Recognised sole practice 9.8
Records
client due diligence 3.36, 3.37
training records 5.6, 9.15
Referral arrangements 20.8
Reliance
meaning of 3.32
problems 3.33
regulated entities 3.34, 3.35
requirements 3.32
Reputational issues 6.11, 7.10, 14.5
Reserved legal activities 9.9
Retired solicitors 10.2
Risk assessment
bribery risk 6.4
tax evasion risk 7.5
see also Client and matter risk assessments; Practice-wide risk assessments
Risk management manual 20.7

Sanctions
checks 3.7, 8.5
definition 8.1
key players 8.2
licences 8.8, 8.9
lists 8.4
non-UK country 8.10
obligation to report to OFSI 8.6
OFAC 8.3
payments into court 8.9
privilege 8.7
types of 8.1
Schools 3.2
Slavery *see* Modern slavery
Solicitors Disciplinary Tribunal (SDT) 9.5
Solicitors Regulation Authority (SRA) 9.3
accounts rules *see* SRA Accounts Rules
annual renewal exercise 10.3, 10.5
authorisation of law firms 9.8, 10.3
bulk renewal process 10.3, 10.5
digital badge 15.3
disciplinary action 9.4
non-lawyers and 9.14
registration of new partners etc 9.12
Source of funds/source of wealth 3.20, 3.21
cannabis growing abroad 4.12
cash payments 3.28
central onboarding team 3.26
criminal conduct overseas 4.12
cryptocurrency 3.24
family member/friend
paying fees 3.30
paying transaction monies 3.31
funds from separate corporate entity 3.29
information/documentation required 3.22
investigating 3.22
lack of clarity 3.23
proceeds of crime 3.25
unsolicited deposit of monies 3.27
SRA Accounts Rules 11.1
completion funds held pending instructions 11.5
donating small balances to charity 11.6
money held in respect of costs 11.4
rounding-up disbursements in bills 11.3
sending monies to in-house solicitor 11.2

third party managed accounts (TPMAs) 11.7
SRA AML visits
likely questions 5.13
possible outcomes 5.15
preparing for 5.14
Suppliers
due diligence on third party suppliers 6.10
screening of 5.3
Suspicion
definition 4.1
reporting to MLRO 4.2
role of MLRO 4.3
timescale for response 4.4
Suspicious activity report (SAR) 4.4
bribery 6.11
change in facts/proposed activity 4.10
criminal conduct overseas 4.11, 4.12
deemed defence/deemed consent 4.8
drafting 4.5
money transfers from China 4.11
NCA not responded 4.8
NCA refuse defence 4.9
no *de minimis* sum 4.13
privilege 4.6
tax evasion 7.10
tipping off 4.7

Tax adviser
applying for supervision 1.11
definition 1.10
types of 7.8
Tax evasion
account freezing order 7.3
amendments to bills 7.13
CFA 2017 offences 7.1
corporate 7.8
family law 7.8
form E omissions 7.12
messaging 7.11
penalties 7.4
policy 7.6
privilege 7.10
property 7.8
readdressing of bills 7.14
risk assessment 7.5
training 7.7, 7.11
unexplained wealth orders 7.2
VAT fraud 7.13
warning notices 7.9
wills and probate 7.8
Terrorism offences 1.5
failure to disclose 1.5.3
defences 1.5.4
funding arrangements 1.5.1
fundraising 1.5.1
money laundering 1.5.1
principal offences 1.5.1
defences 1.5.2
tipping off 1.5.5
use and possession of money/property 1.5.1
Third party managed accounts (TPMAs) 11.7
Tipping off offences
defences 1.5.5
money laundering 1.3
suspicious activity reports 4.7
terrorism 1.5.5
Training
accounts staff 9.13
anti-bribery and corruption 6.7
fee earners/casehandlers 9.13
financial services 13.4
HR staff 9.13
IT staff 9.13
lack of, as defence 1.4
lateral hires 9.13
marketing staff 9.13
methods 5.7
MLRO/MLCO 5.8
qualified lawyers 9.13
records 5.6, 9.15
requirements 5.6
support staff 9.13
tax evasion 7.7, 7.11
temporary staff 9.13
Trusts and estate administration 3.2

Unauthorised business
corresponding with 18.6
Unbundled legal services 18.2
Undertakings in writing 20.6
Unexplained wealth orders (UWOs) 7.2
Universities 3.2
Unrepresented other side 18.4
Unsolicited approaches 19.1

VAT fraud 7.13

Warning notices 7.9
Well-known entities 3.2
Will documents 17.7